# PURITAN CITY

"Leslie's Retreat," North Bridge, Salem, February 25, 1775
A water-color by Bridgman.

# PURITAN CITY

*The Story of Salem*

BY FRANCES WINWAR, pseud. of
Grebanier, Mrs. F. (V.)

849

*Illustrated*

ROBERT M. McBRIDE & COMPANY
*Publishers*                    *New York*

PURITAN CITY

•

COPYRIGHT, 1938, BY
FRANCES WINWAR

•

FIRST EDITION

To Eugene Gise

His life was gentle, and the elements
So mix'd in him that Nature might stand up
And say to all the world, 'This was a man!'

*Julius Caesar*, ACT V SCENE V.

# CONTENTS

# ILLUSTRATIONS

ix

# PURITAN CITY

## NAUMKEAG

"A WORD," wrote the delightful annalist, the Rev. Joseph B. Felt, "is often the source of recollections, feelings and actions. . . . Such, undoubtedly, was the effect produced by the term Naumkeag, when pronounced by the aborigines."

Naumkeag. To the Indian of that section of North American coast which later received the name of Salem, the word called up clear springs and grassy meadows where the heron came to preen its feathers and the far-flying wild ducks darkened the sun with their massed flight. It meant wigwams and cornfields, protected on one side by the ocean and on the other by the forest wall. It meant the camp gathering at night and the friendly fire to frighten away the evil spirit, Abimecho, who walked in the darkness. Naumkeag meant a safe haven. It was the place of rivers skimmed by canoes swift as the flight of a bird; of estuaries where the creatures of the deep sheltered themselves in the shallow waters; of sandy beaches where one walking with bare feet, would call up a thousand little fountains from the hidden clams. Naumkeag was the hunting ground and the place to which the hunter returned to rest. It was home.

To the early colonists Naumkeag was a word of foreboding. For them home lay on the other side of the world, separated by three thousand miles of ocean.

Naumkeag was a wilderness, a mysterious place of which they had vaguely heard from the reports of English navigators. Suspiciously they looked over the side of the ship on the floating chains of yellow blossoms, like gilliflowers, that seemed to lead them to the shore. Beyond that rocky coast, in the shadow of the forest that challenged the sky, they were to build a new hearth and begin a new life. Privation, sickness, perhaps death, faced them—they had already had a foreknowledge of them on the ocean. But they might also find opportunity and spiritual health. They were no adventurers cast off by their native land, but willing exiles, preferring suffering for religious freedom to what they condemned as a comfortable apostasy.

The frail skiffs that landed the early settlers in what was to be the oldest town in the colony of Massachusetts Bay were not the first to carry their freight of religious rebels to foreign shores. As early as 1608 the exodus had begun, when bands of Pilgrims registered their protest against the King and the Church of England by emigrating to Holland. There, they had heard, men could live in peace and worship God as they thought right. Since the beginning of the century they had been persecuted for differing with the practices of the established church. They were deprived of the right to earn a livelihood and, in some cases, they were thrown into prison. The dissenters fell into two parties—the Pilgrims, so called from their wanderings, and the Puritans who remained in the church in the hope of purifying it of Catholic influences. According to both Pilgrim and Puritan, there was still much left to reform since

1534, when Henry VIII broke with the Pope and declared himself the head of the Church of England.

Difficulties beset the Pilgrims at every step. As the English ports were closed to them, they were forced to bribe the mariners to take them to Leyden, often paying out most of their money before they went aboard. Some, less successful, were betrayed to the authorities. Then, instead of a ship bringing them to freedom, they found a prison cell and months, sometimes years, of captivity. Nevertheless, in spite of the many obstacles, a considerable colony of Pilgrims established itself in Holland. But not for long. The busy little commercial nation could not assimilate the English foreigners who had nothing to offer but their willingness to work. Besides, the war which had been threatening between Holland and Spain was about to break out. Once more the wanderers who had neither land nor home, found themselves adrift. Hopefully they looked toward America.

For years the various countries of Europe had been sending out fearless spirits to establish colonies in the new continent but, except for Spain, with meager success. Strange tales had come back, of unheard-of perils and tortures at the hands of the wild tribes who inhabited that unknown world. The merchants, however, and the trade companies that had obtained foreign monopolies from the State, still issued glowing prospectuses that painted the Western continent as the new earthly paradise. Volunteer colonists were wooed by the rival companies who played upon the imagination of the adventurous and took advantage of the needy. After all, by extending colonial trade for their country they were doing a service to the State and amassing fortunes for themselves. And so monopolies were formed for every conceivable article of consumption—salt, leather, wine, starch, tobacco, fish, saltpetre, furs, glass. The new country offered a mine of treasure that needed but the manpower to bring it to light.

News came to London that a band of English Pilgrims was stranded in Holland and looking for a place of refuge. Thomas Weston, an enterprising merchant, saw his chance. The Virginia Company had already established a profitable colony in America: yet the vast eastern coast of the continent had barely been explored. After conferring with a number of fellow merchants, Weston hastened to Leyden with a proposal for the Pilgrims. If, he said, they would enter into an agreement with him to found a trading and fishing town near the Virginia colony, he would provide their passage across the ocean and, after seven years, make them part sharers in the profits of the company.

The Pilgrims had nothing to lose. Perhaps in a virgin country their sons might see realized a new Zion, though the King still refused their demand for freedom of worship. They might even befriend the Indians and bring them to a knowledge of the true God. Thus, with their eyes turned heavenward, they signed the agreement with the London merchants whose thoughts were fixed on the prospective cargoes that would eventually swell their moneybags. Most of them were members of the Church of England; the conscientious scruples of the Pilgrims concerned them but little.

With the King's permission, if not with his blessing, the Pilgrims embarked at Southampton on the *Speed-*

*well* and the *Mayflower*, the ships provided for their passage. It was cold, for autumn was setting in. On the gray water the two vessels looked like cockleshells. Nevertheless, the Pilgrims entrusted themselves to the mercy of Providence and made for the promised land. Soon it was discovered that the *Speedwell* had sprung a leak. To repair it would have delayed them. Sailing back to Plymouth, the *Speedwell* loaded her passengers and their belongings onto the *Mayflower*, and the crowded vessel faced the leagues of ocean alone.

"Hail to thee, poor little ship, *Mayflower* . . . poor common looking ship, hired by common charter-party for coined dollars—caulked with mere oakum and tar— provisioned with vulgarest biscuit and bacon—yet what ship Argo or miraculous epic ship, built by the sea gods, was other than a foolish bumbarge in comparison!"

Two hundred years later Carlyle, who was never generous with praise, thus hailed the heroic *Mayflower*, even though she never reached her destination in Virginia. The voyage was long and difficult. Winter added its hardships. Off the forbidding coast which the Pilgrims called Plymouth, they anchored the *Mayflower* in December, 1620, and founded the first permanent New England colony. But the London merchants were disappointed. The cargoes of salt, fish and furs that they had expected from the New World failed to arrive. Worse, the unskilled colonists, weakened by disease and hardships, met with reverses at every turn. The salt works that they had obediently set up were burnt down; fishing and trading were arts that they did not understand. They had all they could do to keep body and soul together in the hard, bitter winters. Assuredly the Plymouth colony had proved a poor venture.

But the trading companies were not discouraged. There was too much money in colonial speculation for them not to consider occasional losses as part of the game. Each, in its secret ambition, hoped to rival the English East India Company which Queen Elizabeth had incorporated by royal charter twenty years earlier. In that short time the original capital of seventy-two thousand pounds invested by the shareholders had made each speculator a rich man. There was wealth in the Americas as well as in the Indies, if one knew how to get it.

Hence, in spite of the initial failure of Plymouth, a joint stock company was organized in England, and a patent secured from Edmund, Lord Sheffield, for a large tract of land which had been granted to him in the partition of the New England territory. The Dorchester Company thus began its operations under the royal patent of November 3, 1620, which empowered it to make laws, try criminal and civil cases, and enforce order in the event of rebellion or hostile invasion. Without knowing it, the Crown was laying the foundations for future trouble.

Meanwhile, in 1622, Roger Conant, a Puritan, had joined the Pilgrim settlement at Plymouth with his family, but because he did not share the religious views of the founders, had moved on to Nantasket. He was a selfless, high-principled man who firmly believed that America, and especially New England, had been created for those who sought religious freedom. With his followers, therefore, he tried to maintain at Captain Miles

Standish's outpost what he had not found sufficiently exemplified in Plymouth.

But the Dorchester Company had other plans for so good a man and sent him on as governor to Cape Ann, where it had set up a fishing station. Alas, the land proved hostile and the sea ungenerous. Besides, the men, discouraged by their many failures, took little interest in the success of the colony. In spite of the example of Roger Conant and his unceasing efforts to hearten the laggard, the Cape Ann settlement had to be abandoned. At the first opportunity most of the colonists sailed back to England, leaving Conant with a handful of loyal adherents willing to share his uncertain fortunes. It spoke well for the man that even in his defeat he could still inspire confidence.

Since, after this last disastrous venture, the Dorchester Company had sold its ships and gone out of business, Conant was faced with the responsibility of providing for his small band. He knew it was useless to try to wrest even the barest living from the hard soil of Cape Ann. With his men, he set out to explore the coast for a more propitious haven, raising their sinking spirits when they failed and spurring them on with the promise of success. "I was the means," he wrote later, "through grace assisting me, to stop the flight of those few that then were here with me . . . but thereupon stayed to the hazard of our lives."

In 1626, as the trees of the forest were putting on the astounding colors of a New England autumn, Roger Conant and his men laid their first stakes at Naumkeag, just sixteen miles south of their last settlement. It was not the first time that white man had set eyes on the bay and coast of Salem. As early as 1529, Ribero, a Spaniard, had passed that way and sent home a description. But since it held no promise of gold—the Spaniard's bliss, as the old records called it—Ribero's ships sailed on.

Fourteen years later Vallard de Dieppe named it Cape de la Croix, but he, too, made no effort to raise the cross there for France. Then, in May, 1602, Bartholomew Gosnold pushed his vessel, the *Concord*, to shore, and one of his men took notes for the benefit of Sir Walter Raleigh, under whose patronage the party was sailing.

"We made the land," John Brereton wrote, "being full of faire trees, the land somewhat low, certaine hummocks or hilles lying into the land, the shore full of white sand, but very stony or rocky." Six Indians, one of whom wore a sailor's waistcoat and breeches, came aboard in a friendly way, but Gosnold was not tempted to cast anchor for long. There could be no hope of lucre in a shore that was very stony and rocky.

For twelve years no more records were made of the landfall, until John Smith, the inveterate navigator, drew a map covering the coast from Cape Cod to the Penobscot River. Champlain, too, traveling as the companion of the Sieur de Monts, saw the cape and pushed into the harbor. "We named this place Island Cape," he recorded, "near which we saw a canoe containing five or six savages, who came out near our barque, and then went back and danced on the beach. Sieur de Monts sent me on shore to observe them, and to give each one of them a knife and some biscuit, which caused them to dance again better than before."

Unhappily the Indians did not dance long. In the

year 1616 a comet shone red and low in the heavens, striking fear into their hearts; for they knew it was their evil god Squantum, who was giving them a sign of his wrath against them. The following summer whole tribes were wiped out by a strange affliction. The sufferer burned with a terrible heat that made his flesh melt away; his limbs withered and he languished till he died. Neither medicine man nor sacrifice availed against the disease. Young and old, man and woman, all were prey to the plague that swept along the Massachusetts coast till the fields were heaped high with the bodies of the dead.

For three years the disease raged, till there was not one Indian in a hundred left alive. Captain John Smith saw in it the working of a divine will that "provided this Country for our Nation, destroying the natives." He was even more certain of it when he heard that the red men in a body had defied the Christian God. "Not long after such a sicknesse came, that of five or six hundred about the Massachusetts, there remained but thirty on whom their neighbors fell and slew twenty-eight: the two remaining fled their Country till the English came, then they returned and surrendered their Country and title to the English. If this be not true in every particular, excuse me, I pray you, for I am not the Author."

True or not, the fact remained that when the English came to settle in Massachusetts the land was practically deserted except for a few chastened, despondent tribes living in dread of another visitation. They offered no resistance to the white invader, and even saw his coming with a sense of relief.

The section of land which Conant and his men chose for their new settlement lay within the territory of the Agawam and the Massachusetts tribes. They found a town of wigwams pitched on the north side of North River, near where the forest offered game for the hunter. Along the shores there was evidence that the Agawams had learned the art of curing fish—Agawam itself meant the "fish-curing place."

Conant also chose the North River, but he settled on the southeastern shore where the land could be more easily cleared and where thatched cottages could be put up with the help of the clay and the rushes of the marsh that stretched behind the plantation. Soon a row of houses built of logs from the forest and floored with clay sprang up along the shore. The soil about them was prepared for the planting of corn and tobacco, and along the seashore stages were constructed for the curing and salting of the fish that abounded in the waters. Before the end of the year, in the rude cottage of Roger Conant, the first Salem child was born. The father named it Roger after himself.

At last the settlement gave signs of prospering. News of it reached England and before long a new company was organizing itself "for the planting, ruling, ordering and governing of New England."

## CHAPTER II

## COMING OF THE MINISTERS

THE Massachusetts Bay Company grew from the nucleus of the original Dorchester Company, but it was larger and more select. Sir Henry Rosewell and Sir John Young both obtained an interest in it, and it enjoyed besides the support of some half-dozen influential gentlemen, among them Captain John Endecott. Soon a number of well-to-do Londoners joined them by purchasing shares, and all together they proposed not only to extend the plantation of Roger Conant at Naumkeag, but to create a new settlement where religious nonconformists might at last live unmolested. But on a business basis—there were to be no more failures and disasters. From three miles north of the Merrimack to three miles south of the Charles River, the wilderness would be made to flower and bear fruit.

There had to be a forceful leader, however. Although the Company recognized Roger Conant's worth, still, his authority had expired with the dissolution of the Dorchester Company. Moreover, the Massachusetts Bay Company wished to place at the helm a man who had influence in the corporation as well as a personal concern in the success of the enterprise. Captain John Endecott was their choice.

Strong-willed, audacious and authoritarian, he could impose himself upon the refractory and look to the best interests of the corporation to which he was linked by more than one bond: his wife, Anna Gower, was a cousin of Matthew Cradock, the governor of the Company in England. His own people came from Devonshire, where for years they had been working the vast tin mines which they owned. He himself had been educated to medicine and could with justice style himself "chirurgeon." At the time of his association with the Company, he was a hale, handsome man of forty, at the height of his physical and mental powers, not too young still to profit from experience, yet not too old for the prospect of a long and useful career.

Meanwhile, in England, the relations between the Court and the people had been growing worse instead of better, and religious persecution was rampant. Hence when the ship *Abigail* sailed from Weymouth in 1628, she was filled to capacity. Gentlemen and yeomen, Pilgrims and Puritans, all followed Captain Endecott, a "fit instrument to begin this wildernesse-work, of courage bold undaunted," as the old chronicler Edward Johnson put it.

And indeed Captain Endecott asserted himself with the flash of his unsheathed sword. Force ruled where reason did not avail, and insubordination was quelled. It may be that Roger Conant disapproved of the man whose authority had been imposed over his own. If he did, he said nothing, but with the rest of the colonists, now increased to the number of sixty, he pursued his work for the sake of the good which he hoped would be accomplished.

When Captain Endecott portioned out the grants of the settlement, the old Planters, as Conant's men were called, retained their cove in the North River, and received additional lots of land. Some of the newcomers joined them at the cove; others followed Endecott farther up the river. Streets were laid out and houses built as quickly as trees could be felled and men found to build them. In the southeast corner of what is now the junction of Washington and Federal streets, rose "the Governour's fayre house," built from the lumber of the Company's center at Cape Ann. It could have been no splendid or durable structure, for by the end of the century there was no trace left of it; in comparison with the primitive cottages of the settlers, however, it must indeed have been "fayre."

Into this house Captain Endecott brought his wife; but she was not to enjoy it long. Ever since the voyage she had been ailing, and the New England winter that came upon them soon after the *Abigail's* arrival, brought still other hardships. In vain Captain Endecott had Dr. Samuel Fuller sent down from the neighboring colony of Plymouth to minister to the sick. Many died of the scurvy and the malignant fevers which they had caught from one another on the voyage. Before the end of winter, Mistress Endecott lay with them in the rude burial ground on a bluff stretching into South River. Without stones to mark their graves and with no solemn ceremony, the first dead of Naumkeag found rest in the old "Burying Point," now the Charter Street burial ground.

If Roger Conant submitted to the authority of the Massachusetts Bay Company for the ultimate good, not so the old Planters, who looked upon the newcomers as the usurpers of their rights under the Sheffield patent. After all, they had made the first dent in the forest wall;

their spades had been the first to subdue the soil and make it yield. Now that their toil was at last beginning to reward them, others came to deprive them of their fruits. Nevertheless, with the vision of the perfect religious commonwealth still bright, Conant exhorted his men to patience and succeeded in reconciling them to the Endecott group.

At this point, it may be, the name of Naumkeag was changed to Salem in celebration of the peace between the two factions. At least that is what the *Planters' Plea*, printed in London in 1630, would lead one to believe, according to its author, the Rev. John White, who sought the word of God even in the rude phonetics of the red men. "It fals out," he wrote, "that the name of the place, which our late Colony hath chosen for their seat, prooves to be perfect Hebrew, being called Nahum Keike; by interpretation, the bosom of consolation; which it were a pitty that those, which observed it not, should change into the name of Salem, though upon a faire ground, in remembrance of a peace setled upon a conference at a generall meeting betweene them and their neighbours, after expectance of some dangerous jarre." In his *New England*, on the other hand, the Rev. William Hubbard, who wrote in 1680, said that Salem was named by a minister who took his inspiration from the Psalms. He may have meant the Rev. Francis Higginson, who came to the colony in 1629.

If the old Planters were made to see the light, other factions under the jurisdiction of the Massachusetts Bay Company were not so easily subdued. Some years earlier, perhaps in 1626, a small band of adventurers headed by a Captain Wollaston had made a settlement in what is now the city of Quincy and called it after the leader. It was a picturesque hill, sloping gently to the sea and commanding a view of the sails which passed that way.

Little is known of Wollaston. Some said he was a man of rank and of "pretie parts." Whatever his origin, it was certain that he had no official charter for establishing a trading base on any part of the New England territory. But he asked no one's permission. With his associates and some fifty indentured servants, he took possession of the hill and carried on a lucrative trade with the Indians, to whom he gave firearms and ammunition in exchange for valuable skins. After a year or so, lured perhaps by stories of commercial ventures in Virginia, he appointed one of his men to act as his agent and left the mount with a good part of his servants, whom he sold in the South at a great profit.

Thomas Morton, a man who had followed Wollaston through his many shady adventures, remained behind with a few cronies, who only needed his word to send the agent about his business and take matters into their own hands. No sooner said than done. The name of the hill was changed from Wollaston to Merry Mount, and Morton established himself as "Lord of Misrule."

Morton's origin was, if anything, more obscure than his predecessor's, though from his own account he had been a lawyer of Clifford's Inn. To the neighboring Plymouth colonists he was anathema. Day by day tales of the practices of Merry Mount reached their scandalized ears; they began living in dread of the dissolute company which, they feared, would in time become the center of all that was lawless in the colony. Runaway servants would find refuge there, and reckless characters, and pirates who would establish it as a station for their nefarious deeds.

After much deliberation, a few brave spirits among the settlers remonstrated with Morton, to no avail. He was more than a match for reason, with force, and lawless force, on his side. Finally, in the spring of 1628, Miles Standish was sent by the Plymouth authorities to put Morton under arrest.

It was May. Most of the men had gone to the interior to hunt for furs, but Morton had remained behind, carousing and making merry to celebrate May Day in the traditional English fashion with his boon companions —and others upon whom the grave elders looked with horror. Even Governor Bradford could not refrain from writing an account of Merry Mount in his journal. The dissolute band, he recorded in words that did not conceal his displeasure, "set up a May-pole, drinking and dancing aboute it many days togeather, inviting the Indean women for their consorts, dancing and frisking togither (like so many fairies, or furies rather), and worse practises."

It was not long before the noise of Morton's doings reached the ears of Captain Endecott. Boarding a small boat, he sailed the thirty miles to Merry Mount, his wrath increasing as he neared the place. Not for nothing was Whittier to describe him as

> Earnest and honest, a man at need
> To burn like a torch for his own harsh creed;
> He kept with the flaming brand of his zeal
> The gate of the holy commonweal.

Now that commonweal was being imperiled by a band of godless outlaws.

He had expected to find a disorderly crowd. What was his consternation when, in the midst of a clearing, he saw a Maypole, more than eighty feet high, forming the axis of a riotous group. For years the Maypole had been forbidden by the church in England. And now here it was, with a pair of buck's horns nailed on its crest, and its trunk streaming with ribbons flaunting indecent verses of Morton's own composition! In the very bosom of Puritanism the Bacchanalians had set their symbol!

With his usual directness Endecott ordered the pole cut down and disbanded the merrymakers, admonishing them with vigorous words "to look to it that they walked better." As for Morton, he was compelled to leave the settlement, but if anything, he "walked" worse. In his resentment against the colonists, he lived among the Indians, teaching them the use of pistols and powder and starting a mischief from which the colonists were to suffer as the friendliness of the red men turned to hatred. But that was still in the future.

For the present the Massachusetts Bay Company assumed that the Indians not only welcomed, but implored, their white brothers to come to them. At least that was what could be inferred from the seal that was sent to Endecott in 1629 with his governorship. In the silver oval stands a thick-thighed, paunched son of the wilderness with a bow in one hand, an arrow in the other, and a broad girdle of leaves about his middle. Two trees, conifers by their shape, rise on either side of him. Another is in the middle distance, much reduced in a naive attempt at perspective. From the red man's mouth swirls the legend in bold capitals: "Come over and help us," signifying the Indian's eagerness to be Christianized.

Meanwhile the row of thatched houses along the river, built of round logs, was whitened under a foot of snow. The *Abigail* had sailed back to England, and in the ensuing months the discouraged colonists had to agree with the old chronicler that "the ditch between England and their now place of abode was so wide, that they could not leap over with a lope-staff." Many of them wished they could, especially when the food stores ran low, and the Indians, upon whom they had counted for maize, came over to share their own acorns. However, "they made shift to rub out the winters cold by the fireside, having fuell enough growing at their very doores, turning down many a drop of the bottel, and burning tobacco with all the ease they could, discoursing betweene one while and another, of the great progresse they would make after the summers sun had changed the earthe white furr'd gowne into a greene mantell." How anxiously they watched the forest for the first leaf-bud, and scanned the ocean for the sail that meant food and clothes!

In his lonely house, with only a needlework sampler[1] to remind him of the wife he had lost, Endecott thought of the price in life and suffering that the colony demanded. But he did not waver. He knew then, as in the many years of his service, that the end was worthy of the sacrifice.

With the coming of summer, the fleet of ships sent by the Company with provisions for the colonists began

[1] Now in the Museum of the Essex Institute.

to appear, days and weeks apart, though they had left Gravesend together. This time the Company provided both for the spiritual and material needs of the settlers, for on the ship *Talbot* sailed the Rev. Francis Higginson who, with the Rev. Samuel Skelton, was to found the first Congregational Society in America.

For many years, after coming in contact with Thomas Hooker, Higginson had been a conscientious non-conformist. With the rest, he suffered the consequences. Before long he was deprived of his ministry in Leicester and had to depend for support upon the voluntary contributions of his adherents. He did not give up preaching, however, going from parish to parish at the invitation of sympathizers, even when information was presented against him to Bishop Laud and he faced the penalty of life imprisonment.

It was then that the Massachusetts Bay Company called him to the colony. With his wife and eight children, at the age of forty-two, he stood at the stern of the vessel and looked his last on England. "We will not say . . . 'Farewell Babylon! Farewell Rome!'" he cried, as his homeland receded from his gaze. "We do not go to New England as separatists from the church of England, though we cannot but separate from the corruptions in it; but we go to practice the positive part of church reformation."

The voyage was long, painful and adventurous, like all voyages in those brave days. A hundred men and women were crowded into the *Talbot*, sharing its meager accommodations with goats and cattle, and stumbling on the rough seas among the sacks of provisions and the pieces of ordnance that were being sent for the protection of the colony. Storms tormented them in mid-ocean, and calms gripped the ship that lay for days with dead sails under the broiling sun. Smallpox broke out. One night the body of Mary, Mr. Higginson's five-year-old daughter, was buried in the sea. There was hardly a crossing without its toll of death.

Then, as they neared the western shores, they saw grampus fish, more than two yards long, "and bonny fishes and porpoises pursuing one another and leaping a yard above the water." A whale, one day, entertained them by spouting water not far from the ship, and a huge sea turtle swam for a time alongside. At length they saw a mountain of ice shining white and moveless like a cliff on the shore. Taking the soundings, they found themselves in a depth of forty fathoms. Land could not be far off. With what joy they perceived the faint shoreline on the horizon, and saw the ropes of weeds and yellow flowers floating on the sea! Finally, one morning, piloted by a boat sent out by Governor Endecott to meet them, they entered the waters of the bay of Naumkeag. "Marvel harbor," Higginson called it.

Near the shore was anchored a sister ship, the *George*, that had arrived a week earlier, bearing the handsomely engrossed Charter from the King which incorporated the Company into a body politic, with authority for self-government in the limits of its territory. The ruling body was to be known as the Governor and Company of Massachusetts Bay, and its legislature was to be composed of a governor, a deputy and thirteen assistants, elected every spring among the freemen of the colony. Past dis-

*Essex Institute*

OVERNOR SIMON BRADSTREET        GOVERNOR JOHN ENDECOTT

V. WILLIAM BENTLEY, D. D.        ROGER WILLIAMS
*useum*                                           *Essex Institute*

tinctions of wealth and rank were laid aside, and one and all united in a common purpose, to further a common good that had democracy for its guiding principle. A new political experiment, unknown to the Old World, was about to be carried out in the New.

## CHAPTER III

## LIFE IN OLD SALEM

THE Rev. Francis Higginson was so well impressed with what he found in the young settlement that he wrote home about it in glowing terms. The Company had no trouble finding passengers for its fleet which from now on plied regularly across the Atlantic. The land, the teeming waters, the Indians, the plants and animals, all were a source of wonder to the settlers, many of whom were city-bred and had never seen anything more primitive than the gentle English countryside.

"The grapes in this country are four inches about!" wrote one marveling Englishman. As for cherries, "I have never seen so many but in Kent!" exclaimed another.

In the sea banks, oysters and clams measured one foot in length. Lobsters weighed sometimes twenty pounds; but there was such abundance of excellent fish that, with clams and oysters, lobsters were fed to the pigs. But not by the hardworking Indian squaw who, according to the lively William Wood's *New Englands Prospect*,

> to the flats daunce many a winters Jigge,
> To dive for Cocles, and to digge for Clamms,
> Whereby her lazie husbands guts she cramms.

Often the hauls were so plentiful that the fish were more than the colonists knew what to do with. The In-

dians soon taught them. "In Virginia they never manure
their overworn fields," noted the observant John Smith,
"but in New England they do, striking at every plant
of corn a herring or two." The Pilgrims called it "fishing" the field.

Tall trees for spars and lumber grew thick in the forests, and as the Company sent sawyers and carpenters
to the New World, the cabins of round logs gave way
to houses of boards. Ships began to be built—first the
small rowboat, then the masted ship for coastwise sailing. From the Indians they learned that from the trunk
of birch trees they could make canoes so light that they
could be carried with ease for miles until they were
needed for crossing the rivers.

There grew everything that man could want for shelter, warmth—and light. Fish oil, since there was no tal-
low, was the chief fuel for the lamps. But a simpler candle
was provided by the pine tree. "They are such candles
as the Indians commonly use, having no other," Higginson informed his friends in the old country, "and they
are nothing else but the wood of the pine tree cloven
in two little slices, something thin, which are so full of
the moysture of turpentine and pitch, that they burne
as cleere as a torch. . . ." He sent along a few splices
of pine to prove it.

As the back lots began to be cultivated with seed and
grain imported from old England, the diet of the colonists gained in variety. Now with the "pumpions and
cowcumbers" that thrived with the native maize, they
had beans and peas, and even orchard fruit for dessert.
On Endecott Street, in Danvers, is still growing the pear
tree that Governor Endecott planted in his orchard more

than three hundred years ago. A gnarled patriarch, it still bears fruit, itself a vestige of that ancient hardihood that survives in many another monument not made with hands. The labor, however, had not been entirely one of love, for with shrewd forethought the good governor had sought worldly returns for his husbandry. Thus, in 1648 we find recorded that he sold five hundred apple trees from his nursery to William Trask, who considered them a bargain at the rate of an acre of land for every two trees.

At first the Company's court in London discouraged the cultivation of tobacco, except as a physic or for the comfort of old men, who were cautioned to indulge in it privately. However, the "drinking" of tobacco, as it was then called, had taken such a hold that the Indian weed was planted on a large scale, both for export and domestic use. Back of the old Planters' houses the fields were lush with the peculiar green of its leaves.

Many another plant was native to the soil of New England—adder's tongue, alexander, angelica, arsmart, catmint, cinkfoil, clotbur, dogstones, fussballs, pellamount, purcelane, Solomon's seal, speedwell, tormentile, woodwax—names that gladden the pages of John Josselyn, who set down his contemporaries' awakened sense of wonder in his *New England's Rarities Discovered*. For the first time, so long ago, was described that native harbinger of spring, that ear thrust out of the soil as if listening for its time—the humble skunkcabbage, for which Josselyn could find no name. Later, when he revisited the New World, he found another weed sprung up after the English had planted and kept cattle there—the plan-tain, which the Indian called "Englishman's foot," as if it were produced by their treading.

More than the works of nature, the red men both amazed and dismayed the settlers. From the earliest time, descriptions of them abounded in letters and journals. Some savages had been brought to Europe by Columbus, and Princess Pocahontas had walked the streets of London; but in their native woods, the Indians were always a surprise. Mr. Higginson did not fail to respond. With Puritan exactness he described them, commented on their ways of living, and ended with an astounding fashion note: "Their haire is generally blacke, and cut before, like our gentele women, and one lock longer than the rest, much like to our gentlemen, which fashion, I thinke, came hence into England." In his day, the Indian wore nothing but a loin cloth, and a beast's skin flung over his shoulder, much to the scandal of the Planters. Nothing availed to teach the savages better manners, however, for toward the end of the century John Holme declared with more wit than verse:

> What clothes they wear are quickly made,
> They do not help the tailors' trade.

Often at mealtime half a dozen or more Indians would come to the cottages and stand gravely near the kitchen door, saying not a word, though they accepted readily anything that was offered them. They spoke little as a rule and rarely laughed, showing the greatest regard for the man of few words. But they could be noisy enough at their games. After the hunt, while the squaws, who did all the hardest work, were preparing the common meal, groups of Indians would gather together and play *puim* with a bundle of short reeds which they shuffled and distributed like playing cards. Or they played at *hubbub* with five small painted dice on a wooden plate, which they laid on the ground in the middle of their circle and struck at intervals, making the pieces fly up into the air and change their position.

It was an exciting game. As their beady eyes followed the motions of the dice, they slapped their thighs, repeating as loudly as they could, "Hub, hub, hub, hub," so that their voices could be heard all over the settlement, making the women and children tremble with fear. For them, the Indians, with their painted faces and savage decorations, with their greased, foul-smelling bodies and incomprehensible grunts, were the sons of Satan to be kept at a distance, even though the Company advised friendly relations, that even they might be brought to the knowledge of God.

In their wigwam camps, the Indians had their own notions of the white man. Ever since the first had set foot on their continent, things had gone ill with them. Comets had flared in the sky and plagues had swept the land, as if their god of dread, Squantum, were punishing them for showing friendship to the invader. In vain they propitiated Ketan, their good god, with sacrifices after the harvest. In vain they tried to understand the mystery by sitting grimly during the religious services of the settlers. They were puzzled and mistrustful. But not so mistrustful as they were of the neighboring Indian tribes with whom they carried on a ceaseless war. Rather than fall to the mercy of the Tarrantines, the Agawams made friends of the white invaders.

And so the little town of Salem flourished, at peace

with the old Planters and on not too dangerous terms with the Indians, whom they took as their wards by enacting laws for the protection of their corn and land. Every boat from England brought new settlers, and every year saw new houses springing up on the town lots which Endecott awarded to each family, according to its needs.

Now and then a knotty problem presented itself, as when a maid arrived alone. At such times the governor and his selectmen would get together to disentangle it. Should the maid be allotted land and house to her own use, or should she be placed as a ward with a family until she found a husband? If she were not given land, like the rest of the settlers, other maids would be discouraged from crossing the ocean; and then what would marriage-able youths do for wives while the new generation came of age? After weighing advantages and disadvantages, Governor Endecott decided against the granting of land to single maids, as it would be "a bad president to keep hous alone." Instead, the maids consoled themselves as best they could with the award of a bushel of corn each.

How did the settlers live in those first few decades? Not too uncomfortably. The houses built near springs of clear water provided the housewives with one prime necessity; their husbands brought them fuel from the forests. In the kitchen, the principal room, iron or copper pans hung from nails over the hearth in which all the meals were prepared. Sometimes well-polished pieces of pewter stood on the mantel—bowls and ornate por-ringers brought with other precious treasures from Old England. There was also an occasional candlestick or two, but since candles were not generally in use till later, oil lamps lighted the evening meal at the plain boards set with wooden trenchers.

Homely forms took the place of chairs, which only the wealthy could afford to bring with them, and crates or roughly-made cradles stood by the fire for the new-born infant. Luxuries were unknown, though there was scarcely a house that did not own a large wooden chest, sometimes elaborately inlaid with woods of different kinds. It was the housewife's pride and the stronghold of her few treasures of linens and clothing. It had brought the household goods across the ocean, and it would descend, a precious heirloom, to the children born in the new country. Lovingly it was kept dusted and polished, and protected with a fringed cloth.

In the beginning, the family slept on blankets on the floor with only a sheet or a few garments hung between for privacy. Then beds began to be made—plain wooden frames strung across with cords and provided with trundles that fitted under them like a drawer. In these the children slept, on rough mattresses filled with straw, coarse wool and sometimes with the down of the cat-tails from the marshes. As the colonists exerted themselves and sent back to the Company shiploads of fish, timber, "silk grass" and sumac, they received in return articles which they sorely needed. Here and there a family owned a huge canopied bed, fitted with curtains and ruffled valances. Like the chest, such a bed was destined for futurity, and a solid heirloom it was, taking several men to move its separate pieces.

As a younger generation began to grow up, the people of Salem turned their minds to education. In 1636 the general court for the New England colonies made a grant of four hundred pounds to establish a college, and the people of Salem, with the rest, contributed their share. Yet, though Harvard College was thus established with their help in Cambridge, their own town had no provision whatever for a school. In the same year, when with pomp and solemnity the college was named for its chief benefactor, the Salem town recorder made an eloquent little note: "Yong Mr. Norris chose by this assemblie to teach skoole."

But there was no schoolhouse, and no money for the schoolmaster, the son of the Rev. Edward Norris. However, if Salem could afford to contribute toward a college, it could raise enough means to build a school. In those days, the want of currency was felt even at Harvard, where President Dunster's homespun scholars not infrequently paid their tuition in whatever their parents had to offer. One lad brought with him a "lyttell browne cow" and four bushels of barley malt for his first semester. Another, the son of a trader, went through his academic career on the boots and shoes which his father sent to the college steward. In the depression of the 1640's even paper money was at a premium, and not till twelve years later, when the General Court issued an order for minting a new coin, which came to be known as the pine-tree shilling, did the colony enjoy again the feel of silver.

Nevertheless, in Salem, a tiny schoolhouse was soon constructed for young Mr. Norris on a lot of land near Higginson Place. Early in the morning, soon after the town cowherd had gathered the kine together for the common pasture, the children of Salem with their faces new-washed and their hornbooks like little banners in their hands, would troop to school, where Mr. Norris greeted them at the door and saw that no dog or other animal was smuggled in to break the peace.

Schoolbooks were few—perhaps some tattered primer that had found its way across the Atlantic among the household possessions, or an old arithmetic copy book, carefully done by hand, or a well-worn psalmbook with black letters running irregularly across the pages and the margins stained where generations of thumbs had held down the place. Any book that had not the brand of the Church of England could be put to use for the improvement of the young. John Cotton's school catechism, *Spiritual Milk for Babes . . . drawn out of the Breasts of Both Testaments*, was to nourish and edify a later generation.

At first only the children of those who could afford to pay so much a year had the privilege of going to the town school. There was something not right in this, and the grave elders put their heads together. In 1644 the town voted that the school be made partially free—in other words, that those who could pay should continue to do so, but that "if any poore body hath children or a childe to be put to schoole and not able to pay for their schooling, that the Town will pay it by rate."

Several years before the building of the schoolhouse, another small wooden structure had been raised by the town on the corner of the present Washington and Essex streets, where it stood for nearly three hundred years. During the middle of the last century a heated controversy was carried on by a number of zealous antiquarians over the question of whether or not the building behind Plummer Hall contained the original frame of the first church. Nothing was definitely determined, but the consensus of opinion seemed to be that, though it may not be the original church, it is at least an accurate restoration.

In 1638, four years after the church was built, it was evidently found insufficient for the needs of the community, whereupon Governor Endecott, with a number of the town elders, ordered it to be enlarged. According to the specifications given to John Pickering, the carpenter, the building was twenty-five feet long, with a gallery, six windows, and a pair of stairs where the boys sat during the service, well within sight of the tithingman, who brooked no mischief. From its rude pulpit preached such men as Roger Williams and Hugh Peter.

Unlike the later churches of the Puritans, who seemed to hold the belief that the discomfort of the body uplifted the soul, an ample fireplace was provided for the comfort of the congregation—at least until 1677, whereafter, until fairly recently, it continued to be looked upon as a luxury and a sign that the generation had sunk to decay. How familiar to the ears of the ministers became the general knocking of feet toward the end of the sermon, when the congealing faithful brought life to their limbs in the only way they knew! Salemites of the last century could still recall the exhortations of the Rev. Dr. Hopkins, famous for his long sermons: "My hearers, have a little patience, and I will soon close."

In the beginning, following the Hebrew tradition, men and women sat apart in different sections of the church, with the places assigned according to the importance of the members. Many was the headache suffered by the selectmen whose duty it was to see that

Mrs. Hathorne and Mrs. Browne were seated next to the second Mrs. Endecott, and that the places of Mr. Hathorne and Mr. Corwin showed no undue distinction in the matter of inches! Respect for precedence had to be observed, especially when the town notables were given the liberty to erect family pews at their own expense.

With the building of the meetinghouse came the need for someone to keep it in good order; therefore a man was employed for fifty shillings a year to sweep it and ring the bell for the services. For ringing it at funerals he received three pence extra.

Deaths and burials became important events in the young town. They were the only excuse for the people's getting together socially, even if the occasion was not altogether joyful. Then the bier, which the town had provided, was taken out of the meetinghouse chimney, where it stood except during the winter months, and the corpse was carried to the burial ground, followed by friends and neighbors and also by the minister, though in the early days he did not officiate over the grave. Evidently there must have been a scuffle for prominent places near the bier, since the town had finally to decree: "Hereafter, when any corpse belonging to this town is to be interred . . . all persons, with the corpse, are to move and walk orderly. . . . If a man is buried, the men follow first; if a woman, the women first. No person shall presume to run or go before or abreast with the corpse or relations."

Stronger, perhaps, than the desire to be conspicuous on such a public occasion, was the eagerness to be first when the funeral gifts of gloves, rings, spices and wine were distributed, in observance of a custom so well established that the town itself went to the expense of providing liquor at the burial of a pauper. Mourning rings, which were sometimes of gold, with a carved or enameled death's head and the inscription *"Live to die,"* were given to friends and near relations, to be bequeathed in their wills with other valuable personal property. The attendants received gloves, and sometimes scarves. The wine, cider, ale and "hott waters," as occasion offered, were dispensed to the populace. Sometimes funerals were such lavish affairs, and so disturbing to the public peace, that laws were made to curb them, but without success. As late as 1736, when the wife of Governor Belcher was carried to the grave, more than a thousand pairs of gloves were given away.

The founders of God's commonwealth had no illusions about the innate goodness of man, knowing him vile, corrupt and full of sin; hence the Massachusetts Bay Company early extolled the efficacy of chastisement with the apothegm: "Correction is ordained for the fool's back as necessary as food and rayment." Whipping, therefore, was practiced as ordained.

For punishment that was more moral than physical, a pair of stocks was put up in the public square, where the culprit, sitting on a stool with his hands and feet passed through holes in the boards that fenced him like a horse in a paddock, suffered the jeers and scorn of the passers-by. In 1642, the pillory was erected for more serious offenders; and finally, in 1657, when the Quakers were becoming a menace, the whipping post. The selectmen decreed a payment of two shillings and sixpence to the constable for each person he whipped. He did not fare badly. *16765*

Besides, there was a system of fines imposed on men and women who disregarded the many sumptuary laws that established what every good Puritan should wear. Luxury, even if one could afford it, set one apart for condemnation; eccentricity would not be tolerated. Thus we find in the Salem records that John Gatchell was fined ten shillings for an offense, but "in case he shall cutt of his long hair of his head into a sevill frame in the meantime, shall have abated a shilling of his fine." In 1652 two women of the county were fined for wearing silks and tiffany, while Alice Flint, of Salem, was arraigned for succumbing to the vanity of a silk hood.

More and more often such citations appear, till one wonders whether good old cantankerous Nathanael Ward was not justified in the thunder he discharged on feminine heads in 1645. "To speak moderately (!) I truly confess it is beyond the ken of my understanding to conceive how those women should have any true grace or valuable virtue that have so little wit as to disfigure themselves with such exotic garbs as not only dismantles their native, lovely lustre, but transclouts (and this before Carlyle!) them into gaunt bar-geese, ill-shapen, shotten shell-fish, Egyptian hieroglyphics, or at the best into French flirts of pastry, which a proper English woman would scorn with her heels. It is no marvel they wear drails on the hinder part of their heads, having nothing, it seems, in the forepart, but a few squirrels' brains to help them frisk from one ill-favored fashion to another. . . ."

After such a storm what can a frail mortal woman do but take shelter in silence?

## CHAPTER IV

## THE PURITAN COMMONWEALTH

CHARLES I was riding high, yet it needed no prophet to see that he was vaulting toward a fall. With the royal expenditures mounting and the State coffers empty, it was obvious that something had to be done to keep the divine right undiminished. In the beginning of the seventeenth century the deficit of the State budget had reached three hundred thousand pounds; the government debts were three times as much again. And there was no money. As no system of permanent taxation had as yet been devised, the State tried all ways to replenish the royal stores. Titles, monopolies and government offices were sold to the highest bidders. But the money was no sooner gained than it was swallowed up by other expenditures, newer extravagances. The most lucrative source of income was the levying of a direct tax, like the poll tax, forced upon the entire population during the worst of the financial crisis.

As such a tax could not be imposed without the consent of Parliament, which would then grant the King what was known as a subsidy, the relations between the royal government and that restrictive body became strained, especially when the King's demands were not acceded to. The divine right, asserted by Laud for his Majesty, implied prerogatives greater than those of Parliament. Illegal taxes were at once extorted, new loans forced; and then, the better to carry out his absolute rule, the King declared his intention of governing without the help of Parliament. In 1629 that body was dissolved and the functions of government were vested in the Star Chamber and the High Commission Courts. Laud, then Bishop of London and virtually Primate of England, took over the power of the Church, while Strafford, undismayed by the assassination of his predecessor, Buckingham, aligned himself with despotism.

Free speech was muzzled. The Gate-House and Marshalsea teemed with prisoners, among them the brave Sir John Eliot who was to close his exemplary life in the Tower. Absolutism reigned.

Among those most affected were, of course, the Puritans, now that Parliament, which had opposed the King in the church question, could no longer be counted upon for help. It was no wonder that in the same year which saw the dissolution of Parliament, a group of wealthy and influential Puritans determined to leave England forever, to join their brothers in America. But they would not go on the old conditions. They had had enough of despotism at home, and required the assurance of self-government before they would take the step. They were no adventurers, like those to whom royal patents had been granted for personal profit, but men who demanded the right to shape their own lives on the highest moral and spiritual examples.

It was with some surprise, therefore, that the Massachusetts Bay Company read an interesting proposal, undersigned by twelve of the foremost Puritans at the university town of Cambridge, on August 26, 1629. Briefly, the twelve men, who included John Winthrop, Thomas Dudley, Richard Saltonstall and Isaac Johnson,

THE PORTRAICTUER OF CAPTAYNE IOHN SMITH ADMIRALL OF NEW ENGLAND.

Aetatis 37
A° 1616

These are the Lines that shew thy Face; but those
That shew thy Grace and Glory, brighter bee:
Thy Faire-Discoueries and Fowle-Overthrowes
Of Salvages, much Civilliz'd by thee
Best shew thy Spirit; and to it Glory Wyn;
So, thou art Brasse without, but Golde within.

agreed to transfer themselves and their families at their own expense to any port in the Plantation designated by the Company, "*provided* always, that . . . the whole Government, together with the patent for the said Plantation, be first, by an order of Court, *legally transferred and established to remain with us and others which shall inhabit upon the said Plantation.*"

It was a declaration of independence, and one that the Company had to take or leave. It decided to take it, and proceeded, accordingly, to elect a new administrative body of governor, deputy and assistants. John Winthrop, both for his integrity and sufficiency, was elected governor by unanimous vote for the term of a year; John Humfrey deputy-governor, while John Endecott, with seventeen others, comprised the Court of Assistants.

When Endecott learned of his demotion he did not complain. For a year he had been a faithful and energetic ruler of the little plantation, and it had managed to survive. As Governor he had been subordinate to the Company Court in London, following its instructions and taking no active step independently. In the new order he would be part of a more powerful body, with unlimited freedom of action and with the prospect of reward for good work at the annual elections. Most important of all, the commonwealth, which had as yet been but vaguely adumbrated, would stand out in the light of God's approval, for surely it was with the blessing of Providence that ship after ship came into Salem harbor, bringing within a year more than two thousand colonists in the wake of Winthrop.

"Salem, where we landed, pleased us not," Dudley

commented on leaving the *Arbella*, which had taken more than seventy days for the voyage. From the glowing reports of the country, he had been led to expect something more than a huddle of cottages as mean as kennels in comparison with the castles he had left behind, peopled by a few score men and women weakened by long months of privation and disease. In spite of the "good venison pasty and good beer" which, as Winthrop noted with some pleasure in his *Journal*, Endecott had made shift to provide for their welcoming, Dudley wondered whether he had done wisely in accepting the deputy-governorship which Humfrey had at the last moment declined.

John Winthrop, on the contrary, knew that he had been chosen for a mighty task, and that the Lord Himself had chosen him. In the narrow cabin of the *Arbella*, in the discomfort and danger of the voyage, he had made his Covenant with God and God had accepted. "We have taken out a commission," he concluded in his discourse, *A Model of Charity*. "The Lord hath given us leave to draw our own articles. . . . We have hereupon besought of Him favour and blessing. Now if the Lord shall please to hear us, and bring us in peace to the place we desire, then hath he ratified this Covenant and sealed our Commission, and will expect a strict performance of the articles contained in it." With the proof of God's acceptance in the safe arrival of the Puritan fleet, Winthrop could have no thought but to further the Covenant.

He was an intensely religious man. To him, his faith was shield and buckler, and also the comfort that helped him on in the face of adversity. As a youth he had been sent by his father to Trinity College, Cambridge, but he never took his degree, for at eighteen he fell in love with Mary Forth, the only daughter of a wealthy squire, and married her. For some years he lived with his wife's family at Great Stanbridge, Essex, preparing himself for the law, which in time he began to practice. Then suddenly his wife died, leaving him, at the age of twenty-eight, a widower with six children. (Little did he know that the first-born was to become the Governor of Connecticut, besides distinguishing himself as one of New England's pioneer scientists.)

In time he married again, but hardly a year passed when his second wife was buried with her still-born child. This added bereavement, following so close upon the first, plunged him into a deep dejection. God was punishing him; he had no doubt of it. With melancholy foreboding, he began to inquire into his religious state and seriously contemplated abandoning law in favor of the pulpit. His father dissuaded him. For three years, nevertheless, he studied divinity and kept a record of his religious experiences, purging himself of the worldliness that had moved God's hand against him.

In 1618 he married Margaret, the daughter of Sir John Tyndal. He was at peace with God once more, but the world distressed him. Everywhere he saw evil in the declining times, and was certain that the sinfulness of his fellowmen would bring down a heavy scourge and judgment. "My dear wife," he wrote to Margaret, when with the others at Cambridge he was contemplating going to America, "I am verily persuaded God will bring some heavy affliction upon this land, and that speedily: but be of good comfort. . . . If the Lord seeth it will be good for us, he will provide a shelter and a hiding place for us and others."

Now, in the middle of June, 1630, he and the chosen of God found themselves in the place appointed for the establishment of the Puritan theocracy. It was not to be Salem, however; Salem was only the cornerstone. Thus, the same week of his landing, Winthrop recorded in his *Journal*: "We went to Massachusetts to find out a place for our sitting down."

The previous year a house had been built at what is now Charlestown, in Massachusetts, and it is here that Winthrop, with Dudley, Isaac Johnson and a number of the other patentees, decided to settle. Within a few weeks, houses, booths and tents were set up on Town Hill by the people who had followed them. But not for long. Want of water made a permanent settlement at Charlestown impossible. By the 17th of September, 1630, the colony had migrated to the neighboring peninsula. Other cottages were again erected, and by order of the Court of Assistants, with Governor Winthrop presiding, it was decided that the town be called Boston in memory of St. Botolph's in Lincolnshire, whose noble church tower was now a memory to the transplanted Puritans.

They had already a church of their own, one of which as yet not a stone had been raised, but which in solemn covenant they had founded on a spiritual base more enduring than granite. So far the First Church of Boston was but a written sheet, signed by Winthrop, Isaac Johnson, John Wilson, Thomas Dudley and others who, "being by his most wise and good providence brought together in this part of America, in the Bay of Massachusetts; and desirous to unite into one congregation or church, under the Lord Jesus Christ, our head, into such sort as becometh all those whom he hath redeemed, and sanctified to himself, do hereby solemnly and religiously, as in his most holy presence, promise to bind ourselves to walk in all our ways according to the rule of the Gospel, and in all sincere conformity to his holy ordinances, and in mutual love and respect to each other, so near as God shall give us grace."

The covenant was not only for the town of Boston, but for all the plantations covered by the Charter of the Massachusetts Bay Company. The theocracy was at last established. It had its body of laws, incorporated in the Charter and, more important, its guide in the Old Testament as read and interpreted by the Puritan elders. The commonwealth must be governed by God's people in church covenant.

Although to the founding fathers such a commonwealth was the only one possible, when, in the years that followed, they put their laws into practice, they unwittingly sowed the seeds of the very intolerance which they had come to America to escape. First of all, full civil rights were granted only to church members. They alone, after owning their covenant, were accepted as *freemen* and enjoyed the franchise. Logically, it seemed the most equitable procedure. Not rank, not worldly possessions, gave one a voice in the theocracy, but a whole-hearted belief in the principles on which it was founded. Thus the Puritan church and the Puritan state became united, with the elders forming a spiritual house of peers in the law-making body. Nothing was done, nothing decided, till the reverend elders had set their seal of approval upon it, they being the fittest transmitters for the will of the Almighty.

It is not hard to see the pitfalls to which such absolute power might lead, and the injustices that the condition of the franchise could not avoid. Since civil rights were the privilege of church members alone, there arose from the beginning a disfranchised class not necessarily made up of undesirable elements. Often honorable and conscientious reasons kept upright persons from putting themselves forward before the congregation to declare that they had now attained the conviction which would henceforth make them worthy freemen. Again, since the children of the disfranchised could not be baptized, there grew up in time a new generation of men who had no place in the government. The democratic foundation was early undermined,—though democracy as the ultimate good was far from being sanctioned by the early elders. John Cotton, who soon left the pulpit of St. Botolph's to become the Solon of the Puritan theocracy, could therefore write without fear of contradiction: "Democracy I do not conceive that God ever did ordain as a fit government either for church or commonwealth."

Happily the leveling of distinctions in the new environment, where master and servant were exposed to the same hardships, the same labors, to achieve the bare means of existence, brought about the growth of the democratic spirit, in spite of the resistance of some few. How could it have been otherwise? Everything in the virgin country, the feeling of interdependence under unforeseen conditions, the distance from the homes they had abandoned forever, the common perils and the common needs, and again the sense of their divine election, bound them more than any artificial rule. "God sifted a whole nation that he might send a choice grain over into this wilderness," Stoughton was to declare in a later day. The growth of that grain must not be impeded.

## CHAPTER V

## *HERESIES*

H ARDLY had the choice grain been planted in the wilderness, when unforeseen dangers began to threaten it on every hand. Francis Higginson, the first pastor of the flock in Salem, survived the rigors of the climate only long enough to welcome the new governor, and then made his peace with God. A few days later, the wife of Isaac Johnson, the beautiful and virtuous Lady Arbella, after whom the ship that brought her had been named, was laid in the lonely bluff of Burying Point. Heartbroken, her husband followed Governor Winthrop, but scarcely lived to see the founding of Boston; he, too, was buried in the soil that should have seen the growth of his seed. "He died in sweet peace," wrote Governor Winthrop, "leaving some part of his substance to the colony."

Disease and death were not the only enemies. As the colony grew and more people were encouraged to try their fortunes in the New World, men and women began to appear who, although dissenters from the Church of England, were far from holding the Puritan concept of the choice grain. Such immigrants were to be expected, and the governing Puritans were prepared for them. Their commonwealth saw to it that only freemen comprised it; the rest gained admittance to its privileges by courtesy. If any proved undesirable, there were ways, authorized by the Charter as interpreted by magistrate and elder, to render them innocuous.

Punishment might be applied first. If mischief-makers, lawbreakers and otherwise unruly persons persisted in stirring up trouble, the Charter could be called upon for the severest measures. One clause was explicit: "It shall and may be lawful to and for the chief commanders, governors etc. of the said company, resident in the said part of New England, for their special defence and safety, to incounter, expulse, repell and resist by force of arms, as well by sea as by land, and by all fitting ways and means whatsoever, all such person and persons as shall at any time hereafter attempt or enterprise the destruction, invasion, detriment, or annoyance to the said plantation or inhabitants." Loosely interpreted, it authorized a dangerous assumption of power which was to stain with blood the annals of that first century in New England.

Among the passengers who landed at Nantasket from the *Lion* in February, 1631, bringing direly needed provisions for Governor Winthrop's people, was a man hardly entered into his thirties. The arrival of the *Lion* had preceded by a day the time set for a fast, which turned to thanksgiving as sails were discerned in the horizon; but it was not with thanksgiving that the elders of Boston, in later years, looked back on the landing of Roger Williams. He was known for a conscientious and upright man of God, yet it was this very rectitude that, as time went on, made the reverend elders exercise the Charter clause to the limit of its severity.

Roger Williams had spent his childhood near Cocklane, famous for its ghost, in the neighborhood of Smithfield market, where John Rogers, the religious martyr, was burned at the stake. In the parish of St. Sepulchre, Williams had received his early education, and later at

Cambridge, where his father, a merchant tailor, had been able to send him with the help of a scholarship. The young man had a quick but literal mind, that suffered no deviation from what he conceived to be right. There were no two ways for him. Either a thing was so, or it was not so. If it was as he believed it to be in the sincerity of his mind and conscience, not even the fate of John Rogers would have swerved his belief. He had the long-suffering patience of a martyr. In vain would opposition knock its head at the rock of his endurance.

It was not long before the reverend elders of Boston realized that here was more than a match for their Puritan austerity. The man had not been sent for. He had come independently and without any special mission from the Massachusetts Bay Company, yet he presumed to advance opinions which might lead to mischief. In an ill hour, after his arrival, the church members of Boston invited him to become their teacher. No sooner had the proposal been made, than a cataclysm broke over their heads. Williams accepted, but he could not conscientiously consent to fill the post unless the congregation renounced communion with the Church of England, after a public declaration of their repentance for having had anything to do with its worship while in the old country. Quite understandably, the elders refused, seeing no virtue in antagonizing an institution from which they had broken away.

Williams thereupon went to Plymouth, where he was welcomed by Governor Bradford. For more than a year he preached vivid, apocalyptic sermons, rousing the people to righteousness and winning a number of devout adherents. However, as Governor Bradford wrote, Williams "began to fall into some strange opinions, and from opinions to practice." Plymouth became too small for him. Following a controversy with the church, he left abruptly and made his way to Salem, which, soon after Higginson's death, had invited him to take his place. At this time, Winthrop had vetoed Endecott's appointment of Williams, and had reproved him for acting without authority. Now, however, no objections were raised by the Council, and Williams was suffered to preach before the people of Salem, though in no official capacity. The Puritans knew better than to invest with office a man who, as Cotton Mather deplored later, had a windmill in his head.

Indeed, Williams revolved ideas with the speed of the wind. No sooner was there a lull than he was sure to raise a tempest with some opinion that shocked for its singularity and branded him, in the eyes of elder and magistrate, as unsettled in judgment. For example, he held that a magistrate ought not to punish a person for breaking the First Commandment if the breach did not disturb the civil peace; that he ought not tender an oath to an unregenerate man; that no man should pray with the unregenerate, though wife or child; and finally, that one should not give thanks after the sacrament, nor after meals. Any thinking man could see which way Williams was going. The next step would be Anabaptism—the heresy which maintained that infant baptism was unscriptural and therefore invalid for the adult man, who must be rebaptized as a sign of his Christian profession.

In the light of our day, and with the knowledge of Roger Williams' later life, he emerges as a man far in advance of his times. To the Puritans he was a puzzlement and a thorn, especially when out of a clear sky, and when he seemed to be getting on peaceably in Salem, he sent the Governor and Council a writ full of heresy and sedition. At least that is how it was interpreted. How else could one read a paper that disputed the colonists' rights to the land in America because the grant from the King conferred no title, as the Indians were its rightful owners; and that imputed to King James a "solemn public lie" because in his patent he blessed God that he was the first Christian prince to discover this land?

In December, 1633, the Governor and his assistants met in Boston, together with the elders, to determine upon the punishment of Williams. Leniency won, when Endecott pleaded for the man whose mind exerted a fascination upon his own. The culprit was ordered to appear before the court for censure. Obediently Williams presented himself and gave satisfaction of his penitence. Alas, not for long! In a few months the courts were again busy with him. Once more he was defending the rights of the Indians to the land. Among other absurdities, he was advocating veils for the women of Salem, a practice which so infuriated the Rev. Cotton of Boston that he made the tiresome journey to the center of confusion, preaching to such effect that the women soon put off that emblem of corruption.

Williams' other errors were not so easily corrected. In exasperation, the Governor summoned him to reappear before the General Court on the charge of propounding dangerous opinions against the authority of the magistrates. After a lengthy procedure, he was banished from within its jurisdiction, and given six weeks in which to leave the colony. Williams made the most of his time, preaching and spreading his beliefs until word of his defiance reached the government seat in Boston. Not only had the rebel not been silenced, but he had converted more than twenty men who were ready to follow him to banishment and establish a plantation about Narragansett Bay.

The government could not allow it. From that center the heresy would spread, and who knows who might not be contaminated! A warrant was dispatched for Williams to betake himself at once to Boston, and when he did not come, Captain Underhill was ordered to apprehend him. Now, Captain John Underhill, in spite of his splendid service in his military capacity, was a sad reprobate, over whom the men of Boston had often had to shake their heads. There was even a suspicion of heresy about him, more than justified when, upon his being surprised in gross immorality, he excused himself to the gentle Governor Winthrop, saying, "The Spirit had sent in to me the witness of Free Grace while I was in the moderate enjoyment of the creature called tobacco."

Whether by chance or on purpose, when Captain Underhill and his soldiers called at Williams' house, they found he had been gone three days. Empty-handed, they returned to Boston with no information save that nobody knew whither the bird had flown. Massasoit, the Indian chieftain, could have told them. One night in the bitter cold and the deep snow, a man trembling with fever had staggered toward his wigwam with only a compass to guide him through the untracked forests. For three months Roger Williams remained with the Indians till he was nursed back to health. He had long been their friend, and they trusted him. When finally he was strong enough to go on his way, Canonicus and Miantinomo, the chief sachems of Narragansett, gave him a tract of land in what is now Providence, Rhode Island, and there, with the men of Salem who had promised to follow him, he founded his settlement and his church on Baptist principles.

Roger Williams was not the first to fly to Rhode Island from Puritan intolerance. In 1634 William Blackstone had preceded him for no other reason than that in Boston, where he had lived before its founding, trading with the Indians and cultivating his garden, he had grown as weary of the "lord brethren" as he had been of the "lord bishops" in the old country. He was no religious innovator, unlike many of those who were to come after, but simply a bookish recluse who would not suffer the intellectual atmosphere of his seclusion to be permeated by the fire and brimstone of Puritan disputation. Rhode Island offered him what he sought and there he built his estate, Study Hill, undismayed by the fact that he was the only white inhabitant. The Indians, he knew, were less disturbing than the worthies he had left behind. In study, and in the tending of his orchard, he lived to a ripe old age, leaving to future days his name in the still cultivated Blackstone apple.

Yet, from their point of view, the Puritans were only doing what was right in ridding their commonwealth of dangerous and undesirable elements. Intolerance? It was merely a measure of self-defense, of protecting their infant republic from the failure that was sure to follow if the ancient enemy in a new form were given freedom of action. They had abandoned everything, exposed themselves and all they held dear to the perils of an unknown future in an unfriendly wilderness. With success almost assured, they could not suffer it to be endangered by a band of heretics and visionaries who had nothing to lose but the liberty of wandering about the Massachusetts Bay territory. The land outside of the Puritan jurisdiction offered freedom enough for them and their heresies.

As it was, even the best men among the Puritans were beginning to succumb to the spreading infection. Under the spell of Roger Williams, Endecott, inflamed by the heretic's ideas, had gone so far as to tear out with his sword the red St. George's cross from the corner of the British ensign. The Pope, Endecott defended himself, had given it to the King of England as an emblem of victory, and since the banner was a superstitious thing of the Antichrist, neither he nor the conscientious men of Salem could recognize its authority.

The voice was the voice of Endecott, but the words were the words of Williams. Seeing in Endecott's action a possible construction of treason in England, the court called him to trial and penalized him by depriving him of public office for a year. He was tried during the administration of Governor Thomas Dudley, a champion of intolerance; hence the heaviness of the stroke.

More heavily still it fell upon the sects and factions that shortly after the banishment of Williams converted the colony into a seething caldron of dissension. It almost looked as if Satan had turned loose his hordes to try the patience of the magistrates. First came the trial of Samuel Gorton, who left his tailor shop in London to fill New England with his "damnable heresies," derived from David George of Delft, who called himself the

Messiah and his followers the Family of Love. Gorton was put in irons, condemned to hard labor, whipped and banished from plantation to plantation; yet he always reappeared, until the magistrates looked upon this unregenerate Familist as the incarnation of the Devil. He finally found fertile soil for his Familism in Rhode Island, where he established the Gorton sect, which flourished for more than a century.

Mrs. Anne Hutchinson's, however, was the name that to the Puritans spelled the heresy of heresies,—Antinomianism, the belief that a covenant of faith need not concern itself with a covenant of works. More broadly interpreted, Antinomianism involved the assurance that one in a state of grace need not observe scrupulous fidelity of conduct, since what one *was*, rather than what one *did*, established the measure of salvation. To the Puritans such a creed associated itself with indulgence and licentiousness, immorality and execrable practices, and must therefore be exterminated root and branch.

Mrs. Hutchinson had come to New England in the wake of John Cotton, John Wheelwright and other ministers whose exodus from England had made George Herbert write:

> Religion stands on tip-toe in our land,
> Ready to pass to the American strand.

She had been an admirer of both men, who had quickened her religious nature to such a degree that she could expound the faith with the ablest of theologians.

On board ship she had drawn men and women together, talking to them by the hour till some, understanding her less than others, began to be scandalized by her "peculiar opinions." The noise of them preceded her to Boston, where the Governor was immediately put on his guard against her. However, she made herself so useful to the women with her knowledge of medicine and midwifery, that she soon gathered about her a large following with whom she used to discuss points of doctrine at meetings, which were held twice a week. The gatherings were sometimes so large that there was no room for all the faithful who came to listen to her. The magistrates took alarm, especially when she was heard to defend faith against works—a doctrine which might easily make the unwary run to error and extravagance. She was put under arrest and brought to trial before a full court in November of 1637.

What though Mrs. Hutchinson was a woman of spotless character and praiseworthy life? None showed her any consideration for her virtues. What though she was known for her countless services to the sick and poor of her neighborhood? None was suffered to come to her assistance. She had an alert mind and a ready tongue, quick to the defense of her faith and to the censure of what she thought Puritan bigotry. For this, and for the fact that she often confounded the judges with her apt quotations from Scripture, they could not forgive her. The sentence was passed. With her children she was banished from her home, while a number of her supporters were disfranchised and many others disarmed, ostensibly to prevent a concerted attack on the governing body. A few of Mrs. Hutchinson's followers in Boston recanted, but of her Salem converts none was known to make a show of repentance.

In the brief time allowed her, Anne Hutchinson carried her Antinomianism to another colony and ended tragically in an Indian massacre from which only one of her daughters escaped. To Thomas Dudley, most rabid of heresy hunters, as to many another of his mold, her end was looked upon as an act of God. Tolerance to him was weakness, a conviction which he held to the day of his death, when a few verses, by his or other hands, were found in his pocket.

Let men of God in courts and churches watch,

he warned as from the grave,

> O'er those as do a toleration hatch,
> Lest that ill egg bring forth a cockatrice
> To poison all with heresy and vice.

## CHAPTER VI

# THE INDIAN AROUSED

I T IS said that the first Indian who saw the first white man descend from his winged ship, began by running away. Better for him, perhaps, if he had fled with his tribes across the vast spaces, and left the new arrival to the uncontested possession of the land. A race might have been saved, and the conscience of future generations left untroubled.

However much the Puritan colonists differed from the ruthless Spanish invaders of the American continent, they had one thing in common—the conviction that as Christians and men of God they had priority over the heathen. The Indian's land and goods belonged to them— even his very life, if it came to a choice between Christian welfare and savage rights. Hence the Spanish Romanist raised his cross-hilted sword in the tropical American islands, forcing conversions with its blade of steel; while the Protestant, more reasonable, had the Indian plead upon the seal of the Charter: "Come over and help us."

Unhappily, the Indian preferred to worship his own gods, and looked with horror upon the white man's deity who permitted the wiping out of whole tribes under the ensign of the conquistadores: "Conversion or death!" To the invader, one thing alone was clear: there was no room in the New World, however large, for both civilization and barbarism. One had to yield, and the early conquerors saw to it that they had the upper hand.

First the conquered lands were plundered, and then the people subjected to slavery. Thousands of natives—men, women and children—were taken from their homes and brought to other colonies to be sold into bondage. On Camango Island of the West Indian archipelago, a Spanish captain, Pedro le Caliz, took four thousand natives whom he sought to transfer to the port of Cumann. Most of them died on the way from grief and hunger. Others, weighed down by the iron chains on their necks, arms and ankles, could barely stand on their feet. Whenever one or another of the poor wretches loitered behind, the Spanish soldiers, fearing an attack from the rear, ran their swords through them and left them to die on the wayside. It was in the beginning of the sixteenth century that the first Spaniards planted their cross in Jamaica; in fifty years the whole native population had disappeared. In Columbus' Hispaniola there were more than sixty thousand Indians at the time of its conquest. In 1548, only five hundred of them remained. Heathen life was cheap, so cheap that the conquerors were eventually faced with the problem of not having enough native slave labor for their colonies.

Though the English explorers were less cruel, they did enough, by their own report, to shatter the trust of the Indians. Again and again the chronicles tell of kindness received from the Indians, of stranded white men fed and nursed by the savages, whom they rewarded by luring to their ships and then selling to slavery. It is no wonder the red men were compelled to reciprocate with unmentionable atrocities in the exasperation of their primitive sense of justice.

On the arrival of the Puritans in New England a native

population of about thirty thousand was scattered in tribal settlements throughout the territory. The great plague that for three years had swept the coast had killed off a still larger number. For the first few years of the settlement, the colonists would find amid the rags of wigwams and the rotting palisades, heaps of skulls and unburied bones that told the tale of whole families wiped out. Fortunately, the survivors showed themselves friendly to the white settlers.

In spite of the Charter plea, very little was done at first toward the conversion of the Indians. The colonists had too much to do conquering the wilderness and taking care of the devils of dissentience that sprang up in their own midst. As for the Indians, they were satisfied to be let alone, harassed as they were by constant warfare among themselves for the possession of cornfield and hunting ground. To keep on friendly terms with the white invader, therefore, they readily signed away thousands of acres of land for a few trinkets. So far as they were concerned, signing a deed to the colonists meant that they were willing to let the white folk share the land equally with themselves. What was their dismay on seeing their corn land fenced in and themselves shut off from something which, by all the laws they knew, belonged to them!

Gradually their friendliness grew to mistrust, and their mistrust to hate of the white men who had come to dispossess them. As boat followed boat, bringing greater numbers of the people whom they now recognized as the enemy, they were roused to a desperate resistance. But what were their disunited tribes and their bows and arrows against the steel and firearms of the civilized conqueror? They resorted to the terrorizing strategy of the wilderness. Now and again a Puritan who had penetrated the forest returned no more, struck to the heart by an invisible hunter. Children sleeping in garrets would wake up at a sudden cry of "Fire!" to see the thatched roof in a blaze kindled by a flame-tipped arrow in the dark.

No one could travel beyond the borders of the settlement without coming back with hair-raising accounts of the red men's inhumanity. Along the Connecticut River some Englishmen found the quartered bodies of two of their fellows hanging from the trees. The Indians had slain them. Again, Captain John Tilley, who had been fowling in a canoe, was captured by some members of the Pequot tribe. With ingenious cruelty they cut off his hands and feet, and while he lingered for days under the torture, taunted him for his fortitude. Nobody was safe. Men slept with their guns beside them, and the women slept not at all, listening in the night for the cry that warned of danger.

In 1636 conditions had reached a crisis. Two years earlier the Pilgrims, who found the valley of the Connecticut a suitable place for a plantation, had gone there to settle near the mouth of the river, in the heart of the Pequot Indian territory. A number of Puritans from Dorchester and Newtown soon joined them, emboldened by the fact that the Pequots, a dreaded warlike tribe which had made tributaries of the Mohegans, had been greatly weakened by a raging disease. But the Pequots had no intention of surrendering meadow and woodland, even though the newcomers tried to win them over by fair means.

The usual ambuscades and reprisals followed. In the spring of 1636 John Oldham, a prominent planter of Watertown, was barbarously murdered by some Indians of Block Island. Immediately the Governor and Council of Massachusetts Bay met to advise on the course of action, and it was decided to send out a military expedition against the Block Island Indians. John Endecott was placed in command of ninety volunteers, with instructions to take possession of the island and to kill all the men, but to spare the women and children. From there, they were to proceed on a punitive mission to the Pequot territory.

When Endecott and his men left their three pinnaces off Block Island, they found two native settlements of about sixty wigwams. It was the month of August. In the acres the corn was just being harvested and heaps of it were yellowing in the sun. There was not an Indian to be seen, although on their landing some forty arrows had greeted the men from behind the trees. After looking vainly for Indians to fight, the party set fire to the wigwams and the corn, and destroyed the canoes which they found on the shores. Then they proceeded to the Pequot country. Here, after futile parleying, a skirmish ensued during which thirteen of the Pequots were killed and forty wounded. Again Endecott's soldiers fired the wigwams and burned the corn, and then set off for Boston, where they arrived without the loss of a man.

The Pequots plotted revenge. Their land had been taken from them, their homes destroyed, their harvest ruined and the bravest of their warriors slain. It was life or death for them in any event. They determined not to yield without making the white man pay. That winter no one was safe in the settlement. With appalling frequency, bodies were found mutilated in ways that told how bitter and lasting must have been the agony of death.

Then, in the spring of 1637, the Pequots made a mass attack upon the men and women as they were working in the fields, slaying a great number and vowing to exterminate them one and all. Even at the fort built at the mouth of the river, they took their stand with their bows and long shafts, challenging the white man to a struggle to the death. A messenger was sent to Boston to tell of the disaster. Something drastic had to be done, and quickly.

Smarting under the recent lesson of a massacre in Virginia that had wiped out a whole settlement, young Governor Vane, who had just been elected to office, authorized another punitive expedition, headed by William Trask and Richard Davenport, both of Salem. Plymouth was also approached to join the war against the Pequots, whereupon Governor Bradford of the Pilgrims provided a ship and fifty soldiers. The Narragansetts too, anxious to subdue a rival tribe, joined forces with the white men. Together Puritans, Pilgrims and Indians proceeded against the common enemy. In Boston the General Court appointed a fast day to propitiate the Lord.

In May of that year the Pequots stormed the fort at Saybrook, but by June the Puritan churches were already celebrating days of thanksgiving for the victory of their soldiers. Still, the war was not yet over, for the enemy was vengeful and determined. Both sides, however, were matched in their cruelty. It was not for nothing that the white men had had their experience of savage warfare;

they had learned their lesson. Against the children of the Devil there was but one way to proceed—with the Devil's own methods. Hence Governor Bradford could write of the burning of the Indian fort by the Christian soldiers: "More of the Indians were burnt to death than was otherwise slain. It burnt their bowstrings and made them unserviceable. Those that scaped the fire were slain with the sword; some hewed to pieces, others run through with their rapiers, so as they were quickly dispatched, and very few escaped."

That night over four hundred Pequot men, women and children perished in the burning fort. The soldiers had come to kill, and kill they did without mercy, for they felt none. As their frail wigwams burst into flame, the naked Indians, roused from their sleep, staggered in a frenzy of terror to their enclosure, only to be met with the lead and steel of the infuriated Puritans. Many in their despair to escape were impaled on their palisades, and there they writhed till fire or a merciful sword put an end to their torture.

"It was a fearful sight to see them thus frying in the fire," Bradford continues, "and the streams of blood quenching the same, and horrible was the stink and scent thereof. But the victory seemed a sweet sacrifice, and they gave the praise thereof to God, who had wrought so wonderfully for them, thus to inclose their enemies in their hands and give them so speedy a victory over so proud and insulting an enemy." None felt pity for the wretched race. They were enemies of the Puritans, enemies of God, and therefore to be destroyed.

"Thus was God seen in the Mount, crushing his proud

enemies!" cried the Puritan captain, John Mason, at the sight of his handiwork.

Altogether more than seven hundred Pequots suffered a terrible death in the expedition, while many were wounded, dispersed or taken captive. In all parts of the New England territory Indian tribes, cowed by the bloody victory, shrank farther and farther into the forest, pushed back from their fertile valleys by the guns of the white men. They had done no wrong. Their only crime had been to defend from the usurper their simple life, their gods and their laws, found good by generations of their wise chieftains. They understood nothing of the white man's rights and the white man's God. They demanded only the right to live as their ancestors had lived before them.

Civilization would not tolerate it.

That summer of 1637 the ship *Desire*, which had been built at Marblehead the previous year, set out under the command of Captain William Pierce with a sad cargo of fifteen Pequot boys and two women, all to be sold into slavery or exchanged for other merchandise at Bermuda. The rest of the captives had been scattered in the settlements, the victors dividing the spoils.

Before the *Desire* put to sea, a strange letter with a request and an odd scruple of conscience came to Governor Winthrop from the Rev. Hugh Peter of Salem. "We have heard of a dividence of women and children in the Bay," he began, referring to the Pequot captives, "and would be glad of a share viz. a young woman or girl and a boy if you think good." But there was a problem: what of the corn in the Pequot lands? What was to be done about it? They, the Puritans, could not rightfully seize it. The Rev. Peter voiced his misgivings. It was best, he advised, that it be cut down or left to the Narragansetts, "for we fear it will prove a snare thus to hunt after their goods whilst we come forth pretending only the doing of justice."

Alas, that justice had many consequences in bloody struggles and appalling catastrophes. One was to come with the uprising of King Philip, the son of Massasoit. The other loomed centuries away, although an unsuspected cause came on the return of the *Desire* the following February, when together with her cargo of cotton, tobacco and salt, she brought from Tortugas a number of Negro slaves. Samuel Maverick of Noddle's Island purchased three; the rest were acquired by other planters.

Slave-trading found little encouragement at first in New England, although the bondservant had begun by being almost a cornerstone of the new society. The conditions of life in the wilderness discouraged too great a separation of class. The Puritan might insist upon the leather uniform for his servant, but he could not keep his own gloved hands from handling the spade in the need for manual labor. Hardship had a way of leveling all disparity. The records show that on the arrival of Winthrop to the plantation, nearly two hundred bondservants were emancipated—not from any humane consideration, but simply because their masters could not afford to keep them.

Indeed, there came a time when servants were hard to get and still harder to maintain, in the scarcity of money resulting from the unsteady government in England. A sense of his own importance grew in the mind of the underling, an as yet inarticulate yearning for freedom

which told him that by the laws of nature he was born
no less free than his master. With perhaps less amusement than disapproval, Governor Winthrop found place
for an anecdote in his *Journal*.

A man who had been forced to sell a pair of oxen to
pay his servant's wages dismissed him, saying that he did
not know how to pay him next year. "The servant answered, he would serve him for more of his cattle. 'But
how shall I do,' saith the master, 'when all my cattle
are gone?' The servant replied, 'You shall then serve me,
and you may have your cattle again.' " He was probably
whipped for his insolence, but his rejoinder adorns a tale
of deeper meaning than he knew.

Nevertheless it was the common practice for captives
of war to be sold into slavery. The government of Salem
went even farther in its inclusion when, surely from different motives, it enacted in 1641: "There shall never be
any bond slaverie, villinage or captivitie amongst us, unless it be lawful captives taken in just warres, and such
strangers as willingly selle themselves or are sold to us."
Four years later, when a ship came to Massachusetts Bay
with an importation of Negro slaves from Africa, so
strong a protest was made to the Court by Richard Saltonstall that the shipment was ordered back.

The Indians received no such lenity. The Pequots
were sold into bondage, and after them the prisoners of
King Philip's War, in spite of the pleas of such apostles
as John Eliot. "To sell souls for money seemeth to me a
dangerous merchandise," he exhorted. "If they deserve to
die, it is far better to be put to death. . . ." Unheeded
his prayer, unheeded his warning that such harshness
would only mean a prolongation of hostilities. Against

him were upholders of Old Testament austerity like Cotton Mather, who wrote of the Indians: "These doleful creatures are the veriest ruins of mankind. One might see among them what a hard master the Devil is to the most devoted of his vassals." Their removal alone would guarantee safety to the theocracy.

After the last disastrous conflict with the Indians, the record books of the General Court of Massachusetts were black with the tariff of bounties offered for the scalps of red men taken by surprise or slain in any way by the colonists. As late as 1785, on the walls of the old Town House of Salem still hung, shriveled and dusty, a number of those frightful trophies, which were buried by the town boys when the building was torn down that year. But by that time the Indians were no longer dangerous.

## CHAPTER VII

## THE QUAKERS

ON MAY 14, 1685, the General Court met to appoint a public day of humiliation throughout the colonies of Massachusetts Bay. Those were trying times. In England the Revolution had been followed by the Commonwealth, but with no truce to the internecine wrangles of both Church and State. At every street turning fanatics and Fifth Monarchy men set up their tabernacles, crying out strange gospels that filled the world with the gloom of their prophesying. The Church rocked on its foundations, the trembling reaching the New England Congregationalists, who stood grimly by their meetinghouses daring the heretics to do their worst.

For some years, but for a few calamities and visitations of the Lord, things had been comparatively quiet in New England, as quiet as the land itself after the fearful quaking of 1638 that had shaken the earth as with a rumbling of unseen wheels and made the ships lying in the harbor bob like corks in the boiling sea. The Indians and the Antinomians had been suppressed, the first by force of arms, the others by the will of the majority exercised through the law. The people were more united.

In 1643, the year before Salem was appointed the shire-town of the newly-made Essex County, the New England Confederacy had been formed to bind the various colonies in mutual support against the encroachments of foreigners like the Dutch in New York, and against the possible reawakening of the Indians' fury. Rhode Island, for obvious reasons, was excluded.

"Concerning the Islanders," Governor Bradford wrote candidly to the Governor of Massachusetts, "we have no conversing with them, nor desire to have, further than necessity or humanity may require."

Meanwhile a new generation of native-born New Englanders had come to manhood, and many of the old had been laid in the burying grounds with rough stones to mark their graves, over which the town cows were turned out to pasture in the thrifty providence of the Puritans. It was only at the death of Governor Winthrop that any variance marked the austere progress to the grave, when a quantity of precious powder was shot off as a final tribute to a wise and courageous leader. Governor Winthrop died in 1649, from a cold which was followed by a fever. As he lay on his deathbed, surrounded by the elders whom he had summoned to pray for him, Deputy-Governor Dudley came in with an order for the banishment of a heretic which required Winthrop's signature. The dying man turned away from Dudley's insistence. "I have done too much of that work already," he said.

Little did the good man know that the worst had yet to follow—in trials, persecutions and death. At any rate, the New Englanders were prepared for trouble when, in the summer of 1656, even as they were observing their day of humiliation, a ship was drawing into Boston harbor bearing two female missionaries of the detested Quaker sect.

Some eight years earlier George Fox, the son of a weaver in Drayton, Leicestershire, had called public attention to the Quakers by his inspired preaching, which was as if a divine voice were speaking through him. Indeed, the Friends, as they called themselves, had no doubt that it was the spirit of God manifesting itself through him, its agent, as it might manifest itself through any one of them, even the humblest.

The Church of England had its doubts, while the New England Puritans knew for a certainty that if any voice spoke through that "Quaking" sect, it was assuredly not the voice of the Lord. The Quakers were held the more suspect for having no set creed, no church and no ministers, and for holding their meetings as the spirit prompted them, under the direction of whatever individual member felt upon him the impulse of God. Because at their occasional services the speakers shook and trembled in the fervor of their divine possession, and uttered their messages with the incoherence of inspiration, they were dubbed in scorn "Quakers" or "Ranters."

On the first of July the two Quaker women with their bundles of tracts landed in New England. The Puritans were ready for them. Seizing them before they had a chance to say one heretical word, they clapped them in Boston jail and made a bonfire of their literature in the market place. For five weeks the women remained in prison without anyone to plead for them, and then they were released, to disappear from the scene.

No sooner had they left Boston, than another vessel of Satan came to New England, disgorging no fewer than eight of what the General Court was pleased to describe as the "blasphemouth" sect. They, too, came laden with books, which again were burned in the market place, notwithstanding the fact that some were volumes of the

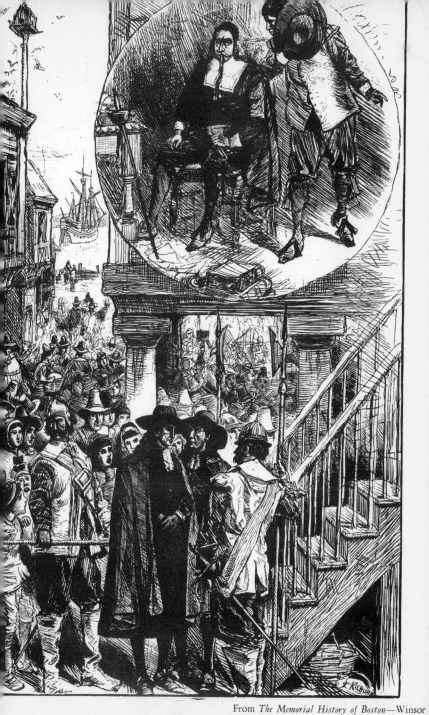

From *The Memorial History of Boston*—Winsor

THE QUAKER'S RELEASE

(Inset) ANNOUNCING THE ARRIVAL OF SHATTOCK WITH THE

Bible. Whatever belonged to the Quakers was damned, and best put out of the way.

The eight men, like the two women before them, found lodging in the prison under the tender mercies of a Quaker-hating jailer. For nearly three months they were kept in confinement, while the elders and magistrates formulated a law to protect their government from this new affliction. By edict of the General Court it was finally decreed that any Quaker who arrived in New England would be immediately committed to the house of correction, whipped and put to hard labor. There was no exception for age or sex—not even for the gray hairs of William Brend who, though nearly seventy, stirred no pity in the hearts of the Puritans. For them he was like his fellows, an enemy of the government and of the order of God in church and commonwealth. No law was too severe against such malefactors. Accordingly, the edict of October 14, 1656, was leniency itself compared with the punitive measures that were soon to follow.

Upon their release, the eight Quakers made their way to the outcast Rhode Island, through unendurable hardships. No one dared help them, for everywhere the dread of them had started up like an epidemic. The Quakers themselves, however, had not come unprepared against the cruelty of their fellowmen. When the righteous spat upon them they turned the other cheek, and when in Pilgrim Plymouth the skin of their backs was furrowed with the scourge, they prayed God to forgive their tormentors for not knowing what they did. "Take no thought for me," young John Copeland had written back home on landing. "The Lord's power hath overshadowed me, and man I do not fear."

Everywhere, in all the towns, the selectmen issued warning against the Quakers, forbidding anyone from entertaining or sheltering the outcasts on pain of punishment. The Quakers themselves could not be intimidated. Rhode Island was too small for the spirit within them. They had to follow its promptings and spread the word of God. One day, therefore, in the late summer of 1657, John Copeland and Christopher Holder were moved to come to Salem. There, as elsewhere, laws had been made against them, but no law could keep their message from reaching the people and converting to their religion many men and women who for one reason or another disagreed with the Puritans.

The two young men were kindly received by Lawrence Southwick and his wife, an aged couple who were members of the church and highly respected for their godly lives. While the strangers were staying with them, they went together to attend the regular services at the meetinghouse where, after the sermon, Holder rose up to speak. He had hardly begun when Edmond Batter, a commissioner with ambitions toward the governor's seat in the court of magistrates, pulled him brutally backward by his long hair and gagged him with his glove and handkerchief. The meeting rose in a panic, as the women screamed and the men, in the presence of authority, stood uncertain of what to do. Holder, in the meantime, struggled to remove the choking gag which Batter continued forcing brutally down his throat. At that Samuel Shattock, also a church member, seized Batter's hand and came to the Quaker's rescue. Batter marked him. No Puritan could oppose authority and get away with it.

With Copeland, Holder and the Southwicks, Shattock

was arrested and sent to Boston jail, as Salem had not yet provided itself with one. The fury of the magistrates knew no bounds. What was the power in these men that made them persist in their preaching in spite of torture and imprisonment, in spite of the lash and the red-hot iron? And what the spell they cast on the soberest of Puritans? There was only one thing to be done—to make the laws more stringent and the punishments more severe. Since the knotted whip had not cast heresy out of the Quakers, they must have it starved out of them. If that would not do, then they must be subjected to the most brutal of punishments, of which the English courts provided many an example to suit all offenses and all degrees. If punishment alone should not suffice, then— But for the extreme measure there was still time.

For nine weeks, in the chill months of October and November, the prisoners were kept in their small rooms without bed, straw, fire or food except for what their sympathizers threw in to them through the windows. The Southwicks and Shattock then returned to Salem, where the church dealt with them. Once more Copeland and Holder resumed their dolorous way to Rhode Island.

Nevertheless the sect grew. In Salem alone there were a number of groups of Friends that met to worship in one anothers' homes, regardless of the dangers they incurred in not attending church meetings. Fines were imposed, whippings administered, and still the doctrine spread, each martyrdom making more converts, till it looked as if half the people had been bewitched.

Edmond Batter, who had been elected to a political office, showed his gratitude by hunting the Quakers as if they were wild beasts. No method was too ruthless. Private homes were burst open, men and women dragged out of their very beds, and marched on foot the many miles to Boston for trial. All New England was in a tumult and, what was worse, divided. Every month saw whole families leaving their homes for the colony of Roger Williams.

Governor Endecott, who had not the forbearance of Winthrop, listened too eagerly to the counsels of the ruling elders. Even at the cost of blood, the commonwealth must be saved. But not yet; not yet. So far the records had been marked with blood only in criminal cases when a murderer had been executed, or a witch hanged, like that Margaret Jones who had mounted the gallows in Boston in 1648.

Every community had had some dreadful example of sin to punish. In Salem there had been Dorothy Talby. Again and again the woman had had to be summoned before the court for laying hands on her husband, and always she offered the plea that God had commanded her so that Talby might mend his evil ways. No one realized that she was insane and that her frequent whippings at the post only deranged her the more. The birth of a daughter in the midst of her troubles came like a warning. "Difficulty" she called her, and by that name the infant was baptized on Christmas Day of 1636. But Dorothy Talby's mind continued to be clouded with strange revelations that urged her to do away with herself and her husband. At last, out of patience with her, the church of Salem cast her out. It was the final blow to the crazed woman. From then on her visions, more frequent and more terrible, gave her no rest. In one of them it seemed to her that God bade her save her child from future misery, and in obedience, she killed her. For that crime she was hanged in Boston, while the Rev. Hugh Peter preached a sermon from the gallows exhorting the people to beware of false revelation.

What tongues of men and of angels should speak now to warn New England against the wily enemy? The courts believed more in deeds than in words. On September 10, 1658, Copeland and Holder, who with other Friends had been unable to resist the call to fulfill their mission in Boston, were seized, led by the marshal to a public place, and there had their right ears cut off as the law decreed. When the knife of the executioner severed the living flesh of Holder, who was the first victim, and the blood began to stream along his neck, the marshal turned away in horror at the sight. "Nay, turn about and see it done!" cried the next man who was awaiting his ordeal.

Meanwhile, in June, there had been a general house-cleaning at the Ship Tavern in Salem where, before the court presided over by Simon Bradstreet of Andover, Major William Hathorne of Salem, and Gen. Daniel Denison and William Hubbard of Ipswich, some twenty prisoners were brought in to answer to the charge of holding a "Quaking" meeting at the house of Nicholas Phelps in the outskirts of the town. The inveterate Batter had led the search, and was proud to see the many firebrands of hell whom he had brought to justice.

The accused looked inoffensive enough. William Brend, his head held high though his frame was bent under his many years, stood by the younger missionary, William Ledra. Both, in the Quaker fashion, wore their hats before authority, till the officers roughly pulled them off. Nearby, Phelps, in whose house the meeting had been surprised, awaited his turn. He was a mild yet courageous man, a hunchback, whose natural affliction had given him plenty of experience in fortitude against the mistrust of his neighbors, who looked on any abnormality as a work of Satan. Lawrence Southwick and his wife, Cassandra, old offenders, awaited the pleasure of the court with their son Josiah, who supported his mother as she grew faint with long standing. Shattock, Samuel Gaskin and Joshua Buffum stood among the rest.

"Why and for what did you come into these parts?" the court asked the two missionaries.

"To seek a godly seed," answered one. "The Lord God said, 'Pass away to New England.'"

The court was not satisfied that it was God who had spoken. By the looks of the accused they were all Quakers, and it was to justify such suspicion that they had been arrested. Words were bandied on either side to establish what constituted a Quaker.

"How wouldst thou know one? By what token?" asked one of the prisoners.

"Why, thou art one, for coming with thy hat on," retorted Bradstreet.

The prisoner looked at him solemnly. "It is a horrible thing," he said, "to make such cruel laws, to whip, and cut off ears, and burn through the tongue for not putting off the hat."

For a moment the court was confounded, and covered itself by changing its tactics. The prisoners were accused of blasphemy, and of preaching heresies at their meetings.

"Prove it!" the missionaries defied. "Come to our

meetings, listen to us and hear, and then make such a thing appear if it be so!"

Denison put the challenge aside. "If ye meet together, and say anything, we may conclude that ye speak blasphemy."

On such pretense of trial the accused were fined, and eight of them, among whom were Brend and Ledra, the Southwicks and Shattock, were remanded to the Boston prison to await the decision of Governor Endecott.

It was obvious to the magistrates that half measures like cutting off the ears of the men and boring the tongues of the women with a hot iron no longer sufficed to keep Hell's minions at bay. There was still the threefold corded whip, made of the dried intestines of animals and knotted with three knots, which, when applied with the full strength of the jailer's arms, laid the flesh bare to the bone. . . . A regular course of it might prove effective in casting out dangerous doctrine, even if life had to go with it.

No sooner were the prisoners brought to the house of correction than the jailer took them in hand, including Cassandra Southwick, who was past sixty. With the rest, she was stripped to the waist and had the stripes laid on her back till she dropped down unconscious. Brend and Ledra as the leaders, were shut up together in a room whose doors and windows had been stopped to prevent their friends from bringing them food. For five days, without light or air and with only a crust of bread and some porridge which had been put before them on their arrival, they lay there without communicating with a single soul. It would have been more merciful had they been left to die. But the law had other plans. On the fifth day the corded whip was applied, and then Brend, who was looked upon as the ringleader, was put in irons, "neck and heels," locked so close together that the bones of his back stuck out of the mangled flesh. Day after day, after he was freed from the irons, he was whipped by the brutal jailer till not an inch of his back was whole; the black flesh was like a pulp and under his arms tissues and blood clotted into bags. At last the staunch spirit gave way and Brend dropped on the floor like one dead.

Ledra clamored for help. The whole prison was in an uproar. In great alarm at the outcry of the people, who on learning what had happened posted papers at the meetinghouse demanding the punishment of the jailer, Endecott sent a doctor to the dying man. It would never do to have a prisoner killed without the court's order. The people would ask questions and demand justice.

After many weeks the dead flesh rotted off and Brend's wounds healed—only that he might have the scars re-opened by still more brutal scourgings. The people of Boston would put up with it no more. In a body they made such vehement protest that Brend and Ledra were released, with the rest of the Quakers. The law, how-ever, had to save its face. The Quakers were released, yes—but to banishment, under pain of death.

"Blasphemers and heretics!" Endecott thundered. "All deserved to be hanged!"

Within three years, four of the eight were dead— Brend in London's Newgate prison for persisting in his faith; Lawrence and Cassandra Southwick in exile, and Ledra in Boston on the gallows tree. There were still other victims. When the Southwicks had been forced to abandon their home, they left two children unprovided for, as whatever small means they had possessed the court had taken in fines. Captain Hathorne thereupon authorized the county treasurer to sell the boy and girl either to Virginia or to Barbadoes to satisfy the court.

The people of Salem had had enough of punishment, and since none came forward to soil his hands with the traffic, Daniel and Provided Southwick were suffered to remain in the town. Some brave souls there were who questioned why people who had done nothing deserving death, banishment or bonds were torn from their homes and treated like the worst of criminals. General Denison answered them. There was no room for both the Quakers and the Puritans. "At present the power is in our hand, and therefore the strongest must fend off."

Boston was busier than ever, fining, imprisoning, whipping and banishing. But no Friend could stay banished. At the risk of life itself he must always return to carry on the work for which heaven had singled him out. As the persecution grew, the Friends' resistance strengthened. Now men and women would hurl their accusations against the New England churches in the very house of God, while the ministers were preaching. In Boston two Quaker women broke a bottle over the head of their arch enemy, the Rev. John Norton, "as a sign of his emptiness." In Salem Deborah Buffum, a pure and modest girl who had just been married, walked through the town naked, her face blackened with ashes, to symbolize the bareness of the religion of the church. Prophets in winding sheets broke in upon lectures, crying out upon the elders as hypocrites and painted sepulchers. One side exasperated the other; the stronger determined to win.

Among Friends who had suffered banishment were

the preachers, William Robinson and Marmaduke Stephenson, and Mary Dyer, of Boston. As usual, after absenting themselves for a while in Rhode Island, they defied the authorities by returning to hold meetings in the Salem woods. So many flocked to hear them that it looked as if the whole town had turned Quaker. Then, taking their lives in their hands, they went back to Boston. This time the court showed no mercy. Robinson, Stephenson and Mary Dyer, "for their rebellion, sedition and . . . as underminers of this government" were sentenced to be hanged by the neck till they died.

It was an audacious sentence, and the court was nervous. For a long time the people had been murmuring, and quite recently, when Robinson had addressed them from an upper window of the prison, the crowd had made resistance against the guards summoned to disperse it. A public demonstration might stand in the way of the execution of justice. To prevent it, it was provided that a hundred soldiers completely armed should conduct the victims to the gallows, while another company remained about the town to prevent any outbreak.

Precautions were not enough. The people must be made to understand, to approve the court's decision. They must be persuaded that by the execution of the Quakers they themselves were being saved. One man alone could be called upon to undertake the task, and to him the justices applied for help. The Rev. John Norton willingly came to their rescue. In a few days a pamphlet defending the sentence was ready for distribution. So cunningly was the defense drawn up that in their gratitude the members of the General Court rewarded its author with a grant of five hundred acres of land.

On October 27, 1659, soldiers with pikes and musketeers with powder and shot stationed themselves before the prison house till the jailer opened the door to let out Stephenson, Robinson and Mary Dyer. Hand in hand the three trudged the way to Boston Common where the ladder and gallows awaited them, amid a concourse of people who had come to see them swung off. Justice and elder, constable and tithingman, came in ceremonial robes to impress with dignity the awful occasion. Even the boys were let off from school to witness the solemn consequence of defying authority.

There were others besides. From Rhode Island and Salem a great number of Friends had come, disregarding personal danger to bring winding sheets for those who were to suffer. Some had been put in prison till the execution was over, but a few followed behind the victims with the linens that were to receive them, dead.

One after the other the two men mounted the ladder and were swung off. For a few moments their bodies quivered, the hands snatched desperately at life, and then the swinging of the rope was stilled. But Mary Dyer did not see. With the rope about her neck and the hood over her head, she was sitting at the foot of the gallows preparing herself to behold God face to face. She had not been told that her son had obtained a reprieve allowing time for her to leave the colony. It was a useless mercy. Eight months later, from the selfsame spot, she was launched into eternity and her body laid somewhere near the others, in a shallow grave in Boston Common.

It is said that the crowd returning from the executions was so great, that the drawbridge on Ann Street (later North) gave way under the weight, injuring a number of people. Again sympathizers of the Quakers saw the hand of Providence in the accident, as they were to see it later when the Rev. Norton died of apoplexy.

William Ledra was the last Friend to yield up his life on the gallows. One cold March day in 1661, the chains that had bound him through sun and snow to a heavy log in the prison yard were knocked off and he was led to the gibbet. Governor Endecott, surrounded by a body of soldiers, stood by to see him die. "I commend my righteous cause unto thee, O God!" the prisoner cried as he stood on the ladder. "Lord Jesus receive my spirit." His words were drowned in the beating of drums.

No one knows to what the persistence of the Quakers, confident of their divine mission, and the righteousness of the Puritans, no less confident of theirs, would have led, with neither side ready to make concessions, had not a letter been brought from no less a personage than the restored King Charles II. Two years earlier, after their banishment, Samuel Shattock and Nicholas Phelps had sailed to plead the cause of the Friends before the home government. In the uncertainty of conditions in England, for a time they had been unable to accomplish their purpose until, through the influence of sympathizers, they were permitted to reach the ear of the King, to whom they told the whole tragic tale of the Quaker persecution.

Charles II listened to them favorably. In November of 1661, therefore, Governor Endecott and the court read with mingled feelings the King's order that the death penalty against the Friends should be no more inflicted, and that further cases of people under judgment or in prison should be tried in England. The monarch's intervention also called for the immediate extension of the franchise to others than freemen, or members of the Puritan church.

The struggle for the franchise lasted long and involved much bitterness, but finally, because of the power wielded by the large body of people entitled to it but hitherto excluded, it ended in the triumph of a greater democracy. The temporal power of the church in New England weakened.

Before the close of the century, at another Quaker trial, the accused was vindicated. Thomas Maule, called "No-Devil Maule" for his opposition to Cotton Mather, had always been openly a Friend. He had stood staunchly by his faith and had built the first Quaker meetinghouse from second-hand lumber in his possession. For years the plain little building sheltered the Quakers, till their name was no longer one of obloquy. Subsequently a later generation, no longer remembering ancient feuds, preserved the original frame in the rear of the Museum building of the Essex Institute, where it was long respected as the first Puritan meetinghouse. It is there to this day, a humble symbol of the triumph of an idea.

In 1695, however, Thomas Maule found himself in trouble for daring to defend the Friends in a volume, *Truth Set Forth and Maintained*, which he had sent out to be published, since Salem had as yet no press of her own. On the charge that his book contained "divers slanders against the churches and government of this Province" Maule was brought to trial in November, 1696, before the Governor and Council in the same court room which four years earlier saw the enacting of Salem's saddest tragedy. It may be that the people had

had enough of the tyranny of the law; it may be, too, that Thomas Maule's own forthright plea had more power over the jury than the arguments of the court. Surely he spoke with conviction as he addressed them.

"If you favor any of the unjust charge [*sic*] of the judges against me, and say there is such matter in the book as they charge me with, you must go to the printer for satisfaction, for I am ignorant of any such matter in the book. . . . My name in the printed book does not in law prove the same to be Thomas Maule, any more than the spectre evidence is in law sufficient to prove a person accused by such evidence to be a witch. Look well, therefore, to your work, for you have sworn trial to make, and just verdict to give."

"Not guilty!" pronounced the jury after deliberation.

It was hardly the conclusion the court had expected, and John Turner, the foreman, was questioned. Ably he defended the verdict. "We were not a jury of divines, which this case required," he answered.

The magistrates must have gone home pondering at such unprecedented independence of judgment.

## CHAPTER VIII

## SALEM GHOSTS

SALEM, early in the spring, today. The great willows whose roots twist about the leaning tombstones of the Charter Street burial ground—old Burying Point—have not yet come to leaf. In the open spaces the grass is brown with the winter, and at the borders of the gravestones charred by a thrifty fire. A fine drizzle is falling; the day casts no shadows.

On the west end of the burying ground the "Grimshawe House," where Nathaniel Hawthorne courted Sophia Peabody, still communicates with the graveyard. Today its lodgers may look out upon the slate tombstones within a few feet of the windows, as did Hawthorne. But in the timeworn place of the dead one does not think of the author, nor of the romance that came to flower at its edge. The "Grimshawe House" is older than yesterday. It is alive with unseen inhabitants. Strange whisperings are heard in it. Hands draw aside the window curtains and ghostly faces peer out at foolish folk who walk among graves in the rain.

In the gray quiet, the dead of a tragical twilight lose their shyness and old Burying Point is peopled with the ghosts of two and a half centuries ago. Governor Bradstreet, who came on the good ship *Arbella*, is here in his four and ninety years; and Captain More, who crossed the leagues of ocean as a boy in the *Mayflower*; and the merchant, Timothy Lindall, who lies under a stone with a skeleton on one side and a Father Time on the other, reminding him that though Death has come, Time trudges on toward the day of final reckoning.

Among them, and older than any of them for the life-weariness upon him, is Nathaniel Mather, the only one of the Mathers who did not live to lay his weight upon the scale of witchcraft. "An aged person that had seen but nineteen winters in the world," says his stone. Perhaps he had not died too soon.

Grim and unrepentant, the shade of Colonel John Hathorne bears the moral burden of nineteen fatal nods from the bench, each one the hanging of a fellow being on the crest of the stony hill on Salem's left. For he was one of the magistrates at the trial of the accused witches. Sober men, wise men, men of God and of the law nodded "death" with him. He knew he had been right; he knew that with the other judges he had fought on the side of God against the Prince of the Power of the Air. Years later, some of those who had sat with him had been smitten in their consciences by the deaths on Gallows Hill. Colonel Hathorne never bowed his head at the reading of a repentance, nor did the Mathers. And they were men of God. After all, had not witchcraft been banished from Essex County with the hanging of those nineteen servants of Satan—and the pressing to death of Giles Corey, the wizard who refused to plead? Somehow the charred grass over Hathorne's grave has a faint smell of brimstone.

Leaving the more conspicuous stones, one wanders among those whose names, half-effaced, have been more enduring than their memories. Good old Salem names they are, but barren of tradition. Elsewhere they appear

on shop windows, on door bells, with no more meaning than many another. Unexpectedly, on the side touching upon the "Grimshawe House," a slate stone reveals a clear inscription. "Samuel Shattock, the son of Samuel and Sarah Shattock, aged 17 years and 14 days. Deceased December 14, 1695."

Samuel Shattock. The name was that of the courageous Quaker who pleaded the cause of the Friends before the King and came back to the Colonies bringing clemency. But the name of young Shattock calls up no happy associations. The image that keeps recurring is that of a puny, sickly boy, sallow of face, dull of eye, perhaps feeble-minded. Persistently the name of Bridget Bishop comes with his, and Bridget Bishop evokes the witchcraft court, the hill of execution, and a poor lone woman giving up her life for a sin she denied with the rope round her neck. Then young Samuel Shattock is identified as one of the players in the witchcraft tragedy.

Salem, 1692. It is late in April. The trees in the forest are about to come to leaf, a glad sign after the dreary winter, and yet one which the people of the little town look upon with something of misgiving. For the Indians live in the forest, and behind the wall of leaves who knows what new mischief may be brewing? The nightmare of their latest and bloodiest uprising to recover their lost lands is still fresh in the minds of the widows and maimed ones of Salem.

The new terror had broken out in the beginning of 1675, when King Philip, chief of the Wamponoags in Rhode Island, had gathered the tribes together in a war for the extermination of the English. In fierce bands the Indians would fall upon a town in the night, and the next morning the sun would light up charred bodies and gutted houses mercifully covered by a pall of smoke. From Plymouth to Connecticut swept the vengeful hordes, destroying everything before them with the finality of lightning. Hardly a house was left standing in the territory from Falmouth to Casco Bay. It was a bloody conflict, brief but not unchronicled.

At least three New Englanders, in the demand for accounts of the Indian war, took up their pens to write about it. But neither the two Mathers, Increase and Cotton, nor William Hubbard achieved the popularity of the homely Mrs. Mary Rowlandson, whose eye-witness report, *The Sovereignty and Goodness of God . . . being a Narrative of the Captivity and Restauration of Mrs. Mary Rowlandson . . .* was published at Cambridge in 1682 at the instance of her friends. And no wonder! Her narrative has all the blood and life of her own experience, told with a vividness that still lures modern publishers to reissue it again and again.

"On the tenth of February, 1675, came the Indians in great number upon Lancaster," begins Mrs. Rowlandson. "Their first coming was about sun-rising. Hearing the noise of some guns, we looked out: several houses were burning. . . . There were five persons taken in one house; the father, the mother, and a sucking child they knocked on the head; the other two they took and carried away alive. . . ."

In the course of the fighting her own house is attacked, —it is on fire, with herself, her children and many others in it. "Now is the dreadful hour come, that I have often heard of . . . but now mine eyes see it. Some in our house are fighting for their lives, others wallowing in their blood, the house on fire over our heads, and the bloody heathen ready to knock us on the head if we stirred out. Now might we hear mothers and children crying out for themselves, and one another, *Lord, what shall we do?* Then I took my children (and one of my sisters hers) to go forth and leave the house: but as soon as we came to the door, and appeared, the Indians shot so thick, that the bullets rattled against the house, as if one had taken a handful of stones and threw them, so that we were fain to give back. . . . But out we must go, the fire increasing, and coming along behind us, roaring, and the Indians gaping before us with their guns, spears, and hatchets, to devour us. No sooner were we out of the house, but my brother-in-law (being before wounded, in defending the house, in or near the throat) fell down dead, whereat the Indians scornfully shouted, and hallooed, and were presently upon him, stripping off his clothes. The bullets flying thick, one went through my side, and the same (as would seem) through the bowels and hand of my dear child in my arms. One of my elder sister's children, named William, had then his leg broken, which the Indians perceiving, they knocked him on the head. Thus we were butchered by those merciless heathens, standing amazed, with the blood running down to our heels . . ."

Besides such innocent victims of assault and carnage, six hundred fighting men fell in battle, and many more were wounded. In the colony's effort to cope with the menace, Salem men and Salem arms were called upon, and the town responded generously. Under Captain Thomas Lathrop, who had once lived with the old Planters on Conant Street but who later removed to that part of Salem which was incorporated as Beverly, a company of foot soldiers drawn largely from the town and its environs, was ordered to the Connecticut Valley. They were all choice youths, not one of them over twenty-two.

For several months they hunted the Indians who had destroyed the settlement of Brookfield, and then marched to Deerfield, where a quantity of grain lay in stack for the suffering towns. Eighteen teamsters heaped the corn into carts and, under the protection of Lathrop's soldiers, started out toward Hadley. It was a hot day in mid-September. The men were thirsty, and weary from the long march. At Muddy Brook, near South Deerfield, they came upon vines laden with clusters of ripening grapes and, seeing themselves safe, separated into groups to gather them for refreshment. Suddenly several hundred Indians who had lain in ambush for the party, leaped out of the shrubbery and with savage whoops fell upon them with their bows and firearms. Of Lathrop's "Flower of Essex" only a few wounded survived to tell the tale. The teamsters were all slain. "A black and fatal day," mourned Increase Mather. Popular sorrow commemorated the place by changing its name to Bloody Brook.

The war continued in attack and reprisal. On August 12, 1676, King Philip's life came to an abrupt end when he was surprised with his followers by a scouting party and shot through the breast. After his death the warring tribes disbanded, many of their women and children were made captive, and the war ended. On a woeful day King Philip's wife and son, with others of their people, boarded a New England ketch and made the sea voyage to the West Indies and to slavery.

"An Indian Princess and her child sold from the cool breezes of Mount Hope, from the wild freedom of a New England forest, to gasp under the lash beneath the blazing sun of the tropics!" Edward Everett was to inveigh in his Bloody Brook address many years later when the nation was facing a grave crisis. "Bitter as death! Ay, bitter as hell."

But not to the people of Salem in 1692. The farther away the Indians, the safer they felt. Ever since the founding of the first New England settlement, the chosen of the Lord had had to fight against the three-fold enemy of the winter, the heretic, and the Devil in the shape of the red man. To the winter they had become inured, for those whom it did not kill it toughened. The heretic was for the moment crushed. The Indian—well, of the Indian one could never be sure.

Thus, when the horn of the cowherd sounded in the early morning from the pen near Mr. Gedney's pale, the people of Salem breathed their relief. Another dawn, dispelling the terrors of the night, another day for them to pass without too much to fear. Then the housewife came out with her pails to fill at the spring, the man of the family looked over the young corn shoots and the great cracks in the furrow made by the first sprouting pumpkin seeds, while the young girls shook out the bed linens or brought their spinning wheels out on the door-step. Furtively the house cat, descendant of those that had been brought from England to war on the squirrels and other small enemies of Puritan welfare, skulked along the stone fences with eyes alert for the unwary chipmunk. Chained to his post, the dog growled at her greater liberty and longed for the time when the master would come with his gun on his shoulder. Then over the marshes they would ramble, and suddenly come to a breathless halt as a covey flew up with a great flapping of wings. Terribly the gun would bark with its mouth of fire, and a bird dropped shrieking from the air. Those days the kitchen hearth was pleasant with smells.

Along the shores where the sea had worn into the land in tidal creeks, the morning awoke with a symphony of noises, for here were the wharves, the ship-building yards and the houses of the smiths, the shipwrights and the seamen. A fine street fourteen feet wide was just being laid out, and here the idle boys and the mariners awaiting their ships spent their days looking out on the distant sail, or standing at the door of the forge where anchors of more than a hundred pounds in weight went through the fire before searching out the depths of the sea. A cheery knocking of mallets resounded through the yards till sundown, when with his bell the crier made his rounds to say that another day had passed, and all was well. Then quiet fell over Creek Street and over Salem Neck, where long ago Richard Hollingworth had founded his shipyard, and over Philip English's house, the wonder of Salem, with its many stories and gables and sturdy chimneys. Night had come again.

Half an hour before dusk the cowherd brought back the kine from the common pastures where they fed every day of the week except on the Sabbath, when as a special treat they were allowed to crop the lush grass on Salem Neck. Their bells sounded in the darkening day, and round their necks the pieces of red flannel that the careful housewives tied as a prevention against witchcraft, fluttered in the brisk April air. For a brief hour lights glimmered in the windows of the houses, then all was dark and still—and fearful.

There were no distractions to keep good folk up at night—none that the ministers would have encouraged. What did the people need beyond the spiritual uplifting of the Thursday lecture and the Sabbath sermon, days when through the main street of the town passed the well-known procession to the meetinghouse—the men on one side, the women and girls on the other and the boys in a group behind, shepherded by the tithingmen who suffered nothing to escape their watchful eye? For boys, in those rigorous days, were as much under suspicion as if they had belonged to some wild species. In Boston an order had even been enacted against them in 1666 for their "irreverent carriage in times of public ordinances of praying and preaching," exhorting the public-spirited to sit in turn before the pews designated for the young scamps. Their natural good spirits betokened the ascendency of the Devil, to be driven out by frequent application of the rod. And used it was, in season and out of season, from the days of the smock to the breeched years of discretion. Had not Henry Dunster, Harvard's first president, set the example by faithfully applying the rod himself on two of his unruly students?

Altogether those were dreary enough days for the respectable members of the community. After sundown they could only go to bed and sleep, with the moral satisfaction that they were preserved from the perils of drunkenness and sin. At the Ship Tavern, however, and in the ordinary of Bridget Bishop on the road between Salem and Beverly, the newly-discovered rum ran freely, and sailors played at shuffleboard till late into the night. Again and again Goody Bishop had been reprimanded by the church, but she persisted in keeping her tavern open. And the powers of evil triumphed, sending the men reeling through the streets till they were brought to their senses by the stocks or a fine or a whipping, their punishment being meted out according to whether they were merely in drink, staggering or railing drunk, or insensible. The only glass which the Puritan looked on without frowning was that which stood by the pulpit and marked with each grain of sand the moments of time improved by God's word. "I know you are good fellows," the ministers were known to say, turning over the hour glass for the second and sometimes the third time. "Stay and take another glass."

The children grew up precocious and unsmiling. No joyous festivals brought them together, for even Christmas had been abolished by Puritan decree—except for the ropemakers of Salem, who cunningly drained their bumpers on December 25 in honor of St. Catherine of Alexandria, patroness of their trade. No wonder Cotton Mather inveighed against all those who had to do with ships and sailing, as he sighed, "It is a matter of saddest complaint that there should be no more serious piety in the sea-faring tribe."

For the children there were no kindly patron saints with whom to hoodwink Puritan sternness, nor were there toys or fairy tales. From the moment they were old enough to toddle they were put to work, first at some simple task, then at employments suited to their years. Early in the life of the colony Endecott had frowned on idleness and kept the youngest hands busy

Increase Mather

Cotton Mather

From The Memorial History of Boston—Winsor

"for the avoiding of absurdities," as he maintained to his death in 1665. With the years, his principles had assumed the rigidity of law. A stern discipline subjected boys and girls to their parents. They had no life but what was forced upon them in long day-tasks and weary hours of church attendance, where they grasped nothing but the terror and gloom of an austere religion that none troubled to bring down to their immature comprehension. The shadows of Puritanism hung over them, unrelieved by the pleasures of a normal childhood.

No wonder they sought distraction in forbidden ways.

## CHAPTER IX

## THE BEWITCHED GIRLS

FOR nearly a month—that is, since the beginning of March, 1692—strange doings had been going on in the little huddle of houses up along Danvers River which was known as Salem Village. Its inhabitants had always been a contentious lot, quarreling amongst themselves and with the people of Salem proper, whether about the pasturing of their cows or matters of church policy. No minister ever lasted long with them. In 1683 the Rev. George Burroughs, after serving the village as pastor for only three years, became involved in a parish feud and thought it best to remove himself to Maine, where he was gladly received by the church of Wells. The Rev. Deodat Lawson succeeded him, but he, too, found the constant disputes too much for him, and finally ceded the pulpit to the Rev. Samuel Parris, its incumbent in 1692. Thomas Putnam and his family watched the changes with sinister satisfaction. They were influential people who knew that no matter what the quarrel, they could always manage to have the upper hand. Had they not driven out Mr. Burroughs—and others?

The Rev. Samuel Parris was neither like Mr. Burroughs nor Mr. Lawson. He had been a merchant in the West Indies trade before he went to Harvard to prepare himself for the ministry, and the marks of his former experience remained with him in cunning and hardness. At forty he was a stubborn, ruthless man who could drive a bargain to his advantage with little scruple for the means he used. If the Putnams wished to play their little game, he could show them that he was past master—even in such expert arts as the detection of witchcraft. For that terrible plague of Satan had broken out once more—there was no doubt about it—and in his own home, the home of a minister of God!

It was not the first time that New England had shuddered at the word. Periodically Satan's minions walked over the land and the courts were busy with trials and convictions. So far in the history of the New England colonies there had been nearly a score of convictions and perhaps a half-dozen executions. The earliest took place in Connecticut in 1647, when Alse Young was hanged for infernal practices; hardly a year passed before Margaret Jones was executed in Boston for the same crime. The latest had occurred in 1688, when Goody Glover, an ignorant Irish washerwoman, climbed the ladder to the rope amid the edification of the ministers.

"Go then, my little book. . . ." Cotton Mather invoked in his *Memorable Providences* that told the history of the Glover case, with which he had been closely associated. "Go tell Mankind that there are Devils and Witches; and that tho those nightbirds least appear where the Day-light of the Gospel comes, yet New England has had Examples of their existence and operation."

No, the Devil was no imaginary evil to the people of New England. He was a real, physical being whom the bewitched described in minute detail, from his blackened skin to his cloven hoof and forked tail. For the Devil had crossed the ocean with the Puritans in remembered witch trials in Old England. James I had fixed the portrait in his *Demonology*, and by zealous witch-hunting had further seared the Evil One in the minds of his subjects; it was no mere abstraction that had sent hundreds of men and women to the flaming pyre. Thus the rites of the cult were familiar to the smallest New England child, who was taught to look out for the Devil with as much real dread as for the enemy Indian.

Elizabeth Parris, the nine-year-old daughter of the minister knew of the Devil, and so did Ann Putnam and Abigail Williams, her closest friends, only a few years older than herself. So did Mercy Lewis, a seventeen-year-old girl who had been a servant in Mr. Burroughs' house and was now employed with the Putnams,—and so did the rest of the dozen maids and women who used to gather in the kitchen of the Parris house to try what they could to raise him with the help of Tituba, a slave bought by the minister in his West Indian merchant days.

Immediately Elizabeth Parris, Abigail Williams and Ann Putnam began to be afflicted with a strange affliction, yet not unfamiliar to those who, like Mr. Parris, had read the *Discourses of the Damned Art of Witchcraft*, written in 1600 by William Perkins, and the nearer *Memorable Providences* of the Boston minister. The girls performed peculiar antics. They screamed without visible provocation, thrust out their tongues, crouched under beds and tables, suffered from horrible convulsions and were unaccountably tortured by unseen beings, who left, nonetheless, obvious marks upon the bodies of the afflicted.

In all respects their malady differed little from that of the Goodwin children who four years earlier had brought Goody Glover to the gallows. The poor old soul had scarcely spoken a word of English, but she had said enough to convince Cotton Mather and the judges that she was a witch. However, though with her execution all the younger Goodwin children were rid of their afflictions, the eldest still persisted in her bewitchment— so stubbornly, indeed, that Cotton Mather lodged her in his house with his newly-wedded wife, the better to examine the symptoms. With the scientific exactness of the former student of medicine, Cotton Mather noted her actions and wrote them down—wrote of how the Devil that possessed her allowed her to read with ease out of Quaker and Popish books, but turned her deaf, dumb and blind whenever a good Puritan text was put before her. So exacting a taste had the Evil One, that though he allowed her to read with ease certain sections of a Church of England book of prayer, he would deprive her of consciousness if the same passages were shown to her in the Bible. However, through the ministrations, the prayers and the fasting of Cotton Mather and his congregation, the girl was finally delivered of her demon, only to have him split into infernal atoms that were to find abode in the bodies of the girls of Salem Village.

Soon people began to be accused, for the girls were mystic and visionary, and could see the specters of witches tormenting them where unafflicted eyes saw nothing but empty air. The contagion spread to the elder members of the group. Mrs. Putnam, the wife of Thomas, fell into trances, together with Mrs. Pope and Mrs. Bibber. Mercy Lewis, Mary Walcott and Elizabeth Hubbard followed suit. It seemed to be a pastime of the Devil to find which of them he could afflict most.

At the very beginning, when the girls were writhing under the first torments, Dr. William Griggs, new to the parish, was summoned by the minister. It was the doctor's first call and he was anxious to make good. As he examined the girls, who promptly fell into fits, stared, gaped and cried out in pain that they were being bitten and pinched, and as he listened to Mr. Parris questioning anxiously whether it was not clearly a case of witchcraft, the doctor did not delay in making up his mind. Yes, the girls were certainly bewitched. For what malady known to medical science could so harass its victims and yet leave them, when out of their fits, as hale and hearty as the healthiest of them?

Meanwhile Tituba, with her husband John Indian, had been consulted for advice on the detection of witches. They willingly offered what help they could. "Bake a witch cake," they said. "Make it with rye and the water of the children. Then bake it in the ashes and feed it to the dog. Soon you will discover the witches."

The charm worked, and by strange irony, Tituba was the first to be accused by the children. Tituba afflicted them; Tituba's shape came to bite and pinch them and draw out their bowels. Soon others began to be cried out upon, at first beggars and homeless women, and then neighbors who somehow had made themselves unpopular to the influential people of Salem Village.

Colonel Hathorne, called upon by Parris, became assiduous in his search for witches. Equally zealous was Jonathan Corwin, in whose house, still standing at the corner of Essex and North streets, the preliminary examinations took place. At the same time, Cotton Mather and other notable witch discoverers were sent for from Boston. Valuable indeed was their learning to the people of Salem, whose knowledge of witchlore came chiefly from the readings of Mr. Parris, and the near, real belief that New England before the colonists, had been tenanted by demons from whom the red men were descended. Had not Cotton Mather obtained first-hand information of a plot of the Devil—"An horrible plot against the country by witchcraft . . . which, if it were not seasonably discovered, would probably blow up, and pull down all the churches in the country"? That plot was just being uncovered in Salem Village.

Samuel Parris watched the developments and found them good. His home had become a center of curiosity and he, by inference, was singled out as a saint. Respectable men came from all over the colonies to see the bewitched children. Days of fasting and prayer were held with great frequency; sermons against the terrible affliction were read from the pulpit by visiting ministers. Salem Village was being put on the map. Surely, as a reward for the visitation upon Mr. Parris, the town should give him that grant of land for which he had been wrangling with his obdurate congregation!

As interest in the affliction grew, greater too became the numbers of the bewitched and the witching. Now not only beggars and demented old women were accused of walking up and down the earth in spectral form to torment the godly. Women of reputed holy living, like Rebecca Nurse and her sisters, Mary Easty and Sarah Cloyse, were cried out upon. From Salem Village the havoc spread to Salem town. Petty enmities assumed diabolic meanings. Dying cattle, perishing harvests, physical ills were ascribed to the malefic influence of neighbors who surely must be witches. Ancient grudges revived. Ten, twenty, thirty years memories journeyed back to give an old mishap a new significance. It was a question of who should cry out first.

The jails overflowed with prisoners awaiting the arrival of the new governor from England for the trials to begin. Salem prison could hold no more; cartloads of the accused were sent to neighboring jails in Ipswich and Boston. Essex County was divided into three parties—the bewitched, the accusers and the judges. There came a time when it was the better part of valor to house a demon in one's body rather than to be oneself lodged in a damp dungeon with chains on hands and feet and Gallows Hill at the end of it all. Next to being afflicted, it was prudent to confess oneself a witch. The examiners became more lenient then, in the hope of discovering more witches from the declarations of the so-called confessors.

Tituba was not too slow to see the wisdom of the procedure, and astounded the examiners by making a full confession.

"Did you ever go to a witch meeting with Sarah Good and Sara Osborn?" they asked, mentioning the old beggar and the bedridden crone who had been among the first to be cried out upon.

"They are very strong and pull me to go with them," Tituba answered.

"Where did you go?"

"Up to Mr. Putnam's and make me hurt the child."

"Who did make you go?"

Painting by Matteson. *Essex Institute.*

*Essex Institute*

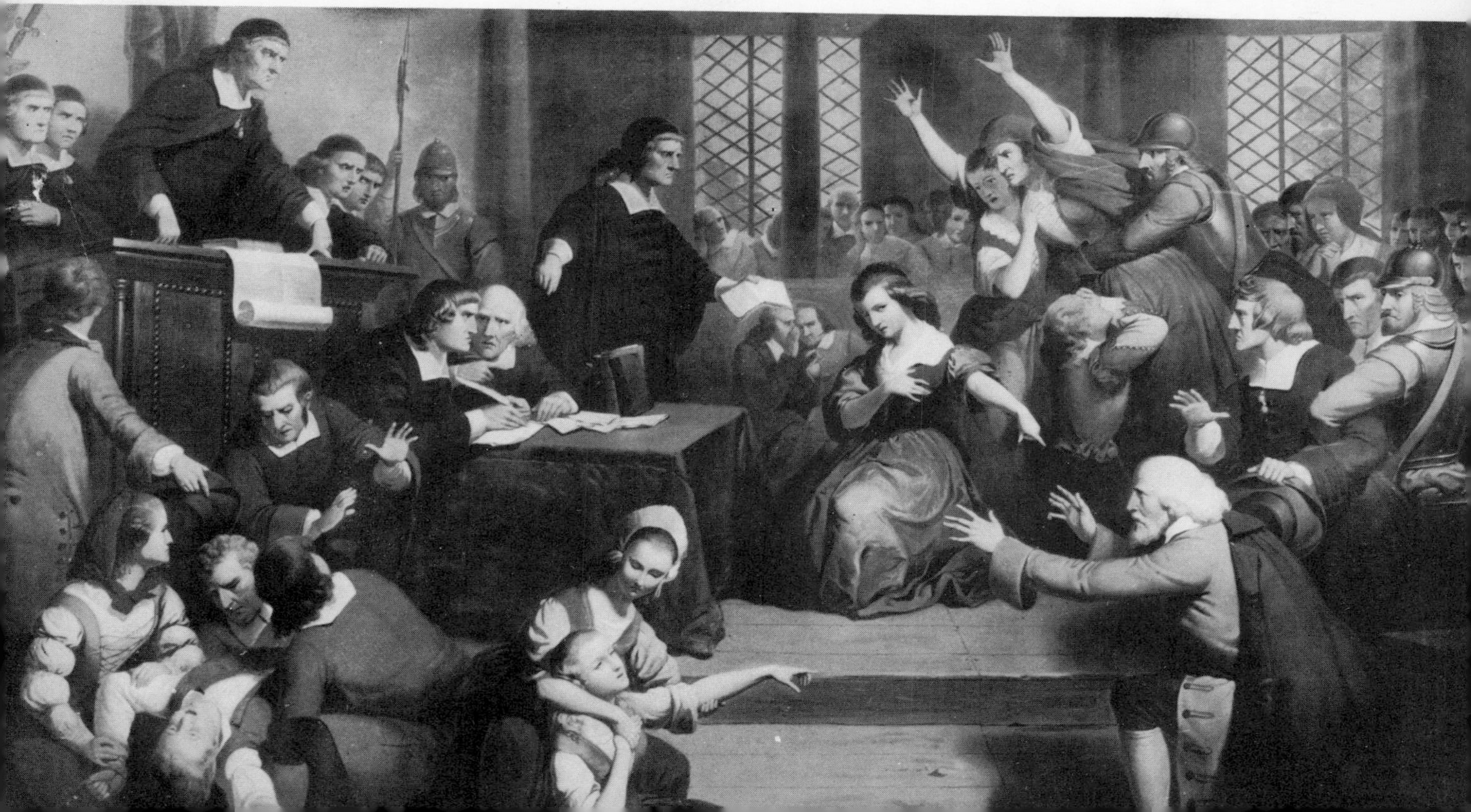

"A man that is very strong, and these two women, Good and Osborn. But I am sorry."

Mr. Putnam saw nothing to displease him in the way things were going. "A man that is very strong—" Certainly the Rev. George Burroughs, with whom he had had a long-standing feud. He was so strong that his feats had long been spoken of with wonder in the village . . .

"How did you go? What do you ride upon?" the questioner proceeded.

"I ride upon a stick or pole, and Good and Osborn behind me. We ride taking hold of one another. I don't know how we go, for I saw no trees or path, but was presently there when we were up."

"And what sights saw you when you went abroad?"

"I see a man, a dog, a hog, and two cats, a black and a red, and the strange monster was Osborn's that I mentioned before. This was the hairy imp. The man would give it to me, but I would not have it."

Obviously the woman was telling the truth. Did she not describe the witch's favorite means of perambulation, and the witch's imp or familiar which she would suckle from her own body so that it would then do her bidding in hurting and tormenting innocent people? Tituba was too valuable a subject to let go. In spite of her confession and repentance she was thrown into prison and chained with the rest.

Seeing how his wife was handled, John Indian was immediately afflicted and fell into strange postures. He was less fortunate than the bewitched children, however, who were pampered and made much of. Though he seemed to suffer untold agonies, his bewitchment was not

taken reverently by those out of the minister's camp.
One day, when he fell into a fit at an inn, Edward
Bishop, a stepson of Bridget Bishop's "so undertook and
managed him" that he was soon brought to. But while
riding home among other accusers, he fell once more
into distraction and, seizing with his teeth the back of
the man who sat before him, thus held himself upon the
horse. Bishop, who had already undertaken and managed him, came again to his rescue, this time with a
stick. By virtue of this simple treatment John Indian
recovered, and promised nevermore to fall into a fit.
His canny doctor answered he doubted not but that if
he had the handling of the children they would have the
devils as speedily driven out of them. Shortly afterwards
he himself was cried out upon, but more fortunate than
the rest, he escaped with his life.

At length the new governor arrived and with him Increase Mather, the father of Cotton, bringing a new
charter from their Majesties, William and Mary, who had
ascended the throne in 1688. Troubled times had preceded their accession, from the death of Charles II, whose
brother, the Duke of York, became King as James II,
to the day when, much to the relief of the colonies,
he was forced to abdicate.

James had been an unwelcome ruler, as unwelcome
as Sir Edmund Andros whom he raised to be governor-
general of all New England. By the time the British
frigate arrived in Boston Harbor on December 20, 1686,
bearing Andros and two companies of royal troops, the
various towns in New England had managed to secure
their lands by obtaining deeds from the Indians. Salem's
was dated October 11, and fairly bristled with poly-

syllabic Indian names that gave it impressiveness if not legality. Now let Andros dare claim that the king owned the soil!

Andros supported his King's claims, nonetheless, making himself detested wherever he went. The people murmured. There was talk of rebellion. Finally, when rumors of the British revolution reached New England, drums were beaten in Boston and the militia of neighboring towns gathered there to overthrow Andros' tyranny. More than twenty companies had trooped to Boston, and fifteen hundred armed men waited in Charlestown till they were needed. New England had uprisen. That day, April 18, 1689, from the gallery of the council house, the declaration of Boston and all adjacent towns was read, naming the grievances of New England against the government of Andros and demanding his surrender.

The people knew that words alone were of little avail. Marching resolutely, they seized the justices whom Andros had appointed and made Andros himself a prisoner in the council house. The revolution succeeded without bloodshed. Eventually Andros was sent back to England and a provisional government established, patterned after the charter government as it had existed until 1686.

Meanwhile Increase Mather had been sent to their Majesties to plead the cause of New England and to seek a restoration of the old charter rights. He did not obtain all that he sought but the new charter had possibilities. Besides, the governor was a friend of his and a convert of his son Cotton who had secured him as a member of his church in Boston.

Governor William Phips, a native of the colonies, was a warring man, unversed in the intricacies of judicature and scarcely of an intellect capable of controlling the situation awaiting him. But Increase and Cotton Mather were able advisers. Before long His Excellency had appointed a commission of Oyer and Terminer to try the accused. Leaving William Stoughton, the deputy-governor, as chief justice, he himself went on his way to fight the French in Quebec and the Indians on the border. These were enemies he understood better.

The first case, that of Bridget Bishop, was brought to trial on June 2, 1692, before the commission of Oyer and Terminer, consisting, among others, of William Stoughton, Major Nathaniel Saltonstall, Major Batholo-mew Gedney, Wait Winthrop, Captain Samuel Sewall and William Sargent, on the accusations of the afflicted girls, and of a number of other witnesses.

## CHAPTER X

## *GALLOWS HILL*

THE courthouse, which stood in the middle of the present Washington Street, was thronged with people who overflowed into the square that Thursday morning when Bridget Bishop appeared before the judges. No one knows why she was selected as the first for trial, when Sarah Good and Mrs. Osborn had been among the earliest accused. But Sarah was then far away in the Boston prison with her five-year-old daughter Dorcas, also accused of bewitching the children, and Mrs. Osborn had died, leaving an unpaid bill for jail maintenance. Bridget Bishop was close at hand; the law could not wait.

Many enemies had the high-handed, sharp-tongued hostelry keeper made for herself among the people of Salem. The women hated her because she scorned the drabness of their garb and disregarded the Puritan laws that fixed the apparel of every sober man and woman. Her bright paragon bodice, braided and looped with many colors, and her cloak of fine cut were the scandal of the town. The late hours she kept at her wayside inn entertaining the sailors at shuffleboard and checkers, horrified the pure in mind. Furthermore, for many years she had been under suspicion of witchcraft because of the accusations brought against her by Wonn, John Ingerson's Negro, who said he saw her shape upon the beam of the hay-house, with an egg in her hand! That had been in 1679, when she was the wife of Thomas Oliver, her second husband. But the good people of her neighborhood had long memories which they exercised zealously when they saw her lands multiply and her tavern thrive.

After a number of Bridget's kindly neighbors had brought in their depositions, the visionary girls were quick to discern her specter among the apparitions of other witches. Even her cloak did not escape their inward eyes. One of them during a preliminary examination cried out that Bridget was coming toward her for no good, whereupon young Jonathan Walcott made as if to run the specter through with his sword. As it was, he struck only the ghostly cloak, making a rent in it, according to the girl. Wonder of wonders, when at Bridget's trial she was asked, "Is not your cloak cut?" and she answered she knew nothing of it, the cloak was spread open and there, for everyone to see, was a rent, neatly mended!

The moment Bridget Bishop was brought into the court room presided over by the justices in great wigs, broad bands and scarlet gowns, the afflicted children fell into fits with loud cries and horrible convulsions. Their limbs were twisted, their faces contorted with grimaces of pain. They rolled on the floor between the justices and the victim. They shrieked unintelligible accusations, drowned by the screaming of Mrs. Putnam, who was even more bewitched than any of them. When Bridget turned her eyes heavenward, knowing that only from God could she expect mercy, the afflicted had their eyeballs rolled up in their sockets. Every motion of her hands or body was repeated by them in a grotesque, a deadly mimicry. She was doomed.

Gradually, through the screaming, like solos in a diabolic symphony, the accusations of the afflicted rose above the general havoc. "Goody Bishop bewitched her husbands to death!" "Oh, Goody Bishop, did you not come to my house last night and did you not tell me that you would torment me?" "You brought us the book to sign, but we would not . . ." "She murdered her husbands!" "She bewitched many persons to death!"

"What do you say to these murders you are charged with?" asked Justice Stoughton.

"I am innocent. I know nothing of them," the poor woman answered.

"What contract have you made with the Devil?"

"I made no contract . . . I never saw him in my life."

The shrieking drowned out her words and the judge's as the children fell into renewed agonies so excruciating that for some minutes the business could not proceed. The woman was working her witchcraft in defiance of the very court.

Meanwhile a written statement had been laid before the judges, signed with the crosses of the nine matrons who, earlier in the morning, had examined Bridget's body for the preternatural mark or teat with which a witch was said to suckle her familiar Devil. Dr. Barton, the chirurgeon, had supervised the proceedings as Bridget was stripped, pricked and prodded in every inch of her body. A mark, "an excrescence of flesh not usual in women" had been discovered on her. Let the Devil help her now if he could.

The court continued with its formal proceedings and acknowledged the indictments wherein Ann Putnam, Mercy Lewis, Abigail Williams, Elizabeth Hubbard and

Mary Walcott charged Bridget Bishop with tormenting them by witchcraft. The room was filled with other witnesses ready to testify against the accused. It seemed as if everyone who had ever known her had turned out to seek her death.

Through the afternoon of that day and through all of the next, accusation after accusation was flung in her face, each charging her with things she could not recall because they had never happened. The judges listened avidly. This was no simple case they were trying. The woman was a minion of the Devil. Had he not tried to come to her help by removing the witch's mark when she had been subjected to a second examination? The court was not duped.

One after the other, the depositions were read. Samuel Shattock, her neighbor, a dyer, charged her with having bewitched his son, the younger Samuel, twelve years earlier. The boy was then about five years old. Often this Bridget would come to his house on foolish errands, bringing him bits of material to dye, queer things, whereof he could not imagine any use. Once after she had come to pay him, the purse and money were unaccountably taken out of a locked box and seen no more. The child was thereupon taken with a fit from which everyone thought he would have died. "Indeed, he did nothing but cry and sleep for several months together, and at length his understanding was utterly taken away." Bridget Bishop had bewitched him. "Among other symptoms of an enchantment upon him, one was that there was a board in the garden, whereon he would walk; and all the invitations in the world would not fetch him off!"

A few years later a stranger came to Shattock's house.

On seeing the half-wit boy he said, "This poor child is bewitched, and you have a neighbor not far off who is a witch," adding, "Your neighbor has had a falling out with your wife and she said in her heart, your wife is a proud woman, and she would bring down her pride in this child." The man then offered a cure. "Let me go with the boy to Bishop's house," said he, "and we will fetch blood of her." He managed only to fetch himself a sound cuff of the ear, which proved that this Bishop was indeed a witch.

Recently the boy had again been taken with fits that the doctors laid to foulest witchcraft. . . .

Another witness was called—Deliverance Hobbs, who had confessed herself a witch and must now speak even though the specters of her sister witches gave her no rest with their tormenting. This Bishop, she declared, tempted her to sign the Devil's book again and to take back her confession, but because she would not do it, Bishop whipped her with iron rods. She knew that it was this Bishop who tormented her, because she had seen her at a witch meeting in Mr. Parris' field, where they all partook of a diabolical sacrament in bread and wine.

Then came Samuel Gray, a man of about forty, speaking with the accents of truth. About fourteen years ago, he testified, he awoke one night to see the room full of light. There, between his child's cradle and the bedside, he saw a woman staring at him. As he rose the apparition vanished, though all the doors were fast locked. When he looked out at the entry door, he saw the same woman. "In God's name, what do you come for?" he asked. The thing made no answer and he went back to bed. No sooner had he lain down, than the shape reappeared near the cradle, whereupon the child "gave a great screech." The woman vanished, but from that moment the child peaked and pined and died after a few months. He knew neither Bishop nor her name at the time, but when he saw her after his child's death, he recognized in her the specter who had bewitched it.

John Bly testified. He said that in an old house which he had pulled down for this Bishop he found witch puppets of rags and hogs' bristles in the cellar wall. She had also bewitched a sow that he had bought of her husband.

Then Richard Coman, John Louder and William Stacy appeared with their testimony against her—and finally, John Hale, the old minister of Beverly. The people turned toward him with one body as he spoke. Even the bewitched seemed relieved of their fits.

Above five or six years earlier, the minister said, Christine Trask, a member of his church, came to desire him not to permit Bridget Bishop to receive the Lord's supper until she ceased entertaining people in her house at unseasonable hours, causing dissensions in people's homes by the drunkenness she encouraged. The next he heard of Christine Trask was that she had become distracted the night after she complained of this Bishop. She continued some time distracted, but did not give over praying and fasting till she was restored to her reason. Now Mr. Hale recalled that her behavior and the fits of the Salem children were much alike. The poor woman continued on and off in her distraction and was finally tempted by the Devil to do away with herself. On examining the corpse Mr. Trask saw that a piece of her windpipe was cut out, and another wound severed the jugular vein, which he believed it impossible for her to have done with a small pair of scissors without the work of the Devil or witchcraft.

Bridget Bishop was condemned. On the tenth of June George Corwin, the sheriff, would take her to the ledge of Gallows Hill, there to hang her by the neck till she was dead. Justice was satisfied—for the moment. Only Nathaniel Saltonstall showed no pleasure. At the end of the session he tendered in his resignation, saying that he would have nothing more to do with proceedings of that nature.

The whole town turned out to see the execution. From Ipswich, Marblehead, Beverly, Topsfield, even from Boston, people flocked to behold the first victory flaunted in the face of the Prince of the Power of the Air. Amid the banks of faces the prison cart left the jail, the lone victim within it, and the sheriff on guard to see that the Devil used none of his arts to wrest her from the hands of justice. Down prison lane, up the main street, past Town Bridge, in and out of narrow ways, the cart lumbered, entering the pasture lands along the road to Boston for a little way only. Then it turned abruptly to the left where, slightly below Gallows Hill, a hillock, ending abruptly in a ledge of rocks, met the road. A few trees were growing on its summit; the rest of the land was rocky and bare. Over one of the branches the sheriff threw the rope he had brought in the cart.

No prayers were said for Bridget. No one had a consoling word for her. She was a witch and she must die. In a shallow hole among the rocks, her poor body was thrown like so much offal.

Contrary to expectation, the afflicted found no release

with her death. Too many other witches remained behind. Within three months, on such testimony as had brought Bridget Bishop to the witch tree, eighteen men and women followed her fatal road to the stony hill.

Now the victims did not go to their death alone. On the nineteenth of July, the second of the Devil's red-letter days, five women were executed at the same time: Sarah Good, whose little Dorcas remained in prison with a small set of chains on her hands and feet, Susanna Martin, Elizabeth How, Sara Wilds and Rebecca Nurse.

An extraordinary thing had happened at the trial of Rebecca Nurse: the jury pronounced her not guilty of the sin of witchcraft. Ever since she had been accused, petition after petition had been brought before the court, signed by her many neighbors who had long known her for her virtuous and saintly life. They were all of no avail before the clamor of the afflicted, who would have her life at any price.

Justice Stoughton, at the jury's unexpected verdict, got up and addressed them. He did not wish to impose upon them, said he, but had they, in their decision, considered a certain expression of Rebecca Nurse's when, on seeing the confessed witches, Mrs. Hobbs and her daughter, brought in to testify against her, she had exclaimed, "What! Do you bring them? They were of our company!"

It was a damning interpretation that he put on the poor woman's words, and the jury, the second time, found her guilty. "I had intended no otherways than as they were prisoners with us, and therefore did then, and yet do judge them, not legal evidence against their fellow-prisoners," Rebecca Nurse explained in her written declaration after Stoughton's move had had its effect. But what cared he to learn that throughout the trial she had hardly known what was happening, she "being something hard of hearing, and full of grief . . ."?

The governor, nevertheless, saw cause to grant a reprieve, even after the minister had publicly excommunicated Rebecca Nurse from the church to which she had been an example of godliness for many years. The afflicted would hear nothing of clemency. Did not the Scriptures say that one must not suffer a witch to live? Rebecca Nurse, too, must die.

Later years have made a shrine of her home in Danvers, and Whittier wrote the epitaph over her pine-shaded grave in the family burial ground on Collins Street, where her body was taken from the hill of execution.

> O Christian Martyr! who for truth could die,
> When all about thee owned the hideous Lie!
> The world, redeemed from Superstition's sway,
> Is breathing freer for thy sake today.

Only those who love to turn over the crumbling pages of old records now remember that she was sacrificed to the rancor of the Putnams for a feud concerning the possession of certain lots of land.

At the next sitting of the court on August 5, six more were tried on the accusations of the same group. They were the Rev. George Burroughs, who had been extradited from his parish in Maine on the instigation of the Putnams and Mr. Parris; John Procter and his wife Elizabeth; John Willard; old George Jacobs of Salem and Martha Carrier of Andover. By the night of August

19, all were dead but Mrs. Procter, whose sentence had been remanded because she pleaded pregnancy.

Never had the testimony been so blood-curdling as at the trial of Burroughs; everything about it seemed calculated to turn the people's hearts to stone. Ann Putnam, the star actress among the afflicted, played her best. Mercy Lewis, who had once been a servant in the household of Mr. Burroughs and consequently bore him many grudges, supported the lead with cunning and shrewdness.

One night, Mercy deposed, Mr. Burroughs came to her and carried her to the top of a high mountain from where he showed her all the kingdoms of the earth, telling her that they should all be hers if she would but sign the Devil's book. If she refused, he would throw her down and break her neck. No, she defied, him, no—not if he threw her down on a hundred pitchforks . . . None cared to inquire why it was that since Burroughs had such power, she was still alive to inform against him.

Other damning depositions followed—from Susanna Sheldon, Mrs. Bibber, Thomas Putnam, Elizabeth Hubbard—from nearly all of the select circle. None equaled the twelve-year-old Ann's. "On May 11," she testified, "I saw the apparition of Mr. George Burroughs who grievously tortured me and urged me to write in his book. (Her father and an obliging neighbor both vouched for the truth of Ann's statements.) I refused. He then told me that his first two wives should appear to me presently and tell me a great many lies, but I should not believe them. There then appeared to me the forms of two women in winding sheets and napkins about their heads . . . They turned their faces toward

Mr. Burroughs and looked very red and angry . . . and told him that their blood did cry for revenge; and also told him that they should be clothed in white robes in heaven when he should be cast into hell; and immediately he vanished away . . . They told me they were Mr. Burroughs' first two wives and that he had murdered them. And one of them told me that she was his first wife, and he stabbed her under the left arm and put a piece of sealing wax on the wound . . . and she pulled aside the winding sheet and showed me the place."

Many came to see Burroughs hanged, even Cotton Mather, who rode among the crowd on his white horse. When Mr. Burroughs was on the ladder with the rope about his neck, he made so noble and moving a speech, in which he protested his innocence and forgave those who wrongfully took his life, that the people murmured and some wept. Cotton Mather deplored such a turn of affairs. What! Should the arts of Satan be made to triumph? Burroughs was no ordained minister, he shouted to the people. Let them beware, for the Devil has often been transformed to an angel of light for his foul purposes!

After the executions the body of Burroughs was cut down and dragged by the halter to a hole among the rocks. His shirt and breeches were pulled off and replaced by an old pair of trousers belonging to another of the victims. In the grave between the rocks the bodies of Willard and Martha Carrier were thrown in with his, and all so hastily covered that one of Burroughs' hands, his chin and a foot of one of the others showed through the soil. No one dared betray compassion or even respect for death. The afflicted were there, ready to cry out upon other victims. The ministers and judges must not be crossed. Late at night, however, Joshua Buffum, from whose house on Boston Street the woeful sight was visible, went to the hill of execution and mercifully threw more soil on the grave. Often before had he helped the friends of the victims to recover the bodies and give them decent burial.

Not yet would the bewitched or the judges cry enough. Here and there a man like the venerable Governor Simon Bradstreet expressed himself against the way the trials were conducted. But his voice was scarcely audible amid the howling of the afflicted for victims and more victims. The delusion had reached the proportions of mass frenzy.

On the sixth of September, six more were tried and received sentence of death; on the seventeenth, nine others were condemned with them. Of the fifteen, only eight made the journey in the cart to execution hill on the twenty-second of the month—Martha Corey, Mary Easty, who was a sister of Rebecca Nurse, Alice Parker, Anne Pudeator, Margaret Scot, Willmet Reed, Samuel Wardwell and Mary Parker. "What a sad thing it is to see eight firebrands of hell hanging there!" cried the self-righteous Stoughton. But for the fact that Martha's husband, Giles Corey, had refused to be tried by the law of the land, there might have been nine.

Giles Corey had not escaped, however. Six days before his wife went to her death, he had been subjected to the *peine forte et dure* provided by English law for those who refused to plead. Blackstone is explicit on the method of procedure. The victim must be brought to a dark chamber of the prison, "and there be laid on

"Witch House," Salem. Occupied before 1675 by Jonathan Corwin, one of the judges of the Witchcraft Court.

Probable site of the execution of the "witches". Photo by Sidney Perley. *Essex Institute.*

his back on the bare floor, naked." The law further pro-
vides "that there be placed upon his body as great a
weight as he could bear, and more, that he hath no sus-
tenance, save only on the first day, three morsels of the
worst bread, and on the second day three draughts of
standing water . . ." The treatment continues till the
sufferer either pleads or dies.

The proud, eighty-year-old Corey was not the man
to yield. Feeling responsible for his wife's death sentence
because of some words he had uttered against her, he bore
the dreadful, lingering punishment until at last he prayed
for death to come. "More! More!" he groaned to the
executioner who laid the weights upon him. As he was
dying and his tongue protruded from his mouth, the
sheriff forced it in with his cane. "About noon at Salem,"
Judge Sewall wrote in his diary under the date of September 19, 1692, "Giles Corey was pressed to death for
standing mute." Robert Calef in his *More Wonders of
the Invisible World* gives the date of Corey's death as
September 16. It had taken the victim three days to die!

The situation grew worse instead of better. Although
twenty had already paid with their lives and eight more
were scheduled for the journey to the hill, there were
still about one hundred and fifty in prison awaiting trial
and two hundred others suspected. From Boston, Andover and the towns round about, men and women
whom the afflicted girls cried out upon were daily being
brought to face their accusers. John Alden, an Indian
fighter and a naval commander, and a son of the famous
John and Priscilla, had already been examined in Salem
and committed to Boston prison. Philip English, the
wealthiest shipowner of Salem, had been cried out upon

with his wife, and their property confiscated. Had they not escaped to New York on the advice of their friends in Boston, their bodies might have lain among those in the crevice. Higher and higher reached the girls in their assurance. At last, after the wife of Governor Phips had been accused, reaction set in. No one was safe any more, the people realized, turning at last a charitable eye on those whom they had been so ready to condemn. Before the end of October, Governor Phips had dismissed the commission of Oyer and Terminer.

Neither Justice Stoughton nor the divines were willing to end the war against Satan—not now, with their work of purification hardly begun. Stoughton, indeed, showed his resentment all too clearly. Swayed by the arguments of the magistrates and divines, Governor Phips permitted a special court to be held in Salem, with Stoughton as the chief judge. Now, however, on the advice of Increase Mather, the court was bidden to remember that it was possible for the Devil to carry on his nefarious work in the shape of an innocent person. In other words, spectral evidence should not be given too much weight.

Of the fifty-two brought to trial before the special court, only three were condemned. But the people had had enough of the evil business and protested, saying that these three were as innocent as the other forty-nine. Stoughton, nevertheless, signed a warrant for their speedy execution, as well as for the death of those who had been condemned at the last session of the commission of Oyer and Terminer.

Then Governor Phips took the matter into his own hands. After sending a letter to King William and Queen Mary, explaining his displeasure at the way in which the trials had been conducted, he issued a reprieve to all those lying under sentence of death. Stoughton fumed and left the special court in a rage. The days of his power were over. The people would have no more of death.

For the last time in New England the battle had been waged between Superstition and Reason. It was a cruel, inhuman fight, with precious lives lost and many more victims made than those who perished on the witch tree. But with the sacrifice of those martyrs, the Puritans emerged painfully from the gloom of superstition and intolerance that had darkened the youth of their commonwealth and stained its annals with blood. New England had come of age.

It is saddening and significant for us to note today that of the many ministers and scholars of New England, none raised his voice to condemn the court which had tried the accused, although many must have known that by their guilty silence innocent people were being done to death. Nothing was written, nothing said to discredit the process of justice. The Commonwealth and the Law could do no wrong.

There was one man, however, who after the Mathers had written their reports and set down their justifications, took up his pen for a severe indictment. But Robert Calef, the English-born merchant, was no one of any account—not in comparison with the powerful Mather dynasty. When, therefore, his answer to Cotton Mather's *Memorable Providences* appeared in 1700, it bore an English imprint. No one in New England had had the courage to publish it. The Mathers and their friends rose up crying vengeance, but since Calef was prepared for all opposition, Increase Mather contented himself with publicly burning the offending book in the Harvard College grounds.

Posthumous defenders, seekers after abstract justice, have now and then taken up their pens for the clearing of Cotton Mather, stressing his intentions rather than his deeds, and charging him, at the most, with being a misguided but sincere man. Of his sincerity there is no doubt. He was ruthlessly, inhumanly sincere, especially in his persecution of the partisans of the Devil, who was so real to him that, like Luther, he saw him with his visual eye. In a superstitious age he added fuel to the flame. In a crisis of intolerance, he did nothing to lead the people toward rationality and mercy. Even after the panic in Salem had died down, he continued his researches in witchcraft, taking as his subjects two ignorant, hysterical wenches who, thinking that the Salem girls had had enough publicity, began to raise the Devil on their own account. They offered a much-wanted opportunity for Cotton Mather to show the judges how *he* would have dealt with the Salem bewitchment—a conclusive experiment, after the fact!

The afflicted, however, seeing that their antics were not making the noise they had anticipated, were soon rid of their bedevilment—but not before Cotton Mather had written the lengthy record of these brands which he had plucked from the burning! Witchcraft was to him as real as the rising of the sun. Had he not experienced the dire effects of it in his own home, a year after the Salem trials when his wife bore him a monstrously malformed child that died soon after its birth?

As time made them see their wrong, the people were bowed with the load of guilt upon their consciences.

Days of humiliation and prayer were held oftener than ever before, and records of the trials which prejudiced the survivors of the victims, were secretly destroyed. In 1703 the General Court made a public gesture of atonement when it voted indemnities to the heirs of all those executed and condemned. The judges, with the notable exception of Hathorne and Stoughton, who died unrepentant, could know no rest. At some time or other of their lives they declared themselves in error, and begged forgiveness of their neighbors for the part they had played in 1692. It was a solemn and dread occasion when, on a fast day in the winter of 1697, Samuel Sewall rose in his pew in the Old South Meetinghouse in Boston and stood with his venerable head bowed, as the minister read his confession of humiliation:

"Samuel Sewall, sensible of the reiterated strokes of God upon himself and family . . . desires to take the blame and shame of it [the witchcraft trial], asking pardon of men, and especially desiring prayers that God . . . would pardon that sin and all other his sins."

.    .    .    .    .    .    .

Gallows Hill, with every springtime, is covered with glossy woodwax, as if to soften the memory of 1692. Trees and shrubs have been planted to relieve its barrenness, and a ball field has been laid out. But over all still hangs a brooding cloud that dims the eye and muffles laughter. Like Hawthorne, we, too, feel that "here, in dark, funereal stone, should rise another monument, sadly commemorative of the errors of an early race, and not to be cast down, while the human heart has one infirmity that may result in crime."

It is a short trolley ride from Salem to Danvers, the

Salem Village of ancient days. The car lets the visitor off in the commercial center of the overgrown village that strives to be a town. On a Sunday not a creature is to be seen in the streets for blocks and blocks except for some stray, droop-tailed dog. Danvers still observes the traditions of the seventeenth century on a Sabbath morn.

A brief walk brings one to the Wadsworth burying ground, the oldest in Danvers. Here Elizabeth, the wife of the Rev. Samuel Parris is buried; here, too, lie many of the Putnams under leaning stones and rank weeds. No one remembers them.

From the cemetery it is but a short diagonal to the very nest of the witchcraft delusion—the site where the parish house stood on the patch of land that made Mr. Parris lust after its possession. Many years ago the Rev. Charles Wentworth Upham, writing about this spot, mentioned a desert place, a barren field. Time has not forgotten. It still sows with salt the once blooming gardens and orchards.

On the corner of Center and Hobart streets a little church rises on what became the new meetinghouse site in 1702, after the unpopular Mr. Parris had been driven out to end an undistinguished life in the frontier towns. The door of the church is open. In the interior there are views of the meetinghouse, showing its progress from a shingled cabin to the present edifice. Voices come from behind a door to the right, and three young men come in, strangely anachronistic in their twentieth century clothes. Did they know anything of the witchcraft delusion—of Mr. Parris, of the Putnams? We might have been speaking a foreign tongue.

Of Samuel Parris all memory has left Salem Village. Only the gray stone that covers the dust of his wife remains, bearing a fading inscription. And a forgotten field, which every recurrent spring mercifully spreads with weeds.

## CHAPTER XI

## THE NEW CENTURY

LORD, with how firm a stroke, with how hard a hand didst thou visit the people of New England! A century ended, another progressed in the march of the years, yet their trials remained undiminished. Every winter brought the same rigors. With every summer came the plagues of insects that devoured the harvests, and the menace of smallpox that threatened to decimate God's people. Happily the Puritans believed in marrying early and often, in obedience to the divine injunction that they increase and multiply. No widows or widowers were suffered to remain long unattached, and from the beginning, if any man came from England without his wife, he was snubbed until he sent for her.

Hence the population was on the ascendant, despite all odds. Moreover, the people had learned many things for their preservation. They knew that cats and dogs carried death with them in time of sickness; therefore with every outbreak they applied Malthusianism before Malthus. They knew, too, of that new method in medicine called inoculation, which had been brought in from the mysterious country of Thessaly where witchcrafts and strange rites flourished. How it had reached Europe no one knows, except that it was told that Lady Mary Montagu, who was traveling in Constantinople, there learned of the practice and recommended it for the preservation of life.

New England was introduced to it through the Mathers, more particularly Cotton, by virtue of his early interest in medicine—though whether inoculation were medicine or merely another piece of the Devil's ingenuity, none could tell. Opposition to it sprang up in all quarters. How could a Christian allow himself to be scratched, to have a humor injected into him for the prevention of the disease—and hope to save his soul? Was it not all in opposition to the will of God?

Cotton Mather did not think so. With the same exaltation with which he had proceeded in the discovery of witchcraft, he entered into the occult art of inoculation. From the pulpit he warned the obdurate and predicted a visitation of the Lord. Had not the sign of God's wrath manifested itself in the skies on the 11th of December, 1719, and did the people still doubt? True, nothing untoward came to justify his premonitions in 1720, but during the summer of 1721 the Lord's hand descended upon New England in another outbreak of the pestilence that raged long and furiously, taking many lives. Then Cotton Mather came to the help of his unwilling people, bolstered up by his title of Member of the Royal Scientific Society and by his never-failing assurance in his divine mission. From door to door, with Dr. Zabdiel Boylston whom he had converted to inoculation, he went, finding subjects for the great test. By the end of the year nearly three hundred had been inoculated.

The experiment seemed to work. Of the many inoculated only six died, whereas the mortality among the others was higher than ever in the violence of the epidemic. Nonetheless Cotton Mather made himself more enemies when he turned to the saving of lives, than in the terrible year when he had labored in the saving of souls. Attacks upon him and his friends appeared in the Boston press, and an attempt was made upon his life when a hand grenade was thrown into his house with the posy, "Damn you, I will inoculate you with this, with a pox to you." God would not allow his minister to be harmed, for when the shell went through the window, the fuse, disconnected by the casement, burned itself out harmlessly. Time proved Cotton Mather right in this instance, and the credit belongs to him for having brought science into what was once the wilderness, several years before it reached France and Germany.

New England had found its place in the world. The mother country saw it, and was pleased. Since the first decade of the great exodus when nearly twenty thousand middle-class Puritans had come to work out their Christian experiment in the New World, a number of other colonies had established themselves about the territory of the Massachusetts Bay Company. Connecticut, Rhode Island, New Haven—all planted their stakes and all prospered.

Farther south Virginia and Maryland, founded still earlier, had developed to an extraordinary degree. By 1660 Virginia alone had a population nearly equal to that of New England. In the ocean wastes, island colonies flourished,—the Barbados, Bermuda and many lesser plantations, all for the glory of Britannia. Then, in 1713, a still vaster territory was ceded to her by the treaty of Utrecht that marked an end, for the moment, to the wars that had ravaged Europe.

For England the conflict had begun under the reign of Queen Anne, although her colonies had carried on a persistent war in the New World to keep the Spanish, the Dutch and the French from encroaching upon her American possessions. It was the French they mistrusted most, those subjects of the profligate Louis XIV who stood for all that the commonwealth abhorred—Catholicism, the divine right of kings, tyranny, pagan culture and aristocracy, as against their solid, honest if grim middle-classness. Not that they despised aristocracy, but it must be of the intellect. Nor did they scorn a humanist culture provided it continued, as in their Harvard, the classical tradition which the Puritan teachers had imbibed at Cambridge in the days when John Milton and Jeremy Taylor had trod the banks of the Cam. Ever since their origin, therefore, the colonies had had to defend their frontiers for the sake of their culture, as well as for the Crown.

In Europe, after the battle of Blenheim, England had driven France to peace, but not for long. Again Queen Anne was forced to send out her great general, Marlborough, to play the war game on the chessboard of the continent. It was an advantageous game for England. When, that April of 1713, the treaty papers were signed at Utrecht, England walked off with Hudson Bay, Nova Scotia, St. Christopher's and Newfoundland. The power of the French in America was drawing to an end.

At the news of the gainful peace there was a general celebration in New England. The colonies, too, had benefited. It meant that the frontiers, always a bar to expansion, could be opened without too great a menace from the enemy and the Indians, everybody's allies in colonial warfare.

On Tuesday morning, August 25, 1713, Col. Samuel

Browne published the news of the peace in Salem and called for a solemnization of the event in the afternoon. Officers in their bright uniforms, soldiers and colonists gathered from all parts to the town, till it teemed as in the old days when other events had drawn the curious. Mounted on a high place, Col. Browne read the proclamation, which was followed by such a volley of triumphal guns from the forts of Salem and Marblehead that much of John Guppy's glass was broken. At the next session the selectmen voted him a sum for damages.

On the whole, England's preoccupation with European and domestic affairs had had a beneficial effect upon the colonies. Free from restrictive interference they developed their resources to the utmost, so that by the end of the century, New England, with a population of well over a hundred thousand, had grown to be almost self-sufficient. A spirit of independence filled every breast—a feeling, however, not unmingled with loyalty toward the mother country, in whose triumphs there was not a back settlement but took personal pride. After all, did they not all contribute, to the least man, with materials—and with life?

Queen Anne did not long survive the triumphs of her general. Hardly a year after the signing of the treaty, she was laid to rest in Westminster Abbey, in the same tomb that contained her husband and children, none of whom had fulfilled her hopes of succession. Dutifully the colonies mourned. Dutifully, too, with a beating of drums and a solemn congress of the dignitaries of Salem, George Louis, elector of Hanover, was proclaimed as King George I. Thrice the ordnance of the fort volleyed. That night the town flared with illuminations, almost as in 1698 when the "great fire," which had started in Timothy Lindall's warehouse, destroyed five dwellings and would have spread to the center had not the Hathorne house been blown up to arrest its course. No mishaps marred the festivities of that night, however, and the citizens of Salem retired, according to the *News Letter*, "with all expressions of joy and entire satisfaction."

Yes, the colonies were loyal, responding to every *luctus* and *gaudium* of the motherland. In the traditionally unfestive New England, where Christmas and May Day had been abolished, November 5 was scrupulously observed in remembrance of 1605, when the royal family had been providentially preserved from being blown up during the Gunpowder Plot. By act of Parliament the date had been set apart as one of public thanksgiving for the churches and subjects of England. The American settlers celebrated it in their own way.

In Salem it was a popular holiday that lasted well into the nineteenth century, though not then, perhaps, in the perfection of detail that is so delightfully described in Henfield's diary. How Guy Fawkes Day became converted to Pope Day is hard to trace through the vicissitudes of tradition in the popular mind. It is definite, however, that without the Pope, who is conceived as the arch-villain in this November pageant, there could have been no holiday.

On the morning of Pope Day groups of boys would go through the streets of Salem parading an image of the dignitary as a reminder of the celebration that was to be held in the evening. Later a sort of circus wagon with two platforms was drawn through the town, bearing on one level the stuffed figures of the Pope, monks and the Devil, and on the other, the actors of the pageant who manipulated the dummies while their spokesman declaimed the lines:

> The fifth of November
> As you will remember,
> Was gunpowder treason and plot . . .

No gentleman at whose door the cart stopped with its following of gleeful boys could resist their appeal, whatever his taste for poetry. Everyone gave something and the contributions were put into a common pot. Finally, when the rounds had been made, the cart with its retinue, which by this time included the whole town, proceeded to some open place and the main celebration was held. It was one to thrill a boy's heart, which, alas, in those days had few legitimate pleasures. In the course of the day a huge pyre had been built of tar barrels, wash tubs, staves—anything that the young marauders had been able to lay their hands on. The images of the Pope, the monks and the Devil were thrown on the heap, and the bonfire was started, to a roaring song and dance that must have made the Indians who came to camp annually on Gallows Hill, wonder whether their old devil Squantum had taken possession of the solemn Puritans. The heads of the figures, however, were preserved from the flames—for the following Pope Day. Meanwhile the proceeds from the collection had been spent on refreshments for the whole party which, what with the fire and an inner glowing, finally went home well warmed.

For a long time another excitement had stirred the blood of Salem boys and youths at the sight of a ship on the sea. Silently their mothers caught the look in their eyes, a look that told of far-off places and strange peoples and marvelous adventure, of rousing fights on the ocean and of ships laden with treasure, of freedom from the narrowness of home and meetinghouse, of a whole vast masculine world in which Salem was but a speck, though dearly beloved because it was home—and yet because it was home, but a springboard to a thrilling universe. Every lad had felt the spell of the sea, from the first, who had taken his place before the mast of Robert Moulton's tiny crafts in 1630, to the proud tar who climbed up the side of Captain Derby's latest schooner, now in the 1750's. That restlessness and that fever had made Salem one of the foremost towns of New England. It was as yet only the dawn of her day.

## CHAPTER XII

## PIRATES AND PRIVATEERING

BEYOND the town proper but distinct from the upper part near North Fields, where the "trade or mystery of distilling spirits" was exercised together with the equally offensive art of "killing all meat," lay the wharves and warehouses of the rising marine dynasties. Before the Revolution they stretched along the upper part of South River, as far as Union Wharf, then called Long Wharf, which spanned the river to a small island known as Jeggle's after William Giggles or Jeggles, who, in 1659, had come there to build ships and send them out to sea. Two more wharves lay at North Bridge, while above them, on North River near Frye's mills, the air resounded with the blows of the shipwright's mallet. In the preceding century Winter Island, too, had been dented with wharves, but before the Revolution they had all disappeared, making way for the warehouse of Richard "King" Derby, and his great wharf, known later as Powder House Wharf.

In the latter part of the seventeenth century most of the shipbuilding was done on the Creek, where a broad bay of the South River floated the new craft to the ocean. Bartholomew Gedney, John Norman, Daniel Bacon and Ebenezer Lambert all had their yards here, west of the Boston and Maine Railroad station, whose granite towers now stand solid where winged ships once found their way to port. Imprisoned in its conduit, the

A MEMBERSHIP CERTIFICATE OF THE SALEM MARINE SOCIETY.

FOREIGN FACTORIES AT CANTON, 1830—1840.

hidden tide still ebbs and flows under the massive structure. As far as the old road to Marblehead, between Norman and High Streets, the ancient bay extended, crossed
by a bridge with a draw of thirty feet for the proud craft
to pass through. Knocker's Hole the region was called,
from the constant hammering of the builders. In 1695
William Becket set up his shipyard at the foot of Becket
Court, where ships were built till 1816; and twenty years
later Joseph Hardy, who was also a trader, established
himself on the cove, now Bertram Park.

Until the Revolution, however, the cod-fishery was
the chief business of the ship-merchants, and many a fortune had been founded on it. Winter Island, from the
earliest colonial days, became the center of the industry,
together with Salem Neck and the bank of the North
River, where the fish were brought in, unladen and
cured. The smell of fish, drying and curing in the open,
hung in the air, but the people of Salem conducted their
industry unashamed. It was an honest business—and profitable. Hence when in 1743 Col. Benjamin Pickman built
his fine house, which is still standing at the rear of 165
Essex Street, he ordered as part of the decoration the
figure of a codfish, carved and gilded, on each riser of
his front stairs. Many a scutcheon of old England had
borne less worthy emblems.

The Rev. Hugh Peter, who had gone back to England
only to be hanged and quartered in 1660 on the charge
of plotting the King's death, had spurred Salem on in
the days of her infant commerce with his cry for ships
and more ships. A few years after the founding of the
town, a thriving coastwise trade began with the Southern ports. Intrepid vessels, no larger than modern barges,

made regular voyages to the West Indies, and dared the hazards of the ocean to trade with Portugal and Spain. Without the help of sextant or Bowditch's *Practical Navigator*, with no map to guide them but some rough chart, meager and incorrect, traced by a skipper on his voyages, the brave masters navigated the perilous seas, often surviving the storms only to run the risk of capture. For the seas, in those days, swarmed with pirates. No cove but might hide a Barbary pirate crew, no ship but might conceal under its canvas the menacing mouth of a cannon.

Nevertheless, to Virginia and the Barbados, St. Christopher's and the Isle of Jersey, the squat little sloops of Philip English and the ketches of other Salem shipmasters carried their cargo of molasses and rum, fish kegs and wooden pails, mackerel and sugar, and brought back wheat and pork, furs and hides, old pewter and iron, brass, copper and goods that they lacked at home. Undaunted, the skippers of New England tacked in all seas, keeping their reckoning, as an old writer tells us, with chalk on a shingle which they stowed away in the binnacle. "By way of observation they held up a hand to the sun. When they got him over four fingers they knew they were straight for Hole-in-the-Wall; three fingers gave them their course to the Double-headed Shop Key and two carried them down to Barbados." In all else they trusted to Providence and their own courage.

Notwithstanding the many dangers and the restrictions of England's navigation acts, a number of wealthy men had arisen in Salem before the end of the seventeenth century. Foremost among them was Philip English, who had come from the Isle of Jersey before 1670. Shortly after his arrival he married Mary, the daughter of William Hollingworth, a well-to-do merchant who owned a wharf at the foot of what later became English Street. In a few years Philip English, who occasionally sailed as skipper in his own vessels, had fared so well that he built one of the handsomest gabled houses in Salem, from whose upper windows he would watch, spyglass in hand, for his ships riding to harbor under a full press of canvas. When the witchcraft panic broke out, implicating him and his wife among the accused, he was perhaps the wealthiest man in New England, with a wharf and warehouse of his own to receive the cargoes of his twenty-one vessels, and with more than a dozen buildings in the town of Salem bringing him rents.[1] On the death of his mother-in-law, the Hollingworth estate fell to Mary English who, in turn, bequeathed it to her son Philip when she died in 1694. In 1748 wharves and warehouses were conveyed by the younger Philip English to Richard Derby, the founder of the eighteenth-century merchant dynasty of his name.

It was in 1671 that Roger Derby, grandfather of Richard, had come from England to try his fortunes in the New World. Like most of the menfolk of Salem, he took to the sea; and his son, Richard's father, followed after him, rising to the cabin by the time Richard was born in 1712. Captain Derby, however, died when his son was still an infant, whose care fell to the charge of the young widow. Mrs. Derby was a woman of the old stamp. Practical and energetic, she brought up the boy to a career on the sea, so that by the time he was twenty-four, he was sailing as master on the sloop *Ranger*, that

[1] For the story of Philip and Mary English see the author's novel, *Gallows Hill*.

crossed the ocean to Cadiz with the staple cargo of fish in exchange for oil, fruit, handkerchiefs and salt. With a crew of half a dozen men he made a number of voyages, directing his course to whatever harbor promised greatest gain, till by the middle of the century he owned a fleet of vessels of from fifty to one hundred tons burden. As "King" Derby he no longer used the docks on Winter Island which had been allowed to him for a farthing a year, but floated his bottoms from his own wharf that made Salem maritime history up until the beginning of the nineteenth century.

For two hundred years the shipwright, the rigger and the sailmaker, the mariner and the skipper still on their sea legs and with the salt in their throats, peopled Derby Street and the harbor front. In the tall sail lofts where the great white wings of the crafts were stretched on the polished floors, silent men sat cross-legged like tailors in the *Arabian Nights*, stitching the canvas with their thimbles fastened to their palms. High above the bustle, they sewed and seamed and tarred the fragrant canvas that was to speed first the quaint sloops and ketches, and then the majestic East Indiamen on their voyages to strange places and newly-discovered inland seas. From the narrow windows they could look out upon the harbor and listen to the distant noises of unlading and shipping. They could recognize by his walk the sailor just landed, and the merchant hurrying from his cargo to the countinghouse where the profits were reckoned. They could hear the rollicking chanteys of the men quenching their thirst in the taverns, and get a whiff of the matting-covered bales of merchandise on the way to the warehouses, giving them, the stay-at-homes, a sense of romance and adventure. They only made the wings, but it was those others who used them—those men with their faces scorched by tropical suns and their eyes hooded from too much gazing on moving waters.

In the warehouses the cargoes changed with the years as, after the Revolution, when England could no longer interfere with navigation laws, the markets were extended and barriers broken through. Then with sugar from the West Indies, there were figs, raisins and almonds from the Mediterranean; ivory and gum-copal from Zanzibar; ginger from India; teas and silks from China; cotton from Bombay, pepper from Sumatra, and from Arabia sacks of coffee. From the west coast of Africa palm oil came in vats, and wine from Portugal and the Madeiras. The very names of the foreign lands were a poem, and the breath of romance hung over the town, with the fragrance of Eastern spices.

Legends arose, and the imagination awakened. The mystery and the solitude of months, sometimes years, passed on the surface of unknowable seas, made the sailors credulous and visionary. Like Coleridge's Ancient Mariner, and like many another before him, they saw strange sights, like phantom ships and weird monsters that came up out of the deep only long enough to fill them with awe. On his first voyage to New England, Josselyn, the traveler, told of "a sea serpent or snake, that lay quoiled up like a cable upon a rock at Cape Ann." Again and again the monster made his appearance, now near Mount Desert, now in the vicinity of Salem as late as 1817, when he revealed himself so clearly that the people could speak of nothing else. Flattered by the attention he received the creature showed himself in the bay almost every year after, till, with familiarity, no one thought any more of him.

Since so much of their life depended on the elements, the people looked everywhere for signs and portents. The logbooks of the navigators were filled with what they saw, while at home those who could write recorded untoward events for future ages. "Three suns [were seen] about the sunsetting," Governor Winthrop wrote in his *Journal* on December 15, 1645. "And about two months after that, two suns at sunrising; the one continued close to the horizon while the other which was the true sun, arose about half an hour."

Many a like wonder Cotton Mather set down in his extraordinary *Magnalia Christi Americana*, together with the yarns he collected from sailors back from their wanderings—stories of miraculous escapes and of ghostly ships riding against the wind and then melting away like clouds in the sky. Salem's phantom ship that sailed on a Friday—hangman's day—with its eerie crew and its two tragic lovers, lived on in the imagination of the people from generation to generation, inspiring the pens of Longfellow, Irving and Whittier.

> It passed away—that vision strange—
> Forever from their sight;
> Yet long shall Naumkeag's annals tell
> The story of that night—
> The phantom-bark—the ghostly crew,
> The pale encircling light.[1]

But these were all supernatural happenings, beyond the control of man, furnishing matter for fireside and fo'c'sle

[1] From Whittier's "The Spectre Ship of Salem."

when real danger did not threaten. There were other, more dreaded, encounters on the sea that made women widows, and children orphans. Not only on the Spanish Main did the Salem vessels have to beware, but also along the familiar New England coast. From the time the first ships started out from the harbor, the logbooks were filled with warnings of perilous areas where every sail meant an enemy. No vessel left shore without arms. At any moment the passing ship might hoist the flag of piracy on the head of its mast and fire without warning.

Other enemies sprang up as New England sails adventured farther from home. Before the close of the seventeenth century Turkish pirate ships were seizing Salem vessels laden with rich cargo, and holding the mariners for ransom in Algiers. In the constant state of warfare in Europe, French frigates and privateers laid hold of anything that flew English colors, and even lay in wait for the New England vessels in their own waters. At the Isle of Shoals, in Salem bay itself, sloops and ketches fell prey to the marauders. "In the year 1689," John Higginson wrote, "I had attained a competent estate. . . . . But since that time I have met with considerable losses. Of sixty-odd fishing ketches belonging to this town but about six are left."

It was therefore with fear and foreboding that mothers and wives saw their men climbing over the ship's side for voyages from which they might never return. Sailors' narratives of the period read like fantastic imaginings, except that they were all too true, as gaunt men, reduced to skin and bone from bondage in Barbary, could testify on their return. Benjamin Alford of Boston and William Bowditch of Salem had been "captives into

Sallee." Robert Carver had been taken nine years before and was still awaiting release. Many disappeared as if they had never been, and time and again the annals of Salem repeated such entries as, "Thomas Purchase went on a voyage in 1681 with Habbakuk Turner, and neither ship nor men were ever heard from." The sea? Pirates? No one ever found out.

Early the New England mariners learned to defend themselves, and many's the tale of bravery that was told over the tankards in the harbor taverns. There was the story of Captain Harradine of Salem,—Andrew Harradine, who taught all marauders a lesson and rid the waters of two notorious rogues. In 1724, after numerous executions in the Boston flats should have taught pirates a lesson, a cloud of suspicious looking topsails appeared off Cape Ann within sight of Salem harbor, and made for Captain Harradine's sloop. A set-to followed, during which the Captain and his crew were seized by Nutt and Phillip, two sea scamps who had been terrorizing the waterways for years. The prisoners were hauled to the outlaw ship, when what was the dismay of the pirates to find their captives turn upon them with the fury of hell-hounds. The affray was brief and deadly. Taken by surprise, the pirates were no match against the righteous ire of Harradine and his men. Before long Nutt and Phillip lay dead on the deck, together with their henchmen; their crew was sardined in the hatches, and Captain Harradine, commanding the helm, turned the vessel toward Boston, to present trophy and prisoners to the authorities.

Salem's most famous pirate case, however, had unfolded earlier in the century. In 1703, the brigantine *Charles Galley* left Boston harbor on a privateering expedition against the offending French. On the voyage the commander was taken ill, whereupon John Quelch, the lieutenant, with a number of the crew, locked the sick man in the cabin until he starved to death, and Quelch himself took command of the vessel—as a pirate. Forsaking the original route, Quelch turned the vessel south toward Brazil, and there engaged in such lucrative exploits that when the *Charles Galley* anchored off Marblehead, the people grew suspicious at the amount of its treasure. Soon the authorities got wind of the rumors, but before any action could be taken, Quelch had admitted his guilt by fleeing with his men.

For many months they were reported here, there and everywhere, now on this ship and now on that, till it was learned definitely that early in June, 1704, they were to sail on a boat from Gloucester. That night Major Stephen Sewall of Salem, with Captain John Turner and forty volunteers, took a shallop and the fort pinnace, and went in search of Quelch and his crew. Several days later Major Sewall returned to Salem, bringing a galley commanded by Thomas Larrimore, and seven of the pirates who had been seized upon it on their way to England. They had still on their persons the booty of their piracy, together with more than forty-five ounces of gold. Two more of the buccaneers, who had been left at Cape Ann, surrendered and were brought a few days later to Salem, from where on the seventeenth of June Sewall escorted them all to Boston for trial.

The Boston authorities did not believe in having sea rovers languish too long in jail. On the nineteenth, therefore, Quelch was tried for piracy, found guilty and sentenced to death. The following day four more of his crew were condemned with him. On the last day of the month, a Friday, all five were provided with hempen necker-chiefs, making a Salem bard burst into righteous numbers:

> The pirates who against God's laws did fight,
> Have all been taken which is very right.
> Some of them were old and others young,
> And on the flats of Boston they were hung.

Meanwhile, England had not been slow to discover that the prowess of her colonial mariners could be put to good use in building up her empire in the West. From the first planting of the colonies, both she and France had been rivals for supremacy; and wars, open or tacit, had brought the colonists into constant clashes with the enemy on land and sea. In Europe, during the summer of 1755, England and France were again on the verge of war. Indeed, without bothering to declare it, England had opened hostilities by taking whatever French boats came in the way of the Union Jack. There were lands she coveted in the West, along the Ohio and the Mississippi; this was as good a way of her acquiring them as any. She had long known that there was virtue in indirection, and George II let things pass. Did he not have the famous Pitt to interpret in his favor the Treaty of Aix-la-Chapelle?

As usual, the war of the mother countries had its counterpart in America, the French banding with their old allies, the Indians, and the English awaiting the arrival of expeditionary forces. They arrived, in brilliant red uniforms, dapper and new, under the leadership of Gen. Edward Braddock. In the middle of July, 1755, with flags waving and the fife and drum sounding martial music, Gen. Braddock's cavalcade and its file of American soldiers marched through the streets of Philadelphia to the frontier, where the French and Indians were awaiting them. They reckoned without the cunning of the enemy. In the forest three hundred frenzied Indians and two hundred Frenchmen fell upon them, slew Braddock and his officers, and massacred the flower of the English army but for the few who considered the better part of valor . . .

Similar disasters met the intrepid New England skippers on the sea. Since commerce, even in times of peace, was a risky business, they took the excuse of the French and Indian War to mount from eight to twelve cannon on their merchantmen, converting them to the not altogether dishonorable class of privateers. The sea always had its risks. What difference whether one fought the pirate flag or the French? Salem merchants were gaining their experience, even if at a cost. Britannia ruled the waves, despite occasional defeats, and New England contributed to her glory—a glory which was soon to turn her shortsightedly against her own.

Perhaps because of the increased hazards to navigation following the French and Indian War, a group of eighteen Salem shipmasters founded the Salem Marine Society in 1766. The request for incorporation, presented in May, 1770, to His Excellency Thomas Hutchinson, made the purposes clear. "The petition of Jonathan Garner junr. and others . . . who are or have been Masters of Vessels, humbly sheweth—That they & sundry other Persons now at Sea, have for a few Years past, united in a voluntary Society for the Purpose of raising a Fund wherewith to relieve such of their Members as thro' Misfortune at Sea, or otherwise, or by Reason of old

Age or Sickness, stand in Need of Relief, & the neces-
sitous Families of deceased Members; and also to com-
municate in Writing, to be lodged with the Society, the
Observations they make at Sea of any Matters which
may render Navigation, particularly on this Coast, easier
& safer."

The Society is still in existence. Of the 617 members
who had joined it up until 1923, when a new edition of
the *Laws of the Marine Society* was issued, only a handful remain,—old men with the bronze of the sea long
faded from their cheeks, but with the yearning for the
ocean still in their eyes as they spin out yarns of the
last time they sailed round the Cape. . . . The names of
father, son, grandson and great-grandson appear from
generation to generation, good old names that made history. One hundred and forty members fought in the
Revolution and in the War of 1812; ten in the Civil War.
In all parts of the world their ashes lie scattered, in
Barbados and Port au Prince; in Canton, Amboyne, Calcutta and Singapore; in wildest Africa, Sumatra and
Zanzibar, in Mozambique and Pulu Penang. But most
often in the death list recurs the requiem: *At sea. Lost at
sea. At sea. Lost at sea.*

Younger than its predecessor, the East India Marine
Society bears 1799 as the date of its founding. Its aims
were more or less the same, but the by-laws also provided for the formation of a museum "of natural and
artificial curiosities, particularly such as are to be found
beyond the Cape of Good Hope or Cape Horn."

Once a year, in the heyday of Salem's glory, the East
India Marine Society held its solemn installation. Then,
with their gifts from the Orient in their hands for the

gaping crowd to see, the members of the society filed
through the streets in the wake of a dignitary in a Chinese
costume and mask, while a handsome palanquin, borne
by Salem Negroes whose faces glowed in the joyousness
of the occasion, exhibited a young Hindoo potentate
whose honest Salem features could scarcely be recognized
in the richness of his borrowed accouterments. In 1848,
perhaps for the last time, the honored palanquin was
taken out when, with the Salem Marine Society, the
East India members enlivened the parade in Boston that
celebrated the carrying of Cochituate water into that
city. "Our two . . . societies made a very fine appearance," says the Salem Marine Society record with commendable frankness. And indeed they must have, with
the Light Infantry and the Salem Brass Band escorting
them, and with the beautiful ship *Friendship* and the
fully panoplied palanquin leading the way. "They also
had a handsome banner and other devices, and attracted
a great deal of notice," resumes the record, to close
abruptly with, "We think they have not marched in procession since that time."

But by then the East India Marine Society members
had more than fulfilled their duty toward their fellow
citizens, and their collection of rarities had grown till it
attracted even scholars from overseas. In 1867, through
the generosity of George Peabody, the museum of the
East India Marine Society was put in charge of the
Peabody Academy of Science—the present Peabody Museum of Salem, where he who wishes may admire the
taste of those salty connoisseurs.

## CHAPTER XIII

## *REVOLUTION*

"THESE are the times that try men's souls: the summer soldier and the sunshine patriot will, in this crisis, shrink from the service of his country; but he that stands it *now*, deserves the love and thanks of man and woman." On a drumhead, by the bivouac fire, Tom Paine penned his first American *Crisis*, read by Washington to hearten his soldiers before the battle of Trenton.

Earlier, on January 10, 1776, Paine had issued his *Common Sense*, the manifesto of the American Revolution. "Let the names of whig and tory be extinct," he pleaded, "and let none other be heard among us, than those of good citizen; an open and resolute friend; and a virtuous supporter of the *rights of mankind* and of the *free and independent states of America*."

When Paine's pamphlet appeared, the Declaration of Independence was still six months away, but the times that try men's souls had been the lot of the American colonies for years under the tyrannous and restrictive measure of the mother country. It was now a time for action, united action, for blood had been shed, first in a massacre on Boston's King Street, and in the outbreak of hostilities on the morning of April 19, 1775, when eight patriots lay dead on the field of Lexington under a volley of British fire.

George III had been sixteen years on the throne. A

stubborn yet foolish monarch with no knowledge of the American continent, but with an overweening ambition for the empire which had been enlarged with the conquest of Canada from the French, he sought to cover an enormous war debt by a system of colonial administration whose sole purpose was the furnishing of revenue. The old and hated Board of Trade was therefore worked overtime passing obnoxious acts and levying taxes to the end, as Palfrey puts it, that the Englishman in America might be employed in making the fortune of the Englishman at home.

In the colonies there were two ways of thinking, with regard to England. In fact, beginning with the long struggle for the maintenance of the first charter, two parties had arisen. There was the party for freedom, insisting on the right of self-government for the colonies under the Monarch; and the party of prerogative, which held that the Crown's authority was alone to be obeyed. In time the terms were to be altered to Patriot and Loyalist.

For more than a hundred years the colonies had borne patiently the navigation acts and other measures that had interfered with the growth of their commerce, and had uncomplainingly supported the soldiers of the Crown that carried on England's endless wars. The crisis came, however, when England proposed to garrison a standing army in the colonies, and, through the three Horatii, Grenville, Egremont and Halifax, devised a Stamp Act to keep the army there. For a year, "out of tenderness to the colonies," as its chief perpetrator declared, the bill was not brought in, but finally, on February 27, 1765, it passed in a full House with a majority of five to one. "The sun of liberty is set," wrote Benjamin Franklin at that time. "The Americans must light the lamps of industry and economy."

The news fell like a thunderbolt on New England. Were they, the sons of liberty, to have taxes levied arbitrarily upon them? Must they submit to trials in the Admiralty Courts for refusal to obey such unjust enactments? Everywhere speeches were made, resolutions carried and petitions submitted. On October 7 the first American Congress opened in New York at a call from Massachusetts, the head and intellect of the Revolution, to find out where the colonies stood in the British scheme of empire, and concluded with the prophetic announcement that they were "a bundle of sticks which could neither be bent nor broken."

In Boston, Salem and other towns the bells tolled and minute guns groaned in demonstrations of grief. In the harbors the flags on the vessels drooped at half-mast. Solemnly, in Boston, effigies of Grenville and other promoters of the Stamp Act were hung on the branches of Liberty Tree where all could see them. Later, they were carried to the Court House as if for trial, and then to the gallows, where they were suspended, cut down, and torn to pieces, all with the gravity of a church meeting. If only the enemies of liberty could have been so easily destroyed!

So bitter was the sentiment against the Stamp Act that Parliament thought it best to repeal it. At the same time it stubbornly held to its prerogative of taxation without representation, and, as if to leave no doubt in the minds of the patriots, exacted an import duty on many commodities, chief of them, tea. The money thus collected was to pay the salaries of the Crown officials in the

# A BLOODY BUTCHER

## BY THE

# BRITISH TROOPS:

### OR, THE

# RUNAWAY FIGHT OF THE REGULAR

Being the PARTICULARS of the VICTORIOUS BATTLE fought at and near CONCORD, situated Twenty Miles from Boston, in the Province

"BLOODY BUTCHERY," A CONTEMPORARY NEWSPAPER ACCOUNT OF THE FIRST ENGAGEMENT WITH THE REDCOATS.

Essex

colonies. England made a fatal mistake. How much better if she had heeded the warning of Pitt, who left a sick bed to address the House of Commons on the Stamp Act. "In a good cause, on a sound bottom, the force of this country can crush America to atoms. . . . But in such a cause your success would be hazardous. America, if she fell, would fall like the strong man; she would embrace the pillars of the State and pull down the constitution along with her."

Yet England could have had no doubt as to the temper of her colonies throughout the proceedings. Benjamin Franklin had given embarrassingly direct answers to the questions which, as an agent for the colonies, he had had to answer before the House of Commons.

"What was the temper of America toward Great Britain before 1763?" queried the interlocutor.

"The best in the world," replied Franklin.

"And what is their temper now?"

"Oh, very much altered."

"What used to be the pride of the Americans?"

"To indulge in the fashions and manufactures of Great Britain."

"What is now their pride?"

"To wear their old clothes over again till they can make new ones."

Many an old coat was turned before the patriot would pay a farthing of the unjust levies. The colonies stood fast against the Townshend Revenue Bill, resolving "to eat nothing, drink nothing, wear nothing, imported from Great Britain."

Governor Francis Bernard, who had early branded himself by declaring that the colonies derived blessings from their subjection to Great Britain, was hardly the man to cope with the rising tide of revolt against the mother country. As yet no word had been spoken of secession or independence, but so strong was the general feeling against the revenue laws, the impressing of New England seamen, and the governor's stubborn refusal to summon the Legislature, that even in spite of themselves, the sister colonies were drawing closer in unity against England.

Samuel Adams drafted petitions to the king, and circulated letters to the colonies discussing the painful issues and guiding leaders to united action. So great was the effect of his writings that the British officials sent a memorial to England, with the result that General Thomas Gage, Commander-in-Chief of the Royal forces in America, was ordered to enforce obedience to the laws and to station a regiment in Boston. More, sloops and frigates were planted in the Massachusetts harbors. The colony was virtually besieged.

"Depend upon it," reproved Hillsborough, the secretary in England for the colonies, "Parliament will not suffer their authority to be trampled upon. We wish to avoid severities toward you; but if you refuse obedience to our laws the whole fleet and army of England shall enforce it."

Indeed, it seemed as if the whole army and navy of the mother country had been sent across the ocean to punish the insubordinate colonies. At least, it looked so to the long-suffering patriots. Everywhere the red coat of the British soldier offended their sight; in the harbors the frigates flaunted the British flag and seized patriot ships. Blood ran high, and frequent clashes occurred be-

tween citizens and the loathed "lobsters." The terms
Patriot and Tory assumed more than their usual significance.

Then, one day in March, 1770, the colonies were horrified by the report of what had happened in Boston,
on the night of the fifth. It was early evening, and a thin
snowfall whitened the houses in the light of a new moon.
Groups of men and boys were roaming the streets in a
state of agitation, for a few days earlier a quarrel had
broken out in Gray's ropewalk between the workmen
and the soldiery, both sides of which had parted with a
promise to renew the fray. At the head of King Street,
soldiers collected for their assignments and walked back
and forth between the main guard and Murray's bar-
racks in Brattle Street. They clutched their clubs and
cutlasses as they passed the groups of citizens, most of
whom were provided with sticks—a precaution that
roused the redcoats to taunts and insults quickly parried
and more quickly returned. Words led to blows, and
soon there was a general clash. In the confusion the
alarm-bell had been rung. People left their houses and
came running to King Street, where they joined the
fight, throwing snowballs against the leveled gun of the
sentry who was shouting, "If they touch me, I'll fire!"

At his cries for help a sergeant with a file of seven
men left the guardhouse, joined by Captain Thomas
Preston of the Twenty-ninth. The sentinel fell into line.
Then the order was given to load the guns.

The crowd could not believe their ears. What! Would
armed soldiers dare to fire on unarmed citizens? They
stood petrified. But only for a moment. The bayonets
of the soldiers pushed them back; their clubs felled the

people right and left. "For God's sake!" cried a by-stander, seizing Preston by the coat. "Take your men back again! If they fire, your life must answer for the consequences."

"I know what I'm about!" snapped the Captain.

No one ever knew whether he gave the order to fire, for in a moment the people's cries of horror were punctuated by blood-curdling musket shots. Panic-stricken, the crowd fell back. The soldiers were ordered to the main guard. In the moonlight, on the blood-darkened snow, five men lay dead.

"On that night, the formation of American Independence was laid," wrote John Adams.

It was true. The people everywhere recognized that from now on they had to deal with an enemy. Leaders sprang up to mold public opinion. Before the end of the year Captain Preston was brought to trial. Pictures of the night on King Street were circulated among the people, with verses to fire their sense of justice.

> Should venal courts, the scandal of the land,
> Snatch the relentless villain from her hand,
> Keen execrations, on this plate inscribed,
> Shall reach a judge who never can be bribed.

Nevertheless, Preston was acquitted.

The Boston Massacre, however, was not forgotten. On its first anniversary, a crowd of patriots gathered in front of Paul Revere's house on North Street and gazed in solemn silence upon the illuminated pictures of the terror in his windows. No, the people must not forget. In Salem, that same day, Samuel Hall's three-year-old *Essex Gazette* appeared with its columns draped in black, "As a solemn and perpetual MEMORIAL:

Of the Tyranny of the British Administration of Government . . .

Of the fatal and destructive Consequences of quartering Armies in Time of Peace in populous cities. . . .

Of the vile Ingratitude and abominable Wickedness of every *American* who abetted and encouraged, either in Thought, Word or Deed, the establishment of a Standing Army among his Countrymen. . . .

Of the unaccountable Conduct of those *Civil Governors*, the immediate Representatives of His Majesty, who, while the Military were triumphantly insulting the whole *Legislative Authority of the State*, and while the blood of the massacred inhabitants was flowing in the Streets, persisted in disclaiming all Authority of relieving the People, by any the least Removal of the Troops;

And of the savage Cruelty of the IMMEDIATE PERPE-TRATORS:

*Be it forever Remembered,*

That this Day, THE FIFTH OF MARCH, is the anniversary of *Preston's Massacre—in King Street—Boston—New England—1770,*

In which Five of His Majesty's Subjects were slain and six wounded,

By the discharge of a Number of Muskets from a Party of Soldiers under the Command of Capt. Thomas Preston.

GOD SAVE THE PEOPLE!

Salem, March 5, 1771."

Alas, the spirited protest went for nothing so far as the home government was concerned. Six months earlier Hutchinson had received an order from His Majesty to give up the fortress in Boston to General Gage—a direct violation of the provincial charter, which placed the command of the militia with the civil governor. Massachusetts was under martial law. Mainly through the efforts of Samuel Adams, committees of correspondence were established in all the colonies. The people were united in spirit, but as yet they had not the strength to assert their unity. By her oppressive measures, England was loosening the most precious jewel in her crown.

For two years no overt act of violence disturbed the colonies. In 1773, however, the East India Company, which found its warehouses overstocked with tea which the colonies refused to buy, applied to Parliament for relief. It came in the form of an odious act, of the same nature as those that had roused the colonies to rebellion. When the East India Company's ships arrived in the harbors of Charleston, Philadelphia, New York, Boston and Salem, they found the government-appointed tea commissioners waiting—but no public to receive their tea. The committees of correspondence had done their work well.

In the port of Boston the *Dartmouth* waited with its hundred and fourteen chests of tea, while the committee of correspondence met to decide on what to do about it.

"Send it back," moved Samuel Adams.

"The only way to get rid of it is to throw it overboard," said Young.

Meanwhile the *Eleanor* and the *Beaver* had arrived, each with its cargo of tea, and moored alongside the *Dartmouth* at Griffin's wharf. For days the three ships lay there with their cargoes, Governor Hutchinson, on the side of the King, taking measures to prevent their sailing before unlading, and the committees stubbornly refusing to clear them. According to the revenue laws of Boston no ship could be cleared with its cargo on board. On the other hand, it could not be re-entered in England. To complicate matters further, after twenty days it was liable to seizure. The committees temporized; the Governor remained adamant. Meanwhile the twentieth day was approaching—the sixteenth of December, 1773.

All morning long, crowds from Boston and the neighboring towns had been milling about the Old South, listening to addresses by Samuel Adams, Young, Rowe and other patriots anxious for the people's will on the tea question. As the afternoon wore on, greater and greater numbers flocked to the meetinghouse, till it seemed as if all Massachusetts were gathered there. Should the tea be landed? What was the people's will? No, no, the tea should not be landed. Almost with one voice the crowd shouted its resolve. "Who knows," asked Rowe at one point, "how tea will mingle with salt water?" Applause drowned the rest.

Meanwhile the December day was drawing to an early close; by six o'clock the wharves were in darkness. In the meetinghouse, however, in the feeble candlelight, anxious faces were still turning toward the speakers' pulpit. Just then the captain of the *Dartmouth* came in to report that the Governor had denied him a pass for his vessel. "Then," said Samuel Adams, rising, "this meeting can do nothing more to save the country."

His words had hardly reached his listeners, when loud war whoops came from the porch, and a band of "Mohawks" with strangely familiar faces under their paint, rushed to Griffin's wharf. Breathless, the crowd followed. Who were they? What were they going to do? Why the disguise? That question they could easily answer.

Down at the wharf the braves clambered over the sides of the three ships, brought up the tea-chests from the hold, and tumbled them into the sea while the people stood by, watching with their usual solemnity. His Majesty had his answer.

When George III was advised of it, he lost his Hanoverian temper, and, in an address to Parliament, accused the colonists of subverting the British constitution. They must be punished to the fullest extent of the law. Promptly a number of penal measures were brought into Parliament, the worst of which, the Boston Port Bill, introduced by Lord North, closed Boston harbor to commerce until His Majesty was appeased, and enforced its various provisions through the army and the fleet. The capital of Massachusetts was ordered removed from Boston to Salem, the Colony's charter was annulled, and General Gage was appointed military and civil governor of the colony.

Massachusetts was not forsaken in her plight. The sister colonies rallied to her support, well knowing that her danger was theirs; all felt punished in her chastisement.

Meanwhile, in Boston, Gage enforced the Regulation Acts and closed the port. In the harbor the ships lay moored, their sails limp, their sides green with weed. The warehouses were silent, and gone was the bustle in ship's tavern and ordinary. Wider and wider grew the division between Patriot and Loyalist, as the one stood staunchly by his constitutional rights, and the other counseled submission to the Crown. It was to patriot Boston, however, that the colonies sent money and supplies, to Boston, the challenger of tyranny, that Salem offered her wharves and stores.

"If Britain by her multiplied oppressions accelerates the independency of her colonies," said Samuel Adams, "whom will she have to blame but herself?"

## CHAPTER XIV

## SALEM PLAYS HER PART

WHEN John Adams visited Salem with his wife before the Revolution, he found a prosperous town with broad, straight, clean streets and the grandest and most elegant houses he had seen in any seaport. Substantial fortunes were being built, and an aristocracy asserted itself in an urbanity of living that amounted to luxury. On Main Street, Col. William Browne's mansion entertained notable guests who arrived in coats of crimson velvet and embroidered waistcoats, with deep lace ruffles at the wrist, silver buckles at toe and knee, and on their heads mountainous white wigs, rising in tiers of curls—the latest fashion from England. He had other houses in the town, and a summer home in Danvers on the crest of Folly Hill, which he called Mount Burnet. Then there were Col. Pickman's mansion with its gilt codfish decorations, Judge Benjamin Lynde's summer residence at Castle Hill, and Thomas Poynton's home, the frame of which he had imported from England on one of his own ships. Many a guest crossed the hospitable threshold with its carved wooden pineapple at the doorhead. And there was the Richard Derby house, solid as the Derby fortune—a fine brick building at the head of Derby Wharf. It was the first house in Salem to be built of brick, against which there was some strange prejudice connected with dampness and declines. Then there were the gambrel-roofed homes of other merchants and ships' captains—all sturdy edifices decorated at the cornices and mantels with knots and rope-friezes, and other devices of the marine wood carver.

How different a life it was from that of the Salemites of 1692, the graves of whose victims on the Hill some pious hand had planted with straggling locust trees! Now, instead of one, there were several places of worship. Where the original meetinghouse of the Puritans had been, rose the three-storied edifice of the First Church, where Mr. Thomas Barnard and Mr. Dunbar preached their sermons. Then there was East Church under the iron law of the Rev. James Diman, a Puritan of the sternest stamp and an ardent patriot. In the latter days of his ministry, after the Revolution, the Unitarian Dr. William Bentley was to succeed him.

At the North meetinghouse, established in 1772 on the corner of Curwen's lane, Thomas Barnard, the son of the pastor of the First Church, held forth. He preached well and was popular, until that hapless day when with a number of the wealthier Tory residents of Salem, he signed an address approving the administration of Governor Hutchinson. None ever knew what the address, presented to Hutchinson on his departure for England, really contained, as it was kept private by the signatories. Their names, however, leaked out, filling the patriots with such zeal for vengeance that, in common with the revolutionaries in other parts of the colony, they treated the Addressers with tar and feathers. Young Mr. Barnard, at heart a patriot, published a recantation in the *Essex Gazette*, begging the Committee of Correspondence "to throw the veil of charity over that incautious act of his."

The veil was thrown, old scores were settled, and in subsequent events Mr. Barnard did his patriot part, unlike the majority of the Addressers who fled the country on the outbreak of the Revolution. There was some talk of their establishing themselves in Australia.

In St. Peter's Church the Episcopalian Rev. William McGilchrist, a Scotchman, served his congregation as rector. He too was one of the Addressers, more out of integrity than opportunism. When the rest of the Tories fled, he stood by his church in spite of scorn and abuse, in spite of tar and feathers, in spite of the stones that were hurled through the windows, and remained firm even after his congregation had wholly forsaken him.

The Rev. Nathaniel Whitaker, Doctor of Divinity, was perhaps the most remarkable clergyman of the town. He had come to Salem practically unknown, but he soon convinced the people of his powers of intellect and oratory, especially after he had succeeded in establishing the Huntington Chapel, as he called his meetinghouse on Main Street. No clergyman had come forward to install him, therefore Timothy Pickering, a zealous Whig, went through the ceremony in favor of a brother Whig who was even more ardent and revolutionary than himself. In the pulpit Dr. Whitaker was fervent and convincing, a sounding trumpet for rebellion. Even before the Boston Massacre he had delivered his fiery sermons, a volume of which, one of the thickest books till then printed in Salem, was issued by Samuel Hall in 1770. Notwithstanding the disapproval of the other churches, the Huntington Chapel society grew to such numbers that, perhaps because of popular sentiment in those critical times, it became the largest in Salem.

Life was more interesting than it had ever been, for with prosperity an aristocracy was rising that wanted scope for its leisure. The merchant class had the ascendant in those days when factories—for sailcloth, rope, glass and a coarse New England wool—were as yet local phenomena. Marine interests formed the backbone of New England; the wealth derived from the sea lay at the base of each solid hearthstone and paid for the imported finery with which both men and women, oblivious of Puritan simplicity, were beginning to adorn themselves. Cocked hat and periwig, scarlet cloak and silk hose, marked the superior standing of the gentleman of the seaport town from that of the lowly inland rustic in his homespun, against which even the barvel of the fisherman was as a badge of honor. Not till after the Revolutionary War did the farmer find any consideration, to judge by the naive comment of a rural Convention member in 1788: "I most tel you I was never treated with so much politeness in my life as I was afterwards by the treadesmen (tradesmen) of Boston, merchants and every other gentlemen."

As for the women, they walked, or rather sailed, in glory if we are to credit the portrayals of the sumptuous creatures on the canvases of Smybert, Blackburn and the fashionable John Singleton Copley. Long since, the olden prohibition which Puritan society put on graven images had been set aside. With the growing taste for luxury it was considered *de rigueur*—for the study of French was not now frowned upon—to have oneself and the members of one's family recorded for the posterity that would eventually inherit household gods as well as goods. Thus, no Boston or Salem matron thought it time ill-spent to give sixteen sittings of six hours each to a Copley or to a Gilbert Stuart. There were Negroes enough to do one's work, and plenty of men and women from the backwoods who were glad of the chance to enter into domestic service.

The tone of good society in Salem was elevated and intellectual, with a thorough polish from Harvard. In 1750 a group of prominent gentlemen formed themselves into a social club for the promotion of polite letters. Ten years later, at a meeting of the club in Mrs. Pratt's "Ship Tavern," which presented a goodly bill for the occasion, a fund was raised to establish what was eventually called the Social Library. Many volumes were contributed by the founders, but most of them were bought in London by the Rev. Jeremy Condy, a minister from Boston, who had been furnished by the members with money and a list of more than three hundred titles. Col. Browne and Col. Pickman, Samuel Curwen, Judge Lynde, who was to be one of the magistrates at the Boston Massacre trial, ministers and doctors, all patronized the Social Library, housed at that time in a room of the brick schoolhouse on School Street. Timothy Orne, who owned fifty-three sails of ships, and Stephen Higginson, another prominent merchant, were also members, and so were the Derbys, the Bowditches, the Nuttings and the Bartons.

Excitement swept the town when it was learned that the seat of government was to be transferred from Boston to Salem. The Loyalists, among whom were public officials and moneyed men, saw in the move a source of advancement for Salem as for themselves; but to the common people, patriots to a man, Gage and his myrmidons were anathema. During the late troubles in Boston they had stood in a body with the sufferers. They had their own "tea-parties," their committees of correspondence, their demonstrations and their courts of justice against offenders who thought more of their own profit than of the common good. At the height of the tea disturbances, John Appleton and Col. Frye were denounced for selling tea, together with the respectable widows, Abigail Epes and Elizabeth Higginson. Deacon Timothy Pickering, who presided, would not be swayed by sentiment. The conduct of the four was pronounced infamous and, as an example to future offenders, it was voted that for seven years their names be read at every town meeting. "When the question is concerning the Liberty or Slavery of America," declared the Committee of Inspection, "the matter is of too much importance to regard the little distinctions of rank, sex, and condition."

To the Tories all such events were merely manifestations of the unquiet times, soon to be remedied by the enforcement of the Crown's authority. They had nothing to lose and much to gain. Accordingly, when General Gage came to Salem on June 2, 1774, with the 64th regiment and two companies of the 65th, some of the foremost men of the town rode out on horseback to meet him. Col. Browne opened wide his mansion to receive him on the day of his arrival, and the following evening, after Gage had sufficiently rested, he was given a magnificent reception at the Assembly Room, built a few years earlier by public subscription when it had been rumored in official circles that Salem would soon be playing a prominent part in diplomatic affairs. Far into the night Salem ladies in rustling silks and sparkling jewels danced with the King's men in gala uniforms decked with gold braid, unheeding in the fever of the music the ominous grumbling of the risen people.

After Governor Gage was settled in the handsome country seat of Robert Hooper in Danvers, the Tories began calling upon him, officially and unofficially. Why should they not seize the moment to bring Salem and their interests to the fore? "We are deeply sensible of His Majesty's care and affection for this Province, in the appointment of a person of your Excellency's experience, wisdom and moderation . . ." they flattered him in an address. "We beg leave to commend to your Excellency's patronage *the trade and commerce of this place*, which from a full protection of the liberties, persons and properties of individuals cannot but flourish." Revolution was no respecter of persons and properties. A little protection from the right quarter would not be amiss.

Gage replied non-committally. No attention, he said, would be wanting on his part to encourage their sentiments of loyalty, "which cannot fail to increase your trade and commerce." He made no promises; he could therefore break none.

The honest patriots of Salem burned with indignation at such Tory maneuvers, and after a meeting at which one hundred and twenty-five merchants and freeholders convened, presented an address of their own, drawn up by the younger Pickering. "We must be lost to every idea of justice—lost to all feelings of humanity—" they declared, "could we indulge one thought to seize on wealth and raise our fortunes on the ruin of our neighbors." Before long, General Gage had to accept the unpleasant fact that these men and not those who had fawned upon him, expressed the true sentiments of Salem.

A battle of wills occurred almost immediately when the Provincial Assembly convened on June 7, 1774. It was no meeting of docile Loyalists, the Governor soon realized when the first resolution passed was a protest against its removal from Boston. For more than a week little of moment happened. Then on the tenth day, resolutions were adopted for a General Congress of the Colonies in Philadelphia "to consult upon measures for the restoration of harmony" between England and America. James Bawdoin, John and Samuel Adams, Thomas Cushing and Robert Treat Paine were appointed delegates, and everything was set. Gage fumed at this blow to his authority and in revenge sent his secretary, Thomas Flucker, with a command to dismiss the Assembly.

Armed with the Governor's proclamation, Flucker posted to Salem Town House, only to find the door closed against him and a crowd of the curious surrounding him to learn his business. Leaping off his horse, he knocked loudly at the door of the hall, demanding in the name of the Governor to be let in. The Assembly grew deaf. Orders were orders, however. Unfolding his proclamation, the exasperated secretary read it aloud from the head of the stairs, hoping that the words would filter in to the mutinous crew. It was the last time that a Provincial Assembly met under a British governor.

Gage was not the man to accept defeat. The situation was growing tense and he must not be caught unprepared. Soon after the dispersal of the Assembly, the patriots of Salem saw with undisguised resentment another company of the King's troops encamped upon the Neck. It was the 59th regiment, under Colonel Hamilton,

PIERCE-NICHOLS HOUSE, DESIGNED BY SAMUEL MCINTIRE, 1782.
Owned by the *Essex Institute*.

PINGREE HOUSE, DESIGNED BY SAMUEL MCINTIRE, 1804.
Owned by the *Essex Institute*.

whom Governor Gage had ordered down from Halifax to cow the rebellious town.

He reckoned without the spirit that defied greater powers than a mere governor's. When, therefore, he prohibited town meetings and appointed councilors of his own, the people persisted in doing as they had always done. Governor Gage held his soldiers in readiness. Early on the morning of August 24, the Town House bell summoned the people to choose a delegation for the convention that was to meet at Ipswich "to determine on such measures as the late Acts of Parliament and our other grievances render necessary."

For days bills of the convention had been posted about the town by the Committee of Correspondence, so that Governor Gage, among others, was informed of it. He did nothing until the hour of the meeting, when he ordered the Committee of Correspondence to appear before him. The assemblage they were calling was unlawful and seditious, the Governor informed them; they must immediately disband it. Very politely the Committee listened to his Excellency, but regretted that since the people were already gathered, they had no power to disperse them.

The Governor then lost his temper, threatening as he had never threatened before. "I am not going to enter into a conversation on the matter," he said sharply. "I came to execute the laws, not to dispute them, and I am determined to execute them. If the people do not disperse, the sheriff will go first. If he is disobeyed and needs support, I will support him."

He did not speak idly. Apprehending that he would meet with difficulties, the Governor had ordered his troops to prepare as for battle and a detachment of red-coats, with muskets loaded, was already marching up Main Street to scatter the meeting. The people had in the meantime elected delegates in the open air, and Richard Derby, John and Timothy Pickering, Jonathan Ropes, Jonathan Gardner and Richard Manning received their orders to attend the Ipswich convention. When the soldiers arrived there was nothing for the Governor to do but to order them back to the fort. Another defeat. Another buffet to authority. Burning with rage, his Excellency ordered the Committee of Correspondence arrested, threatening at the same time to send them to England on the *Scarboro* man-of-war for trial. That night the patriots of Salem slept with loaded muskets, ready to defend their rights with their lives if British soldiers were again marched against them.

Something of this resolve must have reached the Governor, who soon dropped his threats and made ready to return to Boston. With what irony the words of the fawning Tory Addressers must have rung in his mind! "We rejoice that this town is graciously distinguished for that spirit, loyalty and reverence for the laws which is equally our glory and happiness. . . ." Reverence for the laws, forsooth! He had come for peace and had roused a nest of hornets!

The Ipswich Convention met as scheduled without further interference, and proceeded to the order of business, recommending, among other motions, that the General Assembly constitute itself into a Provincial Congress when next it convened. In October, therefore, in spite of his Excellency's displeasure, the Assembly met at Salem Town House, formed itself into the Provincial Congress that was to play such an important rôle in the Revolution, and elected the picturesque John Hancock as President. Richard Derby and Richard Manning were chosen to represent Salem. Now, for both sides, the cards lay on the table. The game remained to be played,—and the game was war.

Sensing their danger amid the embattled patriots, the Tories fled to England and the provinces. Samuel Curwen, Judge of Admiralty and a faithful King's man, forsook wife and home to spend ten dismal years in England—a foreigner in the land to which he had been faithful, and meagerly rewarded, when hostilities were over and he could come back to Salem, with a pension from the Crown. William Browne, too, sailed out of Salem harbor never to return to the handsome mansion that had entertained so many distinguished guests, nevermore to spend a pleasant evening with his old friends of the social club. But he, too, was rewarded. As Governor of Bermuda he had enough to salve his ambition. Yet to the end he was an exile. An exile like Peter Frye, and Andrew Dalglish, and Dr. Dabney, and the many others who could not sympathize with the desire of a people to be free.

While the Provincial Congress had been forming in Salem, a fire broke out whose proportions won for it the distinction of the "great fire" over the previous conflagrations. The damage was indeed considerable for a town of four thousand souls. Besides destroying the Custom House, fourteen shops, eight dwellings and a number of barns, the flames swept over Dr. Whitaker's popular chapel on Main Street and Samuel Hall's printing office, which had been assiduously issuing tracts, almanacs, broadsides, bills, and the *Essex Gazette* since 1768. Neither of the two men allowed himself to be discouraged, however. With his wonted energy, Dr. Whitaker set about raising funds from sympathizing Presbyterians for a new tabernacle, modeled after his friend Whitfield's in London, while Hall brought out his weekly paper, containing "the freshest advices," with hardly a day's delay. Whatever type, blocks and paper he had been able to rescue from the fire, he removed to safer quarters in Mr. Blaney's brick building near the depot.

Since the day the redcoats had come marching down Main Street just before Governor Gage's return to Boston, there had been an uneasy truce between the patriots and that officer of the Crown. Unhappily, in February, 1775, rumors reached his Excellency that the Provincial Congress had been storing cannon and munitions in Salem, whereupon he commanded Col. Leslie to sail to the offending town at the head of a battalion of infantry and confiscate the supply.

No sooner had the troops landed at Marblehead than Major Pedrick, to whom the sight of a British soldier was as a red rag to a bull, mounted his horse and carried the news the two miles to Salem as fast as his steed would go. The redcoats could be there for no good, he reckoned from previous experience, and even though it was the Sabbath, the people must be warned.

Meanwhile Leslie was marching his men toward North Bridge, where he was spied by Col. David Mason, a veteran of the French and Indian wars, who lived near by. Now the colonel, who was not too much distracted by his experiments with lightning and other heavenly phenomena to know what was happening on earth, had more than a suspicion of what the troops came to seek, since he himself had been put in charge of the hidden cannon. On seeing the British drawing near, he burst into North Church where the Rev. Mr. Thomas Barnard was holding the afternoon service, and thundered: "The regulars are coming!"

The alarm brought them all to their feet. In a moment, on a signal from the minister, the people to a man followed Col. Mason to the bridge, the leaves of which had been raised at the first warning to prevent the British from passing. Already a seething crowd of patriots had gathered, with eyes fixed on the advancing block of redcoats. There was Captain Richard Derby, hale and venerable in his powdered white wig, standing as on his own quarterdeck and scowling at the approaching enemy as he had scowled on the pirate colors that had threatened his property. This time it was the people's property as well as his own that was being threatened, for he owned half of the cannon. Then there was Timothy Pickering at the head of forty armed militia men; and Captain John Felt with fire in his eyes; and Col. Orne, who was ready to lead the fighting men of Salem and Marblehead against the British if a single shot were fired.

All were assembled there, all the patriots of Salem, as well as some of the women who had come down to the bridge at the alarm. Mistress Tarrant, whose cottage windows faced the line of march, felt her blood rising as the soldiers passed by. "Go home!" she cried to Col. Leslie. "Go home and tell your master he has sent you on a fool's errand, and broken the peace of our Sabbath! What? Do you think we were born in the woods to be frightened by owls? Fire at me, if you have the courage! But I doubt it!"

It was only the prelude to the defiance which the British colonel was to meet. From his side of the stream he issued orders in the name of the Crown to have the drawbridge lowered so that he and his men might have lawful use of the King's highway and perform their duty in confiscating the hidden arms. From their point of vantage the people declared that the bridge was private property to be taken from them only by force.

"Fire and be damned to you!" shouted some of the most impulsive. But the Rev. Mr. Thomas Barnard stepped forward to allay Leslie's rising wrath. "You cannot commit this violation against innocent people," he pleaded, "here on this holy day, without sinning against God and humanity. Let me entreat you to return."

That was exactly what Col. Leslie would not do. He had orders to pass, and pass he would. The patriots, on their side, were equally determined to bar the way. It looked like the irresistible force meeting the immovable body, each unwilling to be other than itself.

During the parleying the soldiers were becoming restive. At any moment a shot might be fired, and then— Captain Derby took the situation in hand. "Find the cannon if you can!" he challenged across the water in a voice that had silenced the winds. "Take them if you can! They will never be surrendered!"

The poor British colonel was in a quandary. If he forced his way across without permission from higher authority, he might be finding himself in a sorry fix, whereas if he did not obey his original injunction he would be guilty of insubordination. Duty, duty must be done. . . . Ordering his men to the boats, he attempted to make a crossing without the help of the bridge. A number of patriots at once began scuttling the gondolas with cries of defiance, unmindful of the bayonets and the threats to fire. In the skirmish Joseph Whicher, a foreman in Col. Sprague's distillery, was scratched in the breast with a bayonet point—a wound which in after days he was proud to show.

The critical moment had come. With eagle eye Col. Felt watched Leslie, determined to jump upon him and leap with him into the river at the first command to fire. What did it matter if he lost his own life? "I would willingly be drowned myself to be the death of one Englishman," he said.

Fortunately no such sacrifice was necessary. After further deliberation it was agreed that Col. Leslie and his men cross the bridge in obedience to their orders, provided they turn right about and march back again. And so it happened. In orderly formation, headed by their colonel with drawn sword, the redcoats, feeling undoubtedly foolish in their tall pointed hats and overplus of gold braid, footed their way across North Bridge and then sheepishly turned about face without even a glimpse of the cannon they had come to seek. Thus, with no serious bloodshed, the Salem patriots once more outwitted the British lion.

Two months later

> The troops were hastening from the town
> To hold the country for the Crown;
> But through the land the ready thrill
> Of patriot hearts ran swifter still.

Lexington and Concord wrote themselves down in history.

In Salem, the *Essex Gazette* printed a detailed first-hand account of the battle among other matter showing all too clearly where the colonies now stood. It was war, and war for independence. Governor Gage realized it, but he would not alarm His Majesty with the unglossed truth. On the twenty-fourth of April, therefore, by the royal express-packet *Sukey*, he sent an account of the conflict, making it seem more like an unimportant skirmish than the first battle of the Revolution whose shots were heard "round the world."

However, another ship, the schooner *Quero* belonging to Captain Richard Derby, left Marblehead three days later bearing "a full account of the transactions of the troops under General Gage." Young John Derby, the son of Captain Richard, was in command, entrusted with a commission from the Provincial Congress which had met at Concord soon after the battle. Together with letters and dispatches, Captain John Derby carried copies of the *Essex Gazette*.

He sailed under the seal of secrecy. None but the Congress knew his mission and certainly no one in England suspected it when the Yankee *Quero* pulled in at Southampton on the twenty-seventh of May, a crossing of less than a month. Derby's coming was like the bursting of a bomb in the midst of British self-assurance. Diplomatic circles, the press, St. James's palace and the Houses of Parliament buzzed with the disturbing news brought by that mysterious nobody from New England. What was Great Britain to think of Lexington and Concord? Was this not a gigantic hoax perpetrated by the colonists?

Was there really war in America? How was it that General Gage had not yet been heard from when his packet had sailed in advance of the *Quero?*

Few were willing to give Captain John Derby the credence he deserved, though he was questioned for hours and in every detail his narrative agreed with the dispatches from the Provincial Congress. "They that know him," wrote Hutchinson, whom the Tories of Salem had once addressed with servile flattery, "say he deserves credit and that he has a good character; but I think those people would not have been at the expense of a vessel from Marblehead or Salem to England for the sake of telling the truth."(!)

The arrival of the clumsy *Sukey* brought no comfort to John Bull: Captain Derby's accounts were all too true. In vain had the people been urged to suspend judgment till the Government received official tidings. Those tidings were the most damning that could have been imagined. *The London Press* roused itself in the interest of fair play, addressing to the public a letter that minced no words. "We are now in possession of both accounts," it said in part. "The Americans have given their narrative of the massacre; the favorite servants have given a Scotch account of the skirmish. In what one material fact do the two relations, when contrasted with each other, disagree?"

The truth had to be swallowed and, more bitter still, the address to Great Britain and King George contained in the same issue of the *Essex Gazette* that carried the battle accounts.

"Great Britain, adieu! no longer shall we honour you as our mother; you are become cruel; you have not so much bowels as the sea monsters have toward their young ones. . . . Your sword is drawn *offensively*, and the sword of New England *defensively*; by this stroke you have broken us from you, and effectually alienated us from you. O, Britain, see to your own house!

"King George the third, adieu! . . . Your breach of covenant; your violation of faith; your turning a deaf ear to our cries for justice, for covenanted protection and salvation from the oppressive, tyrannical, and bloody measures of the British Parliament, and putting a sanction upon all their measures to enslave and butcher us, have *Dissolved our Allegiance* to your Crown and Government!"

Long years of war had to pass before that independence was won. As fate decreed, when peace was finally deliberated in 1783, it was Captain John Derby, the Salem Mercury, who brought home the first news of it on the ship *Astrea*, in a crossing of twenty-two days. Between the sailing of the *Quero* and the return of the *Astrea* a new nation had been born.

CHAPTER XV

## PRIVATEERS OF THE REVOLUTION

URING the Revolution and the decades that
followed to the War of 1812, maritime Salem
was literally put on the map of the world.
Throughout the struggle her soldiers and officers distinguished themselves in the army. But it was the romantically adventurous side of warfare on the sea that lured the men of Salem. Thus, when the recruiting officer for the navy paraded the streets of Salem with a band playing a spirited tune and the drum beating time, he never failed to collect a crowd. When he found it large enough and containing sturdy youths likely to lend a willing ear to his harangue, he would plant the flag before him and appeal to them in verse.

> All you that have bad masters,
> And cannot get your due,
> Come, come my brave boys,
> And join our ship's crew.

He was usually so persuasive that by the end of the day he had a number of gangling recruits whose mothers pleaded in vain for them "to sleep upon it."

The proclamations issued by the order of Congress and posted on the doors of taverns, ordinaries and other sailors' haunts also played their part. "Great Encouragement for Seamen," tempted one, printed in Danvers by Ezekiel Russell, Hall's successor. "All *Gentlemen Seamen* and able-bodied *Landsmen* who have a mind to distinguish themselves in the *Glorious Cause* of their *Country* and make their Fortunes, an opportunity now offers on board the Ship *Ranger* of Twenty Guns (for France) now laying in *Portsmouth*, in the State of *New Hampshire*, commanded by *John Paul Jones*, Esq; let them repair to the Ship's Rendezvous in Portsmouth, or at the Sign of Commodore *Manley* in *Salem*, where they will be kindly entertained and receive the greatest encouragement. . . ."

And great encouragement it was, with the bowls of punch grog and cherry toddy going the rounds, though Salem's men needed no such persuasive arguments to distinguish themselves in the glorious cause of their country.

Nevertheless the navy offered neither excitement nor profit to the extent of privateering. A mariner sailing on a privateer never knew what he might encounter—and there was the fascination of the adventure. He might never come back to port, once he slipped the cables; and on the other hand, he might return a rich man. The practice, indeed, had had a long and, from the point of view of the men who threw their lives into it, an honorable career. Years before the signing of the Peace of Utrecht in 1713, Yankee privateers had taught enemy devil dogs a lesson in courage and daring, and many the prizes brought home to burn the landlubber with envy. So great was the lure and so fabulous the profit, that in the intervening years of comparative peace which saw the brewing of the Revolution, many a New England seaman engaged in a little privateering on the side, at the risk, if caught, of being hanged in chains on Nix's Mate as an example to other lawbreakers. For Jack, always a simple soul who followed his own brand of extra-terrene logic, could not be convinced by words alone that what was legal enough at certain times became a crime at others.

The articles of privateering contracts made large promises. As a rule the officers and seamen were entitled to one half of the prizes captured by the ship after costs were defrayed. Furthermore, it was agreed that the first who discovered a sail that was later captured, received a reward of five hundred dollars over his share of booty. As for the courageous tar who first boarded an enemy vessel during an engagement, he was given a thousand dollars and the choice of the best firelock on the prize. If such was the bounty offered the sailors, how great must have been the profits of the owners! It is no wonder, therefore, that during the Revolution no fewer than one hundred and fifty-eight ships had been fitted out in Salem alone as privateers, of which more than half were in charge of Elias Hasket Derby, son of the hardy Captain Richard and brother of John. By the time peace was declared, in 1783, Salem privateers had captured four hundred and forty-five prizes. Not without loss, however. Fifty-four of her privateers and letter of marque ships fell into the hands of the enemy.

Like Elias Hasket Derby, who had found commerce ruined by the Revolution, other Salem merchants cast in their lot with the privateers, or, to combine shrewdness with the fortunes of war, converted their ships to letters of marque which carried cargo. Many and strange were the adventures of these fighting craft, manned by dare-devil tars who braved any peril, and so reckless that a frail cockleshell with half a dozen guns—some of them

wooden, or Quaker, guns for mere show—did not hesitate to run into a British man-of-war all of whose cannon
meant death.

A clearer notion of the menaces lurking at sea may be
derived from the catalogue of misfortunes contained in a
marine insurance policy of the 1780's. "Touching the adventures and perils which we the insurers are contented
to bear . . . they are of the seas, men-of-war, fire, enemies, pirates, rovers, thieves, jettisons, letters of mark
and counter-mark, surprisals, takings at sea, arrests, re-
straints and detainments of all kings, princes and people,
of what nation, condition or quality soever, barratry of
the master (unless the assured be owner of said vessel)
and mariners, and of all other perils, losses and misfortunes that have or shall come to the hurt, detriment or
damage of the said ship."

A fearful reckoning, but perforce limited to those
risks which the insurance company was willing to assume. Certainly a completer catalogue of doom could
have been drawn up by the mariners themselves, to whom
acts of God as well as of man, came all in the day's work.
Far from acting as deterrents, the very difficulties became
a spur, and the breath of adventure the only air in which
the hardened sea dog could breathe.

Most famous of the fighting privateersmen, Captain
Jonathan Haraden, who had come as a boy from
Gloucester to follow the sea for John Cabot of Salem,
bore down his prizes like a juggernaut. In one instance,
early in the war, while in command of the *General Pickering*, a letter of marque, he so intimidated a British privateer that its command, at the roar of Haraden's challenge through the speaking trumpet, surrendered without

firing a shot. Again, while off at Bilbao with a cargo of sugar, the redoubtable Haraden, with only sixteen six-pounders and forty-five men, engaged with the British privateer *Achilles*, so huge and well-ordnanced that the *General Pickering* looked like a long boat beside it. In spite of the disparity, or perhaps because of it, Captain Haraden fought as never before, heartened by the crowd of Spaniards who had collected on the seashore in the early dawn, shouting and cheering as they witnessed the gallant fight. When at last he landed with his men after carrying his prize to port, he was borne in triumph to Bilbao by the rejoicing multitude, too human not to enjoy the discomfiture of John Bull, who had so long been lording the seas.

Another of the Cabots' privateersmen indirectly furnished Salem with the nucleus of the Philosophical Library when Captain Joseph Robinson, in command of the *Pilgrim*, captured and brought home from the Irish Channel the four-hundred-and-fifty-ton frigate *Mars*, which in spite of its warlike name and its mounting of twenty-four guns had, among other cargo, a peaceable freight of books addressed to a literary institution in Quebec. They were the property of Richard Kirwan, LL.D., of Dublin, one of whose volumes, *On Climates*, lay among the rest. War was war, however, and a lawful prize shared the fate of all other lawful prizes under the auctioneer's hammer.

Those were golden opportunities for the merchants of Salem, who would often come by a treasure of merchandise through the unpredictable returns of the sea. Ever since the initiation of the war, Joseph Grafton of Salem had found it advantageous to carry on the business

of auctioneer, assisted by the powerful lungs of John
Warden and W. P. Bartlett. On the days scheduled for
the sales, the merchants in their business broadcloth
would congregate at the Salem wharves or at Beverly,
Ipswich and Newburyport, to put in their bids for the
prize and its cargo. The variety of the merchandise spoke
volumes for the privateers' adventurous daring.

"Nov. 19, 1776," reads a contemporary notice. "Sold
by order Capt. Samuel Williams, agent for the privateer
schooner *Dolphin*, Capt. Leach, part of the cargo of the
ship *Sally* taken by the *Dolphin*, viz.: 264 boxes Lisbon
lemons, at £5.10; 47 boxes Portugal onions (not sold);
8 bbls. currants, at 11d. per lb.; 20 cases salad oil, at
£5.5s.; 12 bbls. best velvet corks . . ." Curiously we
wonder at Salem's scorn of onions and at the identity of
the velvet corks.

On the twenty-seventh of the month, hardly two
weeks after this first sale, the *Dolphin* brought in another
prize, the captured schooner *Prosperity*, which must have
lived up to its name as it poured from its hold linen,
crimson tamey, striped cambletee, catgut, silk thread,
spices, cod hooks, gilt paper, tea, sugar, molasses, rum—
and singing books! Again and again the agent for the
doughty *Dolphin* appeared, attesting to its prowess.

Often the boats themselves were sold to Salem ship-
owners, who would purchase shares, as on October 28,
1778, when by order of Captain Edward Gibant the
ship *William and Ann* was sold, one-fourth to Joseph
White for £875 and three-fourths to George Dodge
for £2625.

Six days later, for November 4, we read another en-
lightening notice: "Sold by order of Capt. Silsbee, viz.:—

U. S. Frigate "Essex," built by Enos Briggs at Salem, 1799.

Crowninshield's Wharf in 1806 with the ship "America" at the end of the wharf.

Painting by George Ropes

*Peabody Mu.*

schooner *Congress*, £1275, to E. H. Derby; 2 prs. double fortified three pound cannon, with ladles at £240 per pair . . . powder horns . . . 4 tomahawks. . . ." The son was worthy of his sire.

Then, on November 12, 1778, came the prize of all prizes, when by order of Silsbee and Mason the brig *Otter* was sold to Stephen Roach for £2300. As the name implied, the *Otter* was engaged in fur trading, a most gainful commerce, and she had undoubtedly done well, with her cargo of three hundred pounds of beaver, fifty-eight bags of feathers, her red fox and silver fox skins, her mink and otter and marten. Significantly, she also carried a rat and mouse trap and Hadley's quadrant with a book of directions. And this, ten years before the opening of the fur trade in the Northwest!

And now for our frigate *Mars*. On April 11, 1781, it was offered up at auction together with its contents. The temptation was too great for the literati of Salem. On the initiative of the Rev. Joseph Willard of Beverly, where the sale was taking place, the clergymen Thomas Barnard, John Prince, and Joshua Fisher, together with Dr. Edward Holyoke and a number of other Salem scholars, pooled their resources and became the owners of the Philosophical Library. For one year, until he was called to act as President of Harvard College, the Rev. Mr. Willard served as librarian, when the election fell to the Rev. Mr. Prince.

Now and then the good men's consciences whispered on the way they had acquired their library. They prized their books, however, and they needed them. Besides, had they not rescued the bulky Transactions of the London Philosophical Society and of the French Academy of

Arts and Sciences from the ignominy of being used for wrapping paper? Finally, to quiet their scruples, they wrote to Dr. Kirwan, offering compensation, but like a scholar and a gentleman, he refused it, grateful that his library had fallen into such deserving hands. In the years that followed, the use of the books was extended to other men of Salem, among them a slim, sensitive youth whose chief passions were mathematics and the sea. Nathaniel Bowditch, the greatest benefactor of the seaman with his famous *Practical Navigator*, never forgot the debt he owed to the Philosophical Library. Thus was science served by the fortunes of the sea.

In the same way was marine art benefited when a young Italian painter, Michele Felice Cornè, was rescued from almost certain death and brought by the *Mount Vernon* to Salem. Cornè loved the tall, sparred ships that studded the waters of the busy harbors. He thrilled at the sight of the squared yards and complicated rigging which under his skilful brush retained the life and motion of the vessel speeding in the wind. The Marine Room of the Peabody Museum still shows many of his paintings, while in the garden in the rear of the museum of the Essex Institute is the cupola of the Pickman-Derby mansion, whose ceiling was vibrant with Cornè's fresco of the Derby fleet in its most glorious days.

Notwithstanding the sailor's luck that used to follow the Yankee, it was sometimes his lot to fall captive to the Corsairs, from whom a miracle alone could release him, since all human endeavor seemed futile against the barbarousness of the Dey of Algiers.

As late as 1785, when the young nation was struggling to its feet, two United States vessels were seized by the

Algerines, and their crews, following upon long-estab-
lished precedent, consigned to slavery until friends or
relatives should hear of their plight and furnish ransom.
By 1792 more than a hundred Americans lay in bondage
to the Dey, with countless European hostages, for each
of whom the unscrupulous ruler used to demand ransoms
of from $1800 to $4000.

For years the countries of Europe had been safeguard-
ing their captive subjects by paying the Dey an annual
tribute, and in 1805 the United States, after long de-
murring, joined with them, moved by such pleas as that
of the Salem Marine Society, which voted "That the
Committee of Correspondence be desired to write to
Congress, to know if anything can be done for our poor
brethren prisoners that are confined at Algiers."

The terms of the agreement were as stupendous as his
Deyship's effrontery: for the release of the American
captives he asked a compensation of $800,000; a frigate
worth $100,000, and an annual tribute of $25,000. To
protect American citizens the demands had to be met, and
the government fulfilled them, although, as it later developed, its acquiescence gave no guarantee of the Dey's
honesty. American ships and American sailors proved as
assailable as before, and hundreds of prisoners languished
in bondage, or died of the plague in its frequent visitations
upon Algiers. Not until 1815 did the United States,
through the efforts of Decatur and Bainbridge, put an
end to the humiliation of paying tribute money, with
the treaty following a four-month's war against Algiers.

At the conclusion of the agreement, as the American
squadron lay at Gibraltar, an American officer wrote
home: "You have no idea of the respect which the

American character has gained by our late wars. The Spaniards especially, think we are devils incarnate, as we beat the English, who beat the French, who beat them, whom nobody ever beat before—and the Algerines, whom the devil himself could not beat."

A story is told that the Dey could not get over the loss of his American tribute, and to salve his pride, and at the same time preserve his prestige before other nations, pleaded for a small annual gift,—anything, even a little powder. Decatur answered him to the point. He had no doubt, he observed dryly, that if the Dey insisted upon receiving powder from Americans as a tribute, they would make it complete and send balls along with it. The Dey troubled him no more.

## CHAPTER XVI

## SALEM SAILS ON ALL THE SEAS

AFTER peace was declared and hostilities on the sea had more or less ceased, Massachusetts merchants found themselves with large ships created by the needs of war straining at anchor for more oceans to conquer, and a restless population of mariners hugging the wharves. With privateering once more declared illegal, the seaman could not help feeling perplexed. What had happened to the Continental Congress and the General Court that during the war had issued more than sixteen hundred letters of marque? Where were the grand old days when a merchant would lay down hard cash at the bare prospect of a prize? And what was to become of shipping itself, with Britain's ports closed to the now independent United States, and her colonies barred to American commerce?

True, the harbors of Massachusetts were thronged with vessels, but they were mostly foreign bottoms loaded with all manner of luxuries that they were eager to dump on American shores. And dump they did, knowing that what a nation could not buy with cash under the weight of a staggering war debt, the people would obtain on credit.

There was a rage for luxury. Boston matrons and Salem girls, burgher and merchant, farmer and yokel, all went on a holiday of spending till the lass from the backwoods in her *chapeau Montgolfier* could hardly be distinguished from the Boston damsel but by her twang. Another kind of democracy was coming in, the democracy of class, which culminated in 1800 in the resentful snort of the Boston *Centinel* against what it was pleased to call the shopkeeper beau. "He will spring at one leap over a counter four feet high to pick up a lady customer's handkerchief. He makes the most handsome bow, says the most civil things, and talks surprisingly fast and sensibly about the odor of a roll of pomatum . . . In the daytime he is fully employed in displaying his drawers, boxes, bottles, needles and pins; but in the evening you will find him dancing a minuet with the lady whom he cheated of a half-penny a few hours before."

In spite of the *Centinel's* displeasure, the leveling which it deplored had become a fact whose roots had sunk deep in the growing class consciousness of the people of Massachusetts. Too long the farmer had seen the merchant class control political power. Some even believed that the Revolution had been engineered chiefly by the merchants. Now the day had come for all to have an equal chance at the helm, and farmer Jonathan willingly listened to the voice of the Daniel Shays who, in 1786, urged him to wield spade and pitchfork in a demand for his rights. Maritime Massachusetts quelled the riots, though not the spirit of revolt, and began another chapter of her history in her attempt to utilize the sleeping resources at her ports.

In Elias Hasket Derby's wharf alone there lay four ships of more than three hundred tons burden, too proud and too costly to employ in the ordinary coastwise trade. Like him, Joseph Peabody, William Gray and the Crowninshields, substantial ship owners, had vessels once

manned by seamen for whom the world had suddenly
become too small. And so, taking their luck as it came,
the vessels were sent out at a venture, and trade began
with ports on the other side of the earth, the mysterious
East, a legend that the hardy Massachusetts mariners were
to prove true.

It was a red-letter day for Salem when, on May 22,
1787, Mr. Derby's three-hundred-ton ship, the *Grand
Turk*, Captain Ebenezer West, returned from Canton—
the first New England vessel to make the voyage, though
not the first from America, since three years earlier another had set out for the same port from New York,
under the command of John Green. The *Grand Turk*
had been from home seventeen months and nineteen days,
with no news but what other arrivals brought in. There
were times when she was despaired of—so many months
passed without word of her—but the people had faith in
Captain West and faith too, in the New England timber
that made her. Moreover, she had proved her mettle,
working her twenty-eight guns nobly during the Revolution, and bringing home plenty of prizes. And she was
no stranger to unfamiliar waters, for she had been the
first American vessel to round the Cape of Good Hope.

When the *Grand Turk* came into port at last, the
whole town of Salem was out to greet her. What were
the Chinese like? What was the cargo? What profit? The
store of silks, teas and Chinese ware that was soon to
adorn the homes of Salem, replied to the last question.
The *Grand Turk* had doubled the substantial capital she
had carried out. The other questions were answered at
ease, in long-spun yarns of the mysterious yellow race

that called them "the new people," little knowing how strange they themselves were to the Yankees.

From then on, Massachusetts ships carried on the romantic China trade, past Hawaii, Luzon and Formosa, till, after a stop at Macao, the Portuguese base with its anciently established factory, they sailed the river to Whampoa, the doorstep of ancient Canton, bulwarked by its terraced hongs and warehouses. Hours long the ritual of customs collecting and exchange detained the Yankee traders and the ceremonious Hoppos, the while linguists smoothed out difficulties, and passing Chinese merchants drowned out all negotiation as they cried out their wares from their boats.

The Chinese showed themselves friendly to the "new people." They liked their way of trading, and their merchandise of otter skins, of which the mandarins never seemed to have enough. Before long the Yankees discovered another commodity for which they found a ready market,—the *bêche de mer*, as the French called it, or sea cucumber, which, with edible birds' nests and similar tidbits the Chinese preferred to the most exquisite fare. With the same shrewd economy that had made the first settlers salt down their cod flakes for available markets, their modern descendants put the Fiji islanders to work gathering sea cucumbers, and after boiling and curing the delicacies in special huts set up on the shores, they sailed away with their cargo toward the waiting Cantonese, who paid for them to the tune of thirty thousand dollars a year. Until the middle of the next century, half a dozen Salem vessels had the sole monopoly of this strange fruit of the sea.

With equal zest the wives and sisters of Massachusetts

men delighted in the teas, crapes, silks and nakeens exported by the Chinese, until in time a trade in the millions was established, heaping high the chests of the enterprising merchants. Here is a page of statistics from the records of the Salem Marine Society:

"In 1825 and 1826 a little brig of 223 tons (the *Leander*) brought in cargoes from Canton which paid duties amounting respectively, one to $86,847.47, and the other to $92,392.94. In 1829, 1830 and 1831, a ship of only 287 tons (the *Sumatra*) brought cargoes from the same port, paying respectively duties in the first case of $128,363.13, in the second of $138,480.34, and in the third of $140,761.96,—the five voyages paying to the government an aggregate of nearly $587,000."

Two years after the *Grand Turk's* discovery of the Canton market, the brig *Cadet*, commanded by Jonathan Carnes of Salem, came to Boston from a secret voyage with an incredible cargo of pepper, spices and camphor. A canny son of New England, Captain Carnes kept his exploit to himself until the time came when he communicated his information to the Salem merchant, Jonathan Peele. With remarkable expedition, Mr. Peele started the shipyards buzzing by ordering a fast schooner built from particular specifications. Rival merchants were agog. Why the haste? Why the guns? And why the mystery? They were no wiser when the *Rajah*, trembling with excitement at every sail, left the harbor—for destination unknown to all but her master and her owner.

For a year and a half no word was heard of her. The wiseacres were already imagining her rotting on some ocean bottom, when one day she sailed triumphantly into harbor, every available inch of her crammed with pepper.

Never had Salem seen such a quantity. Pepper in the hold, on deck, in the cabin—precious pepper that was almost worth its weight in gold. Where did it come from? Where had Carnes been? The captain smiled and kept his peace. Mr. Peele beamed and changed the subject. He had good reason to be mightily pleased. After the cargo had been disposed of, he had realized a profit of seven hundred per cent.

For the next two voyages Captain Carnes managed to keep his inquisitive rivals off the trail of Sumatra, on whose western coast he had found the pepper growing wild, but in the end they nosed it out and lost no time in taking advantage of God's bounty. During the half century that followed, Salem became the center of the pepper trade, among other things, re-shipping it to all parts of the world at a profit that kept the Custom House running with wealth.

Other lands and other regions enriched the people of Salem. There were Batavia and Carthagena, Laguira and Tranquebar, Bencoolen and Senegal. And there was Japan, that mixture of beauty and cruelty, of civilization and barbarism, where heathen customs were veiled in such poetry that the simple mariners came home bewildered. Captain James Devereux had been the first to bring a Salem ship to Japan when he entered the *Franklin* into the forbidden ports in 1799, although in 1791 the American flag was seen in a Japanese port when the Boston sloop, *Lady Washington*, and the *Grace* of New York, had tried their luck disposing of a cargo of sea otter. Until then only the Dutch had been permitted to trade with the Japanese. For two centuries they had held a trading base at Deshima, in Nagasaki harbor, carrying on their transactions in a ceremonial that was as humiliating as it was ludicrous. Once every few years their agent was suffered to travel to Yeddo where, in the hall of the Hundred Mats, he was granted an audience by the Shogun, whose august presence remained hidden behind a curtain that he might not be defiled by the gaze of a foreign devil. Later, when the business was over, the Dutchmen had to entertain the court by playing the buffoons at the behest of the Japanese who, by making the Europeans ridiculous, asserted their superiority.

Accident played its part in linking Salem with Japan. While the *Franklin* was lying at Batavia, Captain Devereux was informed that the Dutch East India Company needed a ship to make its periodical voyage to Japan. Seeing the possibility of profit and perhaps of a new market, Captain Devereux offered the *Franklin*. And so the barriers between the West and the obdurate East were overthrown.

What a fairyland revealed itself before the astonished eyes of Salem when on his return Captain Devereux exhibited his cabinets and tea trays of exquisite workmanship, his embroidered silks, his boxes of birds and painted fans, his vases and jade statuettes, his precious inlaid tables and carved screens! It was only the cornerstone, however, of that temple of Oriental art at the Peabody Museum which Prof. Edward Sylvester Morse was to guard so lovingly and explain so sapiently during the latter part of the nineteenth century and the beginning of the twentieth, when he was decorated by the Emperor of Japan with the orders of the Rising Sun and the Sacred Treasure.

For two years, other men and other vessels made their

way to the newly-opened country, bringing back treasures for the imagination as well as for the homes that were being built by the prosperous Salem merchants. Spacious cupboards, of which the lady of the house wore the keys with the pride of a chatelaine, overflowed with ginger in pottery jars encased in baskets of split bamboo, with all kinds of teas in blue and white caddies, with rock sugar in vases the depth of a man's arm, with ivory and jade, and shining black teakwood spice boxes that breathed the romance of the Orient.

Round the smouldering logs in the fireplaces carved with the chisel of the ships' artists, the traveler returning from his voyages told of the dainty ladies of Japan in their kimonos of rich silk made heavy with embroidery, of their glossy blue-black hair framing faces the tint of old ivory, of their long delicate hands, the nails of which shone like jewels. He told of the strange fashion of Japanese men, who wore petticoats like women, who shaved their heads but for a fringe all round which they combed upward and stiffened with gum oil into a little club the size of a man's thumb. He gave word pictures of the temples on the hills against a background of cherry trees that were a wonder to behold—all a mass of blossom with not a leaf to be seen till after the flowers had dropped like a scented rain. And he told of the mysterious ritual of lights in honor of the dead, when, after a feast at which the departed were imagined to be present, lamps were placed in tiny straw boats with paper sails, and floated down the river in the night. Hundreds of these frail barques lighted up the waters, till it looked as if the uncanny St. Elmo's fire that used to flicker from shroud to shroud like the souls of the dead, as the sailors believed,

had summoned all the departed hosts to this eerie celebration.

Suddenly, in 1801, after the Salem ship *Margaret* had
come back with one of her richest cargoes, the harbors
of Japan were closed to American vessels. It was only
when Commodore Perry reopened them that the United
States was readmitted to Nippon trade.

In 1802 Salem again distinguished herself, when the
ship *Minerva*, owned by Clifford Crowninshield and
Nathaniel West, returned from China after circumnavi-
gating the globe. She was the first Salem vessel to perform the circle, achieved by the Boston ship *Columbia*,
Captain Robert Gray, in 1790.

Meanwhile money had been pouring into the Salem
Custom House from the many ships' ventures, in which
even the prudent Salem goodwife made bold enough to
turn an honest penny. "Please to lay out five dollars
which I send by you" reads the memorandum of an
"adventure" for Mrs. Mary Townsend. Miss Harriet Elkins showed still greater enterprise. Her instruction on
the ship *Messenger* from Salem, 1816, directs: "Please to
purchase if at Calcutta two net bead with draperies; if at
Batavia or any spice market, nutmegs and mace, and if at
Canton, two Canton crape shawls of the enclosed colors
at $5. per shawl. Enclosed is $10." Miss Elkins knew her
geography as well as man's inability to choose color simply by its name. Scarcely a vessel left for China or the
East Indies that did not carry some such commission for
the seamen and their friends. Sometimes the "venture"
consisted of nothing more than a humble box of New
England cod; sometimes it amounted to thousands of
dollars, which returned converted into camel's hair

shawls, cornelian necklaces, pottery, screens, Mull Mull finer than cobweb, and many another Oriental luxury.

During the years of Salem's supremacy in trading with the East, more than twenty million dollars in duties alone were paid into the coffers of the stout brick building with its pillared portico and its carved eagle, the work of Samuel McIntire who did not live to see it spread its protective wings over the stronghold of Salem's prosperity. The Custom House was built in 1818, where it still stands at the head of Derby Wharf, after England had been taught her second lesson on the sea. But that had not been till after years of struggle and another clash of arms.

Upon the outbreak of hostilities between England and France at the height of the French Revolution, American vessels no longer found themselves safe from French privateers and from the rapacity of the British who, on the plea that the enemy ports were blockaded, seized upon every ship in sight. Salem was plunged in gloom. "Every day," quotes Felt in his *Annals*, "has brought with it fresh intelligence of insults to our flag, abuse to our seamen, and destruction to our commerce."

A commission from Massachusetts, Virginia and South Carolina was sent to France, but obtained no audience. Money alone, they reported, could buy immunity from attack. Inspired by Pinckney's defiant, "Millions for defence, but not one cent for tribute," a new navy department was created. Twelve frigates, one of which, the *Essex*, was built in Salem, were fitted out, and letters of marque were again granted for privateering. To the tune of "Hail Columbia," first sung in May of 1798, midshipmen manned the decks and fought. Quite different was the temper now from that of 1792 when all of Massachusetts was rejoicing at France's brave struggle for liberty. To the republic still in its teens, the manifestations of freedom in the monarchy that had always symbolized the ultimate in tyranny and corruption, came as an assertion of their own independence. If freedom should spread throughout the world, how wonderful for humanity!

Accordingly, in January of 1793, Boston celebrated the early victories of the French people in a grand public banquet to which the multitude was invited. On a cart twenty feet high, a huge roasted ox with gilt horns, a peace offering to Liberty and Equality, was drawn through the streets by fifteen horses and followed by a retinue of other vehicles containing bread and two hogsheads of punch. Through the principal streets filed the pageant of freedom and goodwill, as the tumultuous crowd warmed itself in the wintry weather with lusty shouts of anticipation. In State Street, from the Old State House, as far as Kirby Street, a long table had been laid, and there, while ladies and gentlemen looked on benignly from the surrounding balconies, the populace partook of the offering to Liberty till only the bones remained in the enthusiasm of their feasting.

Meanwhile, in dignified seclusion at Faneuil Hall, four hundred of the more prosperous friends of Equality dined more elaborately in the shadow of the obelisk erected in the dining hall for the occasion, deriving a comfortable satisfaction as they looked up at the surmounting figure of the goddess Liberty trampling upon crown, scepter and broken chains.

Alas! an evil wind soon wafted across the ocean the news of the execution of Louis XVI. Boston and the whole of Massachusetts were speechless with horror. But not for long, for the Federalist, or conservative, party that held the reins of power, made itself heard. Democracy could be a very dangerous thing in the hands of those who did not understand it; Boston mistrusted its effect upon the growing industrial classes.

In the course of time, feelings rose high against the once celebrated followers of Freedom and Equality, and America took measures for its safety. By 1800, ninety French vessels mounting seven hundred guns had been captured by the United States.

Trouble, however, was not yet over. For some years America's commercial success had given England umbrage. It sought but the least excuse for attack, and found it. More and more American ships became the prey of British cruisers, with subsequent condemnation in the Courts of Admiralty, and the imposition of hateful Orders in Council.

From every port in Amercia resolutions and protests demanding redress were sent to Washington, which had succeeded Philadelphia as the capital in 1800. But the President shuffled and temporized. A critical juncture was reached when the British fired upon the American flag flying upon a national ship. So high flared the people's indignation that if war had then been declared, the country would have backed the declaration to a man. President Jefferson, however, tried to remedy the situation in his own way by forcing the Embargo Act through both houses of Congress.

Its effect was more disastrous than even war would have been. In Salem as in other New England ports, the ships lay idle in the harbor, haunted by idle sailors whose

NATHANIEL BOWDITCH
Navigator and Mathematician

JOSEPH PEABODY
Merchant

JACOB CROWNINSHIELD
Shipmaster and Merchant

*Peabody Museum*

ELIAS HASKET DERBY
Merchant

families cried for bread. Commerce, industry, agriculture
—all were at a standstill, as if the dead calm that had
paralyzed the waters were stagnating the very blood of
the country. Public soup kitchens had to be opened to
feed the starving of the nation, yet the Embargo, far
from being lifted, was pushed forward by the Enforcing
Act.

Sullen crowds of sailors bearing the flag at half-mast as
emblematic of the people's feelings, marched to the mansion of the governor demanding bread. But party factions
carried on their private squabbles, little realizing that
the end would be either a continuance of despotism or
civil war. Already riots and insurrections were reported
. . . In the nick of time, through the efforts of such men
as Joseph Story, the Embargo was repealed, and the
winds of commerce once more blew over the face of
the waters. Unhappily England also resumed her rapa-
cious activities.

In the meantime Elbridge Gerry had supplanted Gore
as Governor of Massachusetts, while James Madison, the
Democratic candidate, succeeded Jefferson as President
in 1808. The governorship of Gerry was important only
in that it gave a new word to the language and strengthened the power of the Federalists, his opponents. During
the Gerry administration the election districts of Essex
County were so hewn and rearranged to favor the Democratic party at the polls, that Gilbert Stuart, the artist,
struck by the peculiar outline of the map, was inspired
to add claws to Salem and Marblehead, a beaked profile
to Salisbury and wings to Andover, converting the whole
to a frightful creature which he said looked like a salamander. "No, not salamander," said Major Benjamin

Russell of the Boston *Centinel*, "but Gerrymander!" The word has survived to our day.

In the ensuing elections an engraving of the Gerry-mander appeared on all handbills and broadsides, as well as in the Boston papers and the Salem *Gazette*. Needless to say, the Federalists won, strengthened as they were by popular sentiment when President Madison declared war against Great Britain on June 18, 1812.

The war that would have been defensive and therefore justifiable in 1807, had changed in character by 1812. New England, which had suffered most under the Em-bargo and the Enforcement Act, had had enough of hardship. Nevertheless, when British ships and British soldiers descended upon her seaports, burning and pillag-ing, she fought—and bravely. At this crisis two hundred and fifty vessels were called for by the navy. Salem alone furnished forty, with the same spontaneous gener-osity with which in 1798 she had drawn upon her forests and her coffers to build the frigate *Essex* at the call of the nation.

On June 1, 1813, the whole town of Salem was sum-moned to the hills overlooking the sea by the roar of the broadsides that meant another engagement between a United States frigate and a British man-of-war. They were not mistaken. So near shore that men and colors could be distinguished, the American frigate *Chesapeake*, commanded by Captain Lawrence, had pulled alongside the British *Shannon*, and the first broadsides had been exchanged. The people cheered for Captain Lawrence. Not so long since, he had given the lie to the boast that any British ship could beat an American frigate, when with the sloop-of-war *Hornet* he had completely anni-

hilated the proud British *Peacock*, a warship of such superior armament that the English could not recover from
the shock of its loss.

Captain Broke of the *Shannon* had been on the lookout
for Lawrence. That fateful day he challenged him to
come out with his new *Chesapeake* and engage with
him. His fighting blood up, Captain Lawrence impul-
sively accepted the challenge. As the people on the shore
were watching, there was a strange commotion on the
sea. Something seemed to be going wrong. Still the broadsides rolled like thunder across the water. Suddenly the
*Chesapeake* fouled with the *Shannon* and got out of
control. In no time the British were swarming over her
side, clearing their way with gunfire. A shot felled Captain Lawrence. "Don't give up the ship!" he shouted as
he fell. "Fight her till she sinks!" His men obeyed. Never
had there been such fighting. In less than fifteen minutes
two hundred and fifty men met their death on both sides.

Some time later, when the bodies could be recovered,
those of Captain Lawrence and of Lieutenant Ludlow
of the *Chesapeake* were brought to Crowninshield's
Wharf near Becket Street. From there, on the twenty-
third of August, with the whole town following, they
were borne to their burial amid honors never before accorded to any heroes in the history of Salem.

Under the direction of Major John Saunders, and escorted by the Salem Light Infantry, the two marine societies and reputable citizens, the hearses, covered with
the colors, were borne to the Rev. Mr. Spaulding's meetinghouse in Howard Street, where the Hon. William
Story pronounced a moving oration. After the funeral
service by the Rev. Mr. Henshaw of Marblehead, the

bodies were temporarily deposited in the tomb of Captain George Crowninshield in the Howard Street cemetery, to the firing of minute guns from Washington Square. At the same time in Boston, whose flags hung at half-mast, the bells tolled, and guns volleyed from the frigate *Constitution* lying in the harbor. Ten days later, a ship conveyed the remains of Lawrence and Ludlow to the Navy Yard at Charlestown, and from there by land they were carried to their final resting place in New York's Trinity churchyard.

## CHAPTER XVII

## SOCIAL LIFE, WONDERS
## AND AMUSEMENTS

IN HIS way the Rev. Dr. William Bentley, whose congregation in the East Church was made up of ships'
captains, sailors and sailors' wives, was himself half a
seaman, although he was seldom to leave his pulpit till
the beginning of the next century when he was chosen
Chaplain of the House of Representatives. He was a
classical scholar and a man of great learning, who read
more than twenty languages and spoke the modern ones
fluently.

It is probable that through his zeal for knowledge and
his love of books, German culture entered New England
when, in 1806, Professor Ebeling of Hamburg, with
whom Dr. Bentley corresponded, sent him a select case
of books from the proceeds of a bag of coffee which the
churchman had invested as a "venture." "The good professor," he noted, "has furnished me with great economy
with some of the best books which his country has
yielded."

The worthy Dr. Bentley returned the compliment
in kind, sending to Hamburg copies of the editions which
from then on began pouring regularly from the printing
presses of New England. By a strange turn of fate, Professor Ebeling's collection which, with the disappearance
of the original editions in America became of considerable value, was finally repurchased by an American, the
merchant Israel Thorndike of Beverly, who presented it
to the Harvard College Library.

Nevertheless, in spite of his cultural interests, Dr. Bentley's life was bound so closely with the fortunes of his people, that to him, too, the sea, more than an expanse of changing water, meant life and death. From a lookout built for him by Captain George Crowninshield, one of his parishioners, he used to scan the horizon for the incoming sail, and the moment his spyglass made sure of the long-awaited ship, he would raise a pennant on the flagstaff of the tower, that all might know the glad tidings. Sometimes he would climb the lookout with a heavy step, to hoist the signal at half-mast, when some mariner brought news of disaster.

His memoranda made dreary reading. "April 24, 1785, Sunday. Notes for Martha Hodgson, sick and brother at sea. Hannah Bushnel, for sister's death and brother at sea. Hannah Archer, death of daughter and friend at sea . . . July 3, 1791. Anna Bowditch, death of Husband, and prayer for her brethren at sea . . . Sarah Batten, sudden death of her only son and for son-in-law at sea . . . Dec. 1786. News of the death of Captain Adam Wellman. There is something singular in this event. Wellman is the third Captain who has been part owner with Captain White in the same vessel and who has died in succession within the space of one year."

Throughout his long life he kept a diary. Nothing escaped him. From the garments of the distinguished visitor—and there were many who came to Salem, from Lafayette in 1784, whose arrival was announced with the ringing of bells, to Peter Pohquonnoppeet, a chief of the Six Nations and a graduate of Dartmouth College —to the peculiarities of the latest curiosity brought by the far-travelers to Salem harbor, his insatiable interest ranged. He was everywhere. Nothing that concerned Salem was too unimportant for him to know.

Hence, when Jacob Crowninshield who was to serve honorably in Congress, brought home from a voyage to India the first live elephant that was ever seen in America, Dr. Bentley was among the earliest arrivals at the Market House, where the monster was exhibited. The closeness of his inspection proves that he got more than his money's worth, although he complained that the crowd of spectators forbade him any but a superficial view. "He was six feet four inches high," he wrote in his diary. "Of large Volume, his skin black as though lately oiled. A short hair was on every part but not sufficient for a covering. His tail hung one third of his height, but without any long hair at the end of it. His legs were still at command at the joints but he could not be persuaded to lie down . . . Bread and hay were given him and he took bread out of the pockets of the spectators. He also drank porter and drew the cork, conveying the liquor from his trunk into his throat. His tusks were just to be seen beyond the flesh and it was said had been broken. We say *his*," he concludes out of deference to truth, "because this is the common language. It is a female, and teats appeared just behind the fore legs."

Later the same pachyderm delighted the sober Bostonians who, less perspicacious than our good Dr. Bentley, allowed it thirty bottles of porter and other spiritous liquor for its daily consumption—a quantity that would never have been countenanced in a lady-elephant. But the announcer's word couldn't be doubted: "He will probably live between two and three hundred years."

With such assurance of its sex and its longevity, they enjoyed its pranks and went home satisfied.

Other quadrupedal marvels were brought to Salem in the course of the years as New England mariners penetrated farther into unknown lands: two camels, male and female, from Arabia, advertised in 1789 in the *Salem Mercury*; an African lion in 1795, "at 9d a visiter"; a bison, in 1797, the same year that brought crowds to see the elephant at the then new Market House; and many another wonder that delighted young and old.

The most marvelous collection, however, came in June, 1834, in time for that other intrepid annalist, the Rev. Joseph B. Felt. "A large number of animals arrive," he notes excitedly. "Twenty wagons containing them, were drawn by sixty horses. A great India elephant, 10 feet high and of 10,000 pounds weight, brought a band of musicians on his back. In the collection were an Asiatic lioness, South American tapir, tigers, camel, leopard, hyaena, margay, lama of Peru, panther, Russian bear, ichneumon, mocos, catamount, kangaroo, jackall and rompor." The animals were shown on a lot by St. Peter's Church near the jail. For the occasion, the children were let off from school so that they could follow the procession through the streets.

But the culminating curiosity came the following year, when the Rev. Mr. Felt wrote: "A collection of animals visit us. In this was the unicorn." Thus, briefly, without comment, he mentioned it, as if after such a spectacle there was nothing more to be said. No wonder! It is probably the first and only time that the fabulous beast was ever known to visit any earthly city.

At the time of the Rev. Mr. Felt's writing, there were

one hundred and eleven Salem vessels engaged in foreign trade. Round the Cape of Good Hope they carried the American flag, to the Isle of France, India, China and Japan. Their masters were among the first to open nego-tiations with St. Petersburg and Zanzibar, Calcutta and Bombay, with Sumatra, the treasure island of the pepper trade, with Batavia, Arabia, Madagascar and Australia.

For decades the name of Salem had been known from one end of the globe to the other. But it was the peak that implied the fall. Long before the close of the cen-tury, all of Salem's great ships would lie where all ships go when they slip their cables for the last time. Had it been ominous when the second *Grand Turk* of 564 tons, which Salem proudly called its Great Ship, had been sold to New York, as "much too large for our port and the method of our trade"?

Unmindful of the shadow of doom, Salem's ship-mer-chant class had made of the town that numbered eight thousand souls at the close of the eighteenth century a rival of Boston in the loftiness of its standards, and its peer, if not its superior, in architectural achievement. Today there is no avenue in New England that can com-pare with the tree-shaded Chestnut Street which Salem's McIntire endowed with the purest heritage of architec-tural art in fanlight and sidelight, in slender column and carved capital, in dignity of line and excellence of execu-tion. Most of the buildings belong to the early nine-teenth century, when McIntire had developed his Adam style to the perfection of which he had proved himself capable in the Peirce-Nicholls house on Federal Street.

Little is known of Samuel McIntire, and less of the nameless builders and carvers who knew so well how to realize his designs. The son of a housewright, McIntire was born in Salem in 1757, and eked out a penurious youth in the shipyards, carving cabin moldings and figureheads. No one had heard of him till he emerged as the architect of the house which the wealthy Jerathmeel Peirce commissioned him to build in 1782. Prudently thrifty, Captain Peirce was in no hurry about completing the interior, so that the house now displays McIntire's development of style to its apex in the Adam parlor, finished in 1801 perhaps to make a setting for the wedding of Sally Peirce to young Captain George Nicholls.

With civic pride Salem began to think of her public as well as of her private buildings; in the Court House, the South Meeting House and the assembly halls, McIntire found full scope for his genius. In 1803, perhaps in envy of the Argand lights which Boston had adopted, some public-spirited citizens set up street lamps to illuminate Salem and offered them to the town. Felt reports the reaction of thrifty New England, even in the matter of a gift: "Their present was accepted on condition, that the cost of lighting and keeping the lamps should not exceed $1500 a year."

How did the people of Salem live after the period that had seen the American and the French revolutions, and had created a wealthy merchant class that made it possible for individual members, like Elias Hasket Derby, to leave a million and a half to his sons at his death in 1799?

Class distinctions, in spite of the two social upheavals, still kept the rich apart from the middle, and the rapidly developing, lower classes, so that although Salem was reckoned as the wealthiest of any Massachusetts town, she had her dilapidated Alms House near the old frog pond of the now beautiful Washington Square. Lords of commerce, the Derbys and the Crowninshields, commanded at quarterdeck and political platform, whether Federalist or Republican; the middle classes chose where their advantage lay; the lower classes made the best of what resulted. For all three, life and prosperity were bound up with the sea; the time had not yet come, though it was near, when cotton mill and leather factory were to utilize the wealth of idle shipmerchants and give employment to an immigrant population that followed the lead of industrialism. Not that the factory was unknown to New England. As early as 1789, Washington, who had seen one in operation in Boston, left its description. "They have twenty-eight looms at work and fourteen girls spinning with both hands . . . Children (girls) turn the wheels for them, and with this assistance each spinner can turn out fourteen pounds of thread per day, when they stick to it; but as they are paid by the piece, or the work they do, there is no other restraint upon them but to come at eight o'clock in the morning and return at six in the evening." Only the daughters of decayed families were given employment.

Social life, while not as brilliant as Boston's, nevertheless was bright enough when cotillion parties gathered in the great parlors where young women in filmy Eastern cottons or voluminous satins pirouetted toward their partners in the French trowsers that most men had adopted—except the old who still clung to buckles and breeches. At the wedding of Sally Peirce, visiting belles were extinguished with envy of her gown, made of the most beautiful striped Bombay muslin ever seen in Massachusetts. Her bridegroom had brought it for her himself across the ocean. During the season, there were formal balls in the assembly halls, enormous dinners that lasted for hours—sleighing in the winter, and pleasure yachting in the summer.

George Crowninshield's *Cleopatra's Barge*, built in 1816, initiated the rage for yachting cruises. On the first voyage, he took her to the Mediterranean, where, with her rainbow-colored sides and her soaring sails, she was the wonder of all who saw her. Prominent visitors drank of her choice liquor and feasted in her magnificent cabin. France and Italy outdid themselves in singing her praises in their papers. Unhappily, while preparing to take her out on a second cruise, George Crowninshield died, and after changing hands, the *Cleopatra's Barge* eventually became the property of the King of the Sandwich Islands who gave for her ninety thousand dollars' worth of sandalwood.

In the meantime, with the many changes in the social order, something had happened to the stern religion that the founding fathers would have rooted forever. With the French upheaval and the preliminary work of enlightenment of the Encyclopaedists, scepticism and infidelity had made inroads even among the Puritans, who followed the trends in philosophy as they followed the imported tonsorial fashion of wearing the hair *à la Brutus*, *à la Titus* and *à la Liberté*. Not that churchgoing suffered in consequence. On the contrary, the meetinghouses were as popular as ever during the Thursday and Sunday lectures. A certain relaxing of discipline, however, had made itself felt, and a largeness of outlook that could treat with levity a subject which once would have brought a Puritan to the stocks, if not worse. Hence, in

1802, the Boston *Centinel* could print, without fear of punishment, a set of light verses on the perennial subject of the limits of the Sabbath:

In Superstition's days, 'tis said,
Hens laid two eggs on Monday,
Because a hen would lose her head
That laid an egg on Sunday.

Now our wise rulers and the law
Say none shall wash on Sunday;
So Boston folks must dirty go,
And wash them twice on Monday.

Religious tolerance had for many years enabled members of the various Christian sects to live in peace, if not harmony, in Massachusetts. At the time we speak of, besides the meetinghouses of the Congregational Society, there were the churches of the Baptists, the Methodist Episcopal and Episcopal, the Unitarian, the Universalist and others. Gone were the days when men and women would have been hanged for dissenting from Puritan belief.

Together with church buildings, other edifices not connected with religion began to embellish the towns, as leisure increased and people hungered for amusement. In Boston, at the Columbian Museum, described as "an elegant temple of fame," David and Goliath, modeled in wax, could be seen side by side with the contemporary notions of female pulchritude in the life-size figurines of the "New York Beauty" and the "Boston Beauty." Salem, too, had her temples of fame on a smaller scale. However, if not satisfied with the amusements at home, the élite could always take a trip Bostonward, to hobnob in theaters and museums with the visiting *beau monde* from the South, or spend a few pleasant days in Mr. Craigie's or Mrs. Carter's boarding house, walking in the gardens or sitting on the grass by moonlight to the strumming of guitars. For that instrument was not unknown to a social class that would sometimes bring home Italian and Spanish wives.

People frequented the theater, although the drama had not long been enjoying popular favor in New England, where the law prohibiting theatrical performances had been re-enacted as late as 1784, notwithstanding the strides in dramatic art already made in other cities, like New York and Philadelphia. After nearly a decade of agitation by liberal gentlemen of Boston, the first theater, or rather, the New Exhibition Room, was opened in Board Alley, a lane redolent of stables and paved with mud. The New Exhibition Room, despite its name, was itself a converted stable. Nevertheless, Garrick's farce of *Lethe* was enjoyed by capacity audiences of New England beaux and gentlemen who, overlooking all manner of discomfort, later sat through *Venice Preserved*, the tragical history of George Barnwell, *Romeo and Juliet*, and *Hamlet* as if they were attending moral lectures. Indeed, the plays were advertised as such, in an attempt to keep the theater within the good graces of a frowning power group.

Four months the Messrs. Harper, Morris, Watts, Murray, Solomon and Redfield, together with Miss Smith, Mrs. Solomon and Mrs. Gray, strode the boards, enacting the passions of their heroes and heroines. Then suddenly the law clamped down upon them with the arrest of Manager Harper and other members of the troupe. A scuffle ensued, with catcalls against authority by the young men who, then as now, swelled the audience, and the night's events closed with the destruction of Governor Hancock's portrait which hung in front of the stage box. His Excellency had always opposed the theater; youth, striding toward progress and liberality, staged its own protest. After a hearing the following day at Faneuil Hall, Harper and his actors were released, and for a few months longer the New Exhibition Room struggled along. Then it was taken down.

But interest in the drama did not die with it. Indeed, having had a taste of its pleasures, the people clamored for more. Thus in 1794, Boston's first real theater, designed as such in fine red brick, with a columned portico and a commodious stage, opened its doors to the performances of *Gustavus Vasa* and *Modern Antiques*, especially imported from England. In time the corner of Federal and Franklin streets became the rendez-vous of Boston, as toward five o'clock in the afternoon, carriages with liveried servants brought the audience to the theater door. Women, little by little, gained admittance to the sanctum, although for a long time their presence, particularly in the third row, continued having an unpleasant connotation.

Other theaters began to be built as need for them grew, but the Boston Theater, till 1827, remained the best and the most popular. Here Boston and the visiting aristocracy of Salem and other towns, heard Cooper and John Howard Payne, the great Edmund Kean, and Macready of the eloquent pause. Here recited Junius Brutus Booth and the elder Charles Matthews. It was for the succeeding decades and the boards of the Tremont Theatre to witness the art of the Kembles, Tyrone Power, Fanny Jarman, Charlotte Cushman, Ellen Tree and John Gibbs Gilbert. By that time the Massachusetts theater had completely emancipated itself.

# THE

# Elephant,

ACCORDING to the account of the celebrated BUFFON, is the most respectable Animal the world. In size he surpasses all other terrestrial creatures; and by his intelligence makes as near an approach to man, as matter can approach spirit. A sufficient proof that the not too much said of the knowledge of this animal is, that the Proprietor having been absent ten weeks, the moment he arrived at the door of his apartment, and spoke to the keeper, the mal's knowledge was beyond any doubt confirmed by the cries he uttered forth, till his Fr came within reach of his trunk, with which he caressed him, to the astonishment of all those saw him. This most curious and surprising animal is just arrived in this town, from Philadel where he will stay but a few weeks. ——————— He is only four years old, and we about 3000 weight, but will not have come to his full growth till he shall be between 30 and years old. He measures from the end of his trunk to the tip of his tail 15 feet 8 inches, round body 10 feet 6 inches, round his head 7 feet 2 inches, round his leg, above the knee, 3 feet 3 inc round his ankle 2 feet 2 inches. He eats 130 weight a day, and drinks all kinds of spiritous liqu some days he has drank 30 bottles of porter, drawing the corks with his trunk. He is so tame he travels loose, and has never attempted to hurt any one. He appeared on the stage, at the Theatre in Philadelphia, to the great satisfaction of a respectable audience.

A respectable and convenient place is fitted up at Mr. VALENTINE's, head of the Ma for the reception of those ladies and gentlemen who may be pleased to view the greatest natural c osity ever presented to the curious, and is to be seen from sun-rise, 'till sun-down, every D the Week, Sundays excepted.

☞ The Elephant having destroyed many papers of consequence, it is recommended to vis not to come near him with such papers.

☞ Admittance, ONE QUARTER OF A DOLLAR.——Children, NINE PENCE.

Boston, August 18th, 1797.

BOSTON: Printed by D. Bowen, at the COLUMBIAN MUSEUM Press, head of the M

BROADSIDE ANNOUNCING THE DISPLAY IN BOSTON IN 1797 OF THE
FIRST LIVING ELEPHANT TO REACH AMERICA BROUGHT BY CAPTAIN
JACOB CROWNINSHIELD IN THE SHIP "AMERICA".

## CHAPTER XVIII

## GOD GOES EASTWARD

AFTER the War of 1812, the people of New England began turning their thoughts to the cultivation of a vineyard which, in their preoccupation first with the gaining of freedom, and then with the preservation of it, they had left to other hands. The world had widened its boundaries. Not a day passed but travelers arrived telling of places where the word of God was unknown and where strange, sometimes cruel, customs prevailed. Many a note did Dr. Bentley make in his diary and many a prayer did he offer up for the benighted of humanity. "Had some information respecting Coromandel coast and Bengal from captains B. Crowninshield and Gibant," he wrote on one occasion. "The first testified that he saw the funeral of a husband in which the wife was consumed. She was feeble, led round the pile by two Brahmins, appeared ill and suspected of taking opium. The fire was quickened by brimstone, etc., and the ashes swept into the River. She was very young."

He cited but a single instance of what was daily happening in those dark lands, yet none in America seemed disturbed by such heathen practices. New England, God's commonwealth, was strangely indifferent to the divine injunction once so important, to spread the Gospel where it was not known, and to conquer the world for God.

Yet New England had already had her missionaries,

if only for the conversion of the Indians. In the middle of the seventeenth century, when John Eliot of Roxbury and Thomas Mayhew of Martha's Vineyard began their Christian work among the savages, their example kindled the fire in other breasts, and, though more than thirty years after the founding of the colony, the original intention was carried out. Gookin, Cotton, Shepard, Bourne and Brainerd took up the labor with laudable zeal and with such results that missionaries like the Rev. Samson Occum, sprang up among the "praying Indians" themselves.

John Eliot, however, was the champion of them all, winning for himself the titles of Apostle and Evangelist. What with his translation of the Bible into the Indian tongue and his large number of followers, he enlisted the support of an English society for the converting and civilizing of Indians, and with the funds that it contributed, laid the cornerstone of the first brick building in Harvard—the Indian College, for the education of native students. He also bought types and a printing press, and it was here at Cambridge that his Indian Bible was printed. For some years the good work continued— till disaster came with the outbreak of King Philip's War.

Not till the beginning of the nineteenth century was there a reawakening of the missionary spirit in America, although England had long been persevering in the Christianizing of her many possessions in the East. Accounts of the dedication of British missionaries reached New England; but none of her godly men was so far inspired as to wish to give up his security for the risks— and they were many—of spreading the Gospel among the heathen.

On August 9, 1788, a son was born at Malden, Massachusetts, to Adoniram Judson, Congregationalist minister. Feeling, perhaps, the dedicatory significance of the name, "the Lord is most high," he gave it to his child. Young Adoniram was one of those astonishing children to whom learning came without effort. When he was three years old his mother taught him to read during the short absence of her husband, who was amazed on his return to hear a chapter of the Bible read out to him with accuracy and solemnity by the child in petticoats. A year later the boy was already preaching to the children of the neighborhood, opening his sermon with the hymn beginning with the words that were to prove prophetic, "Go preach my Gospel, saith the Lord."

Brothers and sisters were born to Adoniram, and the Rev. Mr. Judson, to improve the condition of his growing family, moved first to Wenham, then to Braintree, and again, when Adoniram was fourteen, to Plymouth. In 1804 the boy matriculated at Providence College, later Brown University, and was so assiduous a student, in spite of the time he gave to teaching school in his last term, that he was graduated with the highest honors.

For a year he remained at Plymouth, trying to earn a livelihood by opening a little private academy and publishing two textbooks. Restlessness seized him. Like most of the youth of his generation, he was suffering from the after-effects of the French Revolution. In the class above him at college, a young man for whom he had an adolescent worship had aided in the development of Adoniram's "French infidelity." Together they would discuss the questions that perplexed the age, with the result that Adoniram had come out of the university with doubts which wounded his father in his conviction that his son would be a great man in the service of God. From earliest childhood he had inspired Adoniram with his hopes in him; now it seemed as if they would never be.

They appeared remoter than ever when Adoniram's ardent and adventurous spirit made him close his school at Plymouth and sent him wandering through the Northern states. In search of what? He himself did not know. At Albany, with a number of other intrepid souls, he ventured on the newly-invented Robert Fulton steamer then making her second voyage, and navigated the Hudson down to New York. The beauty of the landscape lived forever in his mind, to be called up again when, far from home and near death, he gained from the remembered vision a few last moments of happiness.

Alone in the big city which even in those days cast its spell over out-of-town youth, Adoniram lost no time in associating himself with the most unconventional group he could find—a company of young, carefree strolling players whose courses were of the gayest and whose morals of the lightest. With them he roamed the state, making merry and with not a care in the world.

But he was not for nothing the son of the Congregationalist minister who had never ceased telling him that he, his firstborn, must be a great man. Sometimes, when in the midst of his rebellion, Adoniram allowed himself to think of home, he wondered why he had ever embarked upon a life which fundamentally he did not enjoy. Adventure and excitement were there. But where the satisfaction, the sense that he was doing the thing for which he was destined? What had happened to him since the days of his boyhood when he had had visions of himself as an eminent divine? In an impulse of repentance he left the players and started back for home.

The inns were crowded, for with the improved means of travel, people went abroad more than before. At one of the houses where he stopped for the night, the landlord apologized for putting him up next door to the room where a young man lay dying. The thought kept Adoniram awake all night. A youth like himself was at that moment about to face his Maker. Was he prepared? Had he so arranged his life that those last hours were not hours of anguish? What if he himself were just then to die? . . . How could he face eternity? Thus wrestling with his soul, he listened for every movement from the next room, his heart beating at every stirring of the bed, at every footfall of the attendants.

Next morning when he saw the landlord his first question was of the dying youth. "Oh, he is dead," the host answered him.

"Dead!"

"Yes, he is gone, poor fellow!"

"Do you know who he was?" Strange, the persistence of his concern for a stranger!

"Oh, yes. It was a young man from Providence College—a very fine fellow. His name was—" And he gave the name of the youth who had been Adoniram's closest friend, the freethinker with whom he had questioned religion and spent profitless hours in undermining his faith.

He arrived at Plymouth another man. In October, 1808, a few weeks after his return, he was admitted to the Theological Institution of Andover as a special favor, since he was not a candidate for the ministry. A month later his diary bore an important entry: "Began to entertain a hope of having received the regenerating influences of the Holy Spirit." In the time which followed, that hope was fulfilled. By the end of the year he had dedicated himself to God, and at the age of twenty-one he joined the Third Congregational Church in Plymouth.

Meanwhile, since 1803, mission societies had been forming in Massachusetts and a periodical *The Massachusetts Missionary Magazine*, was circulated throughout the state to spread the information of the work which European missionaries had been doing among the heathen. It was read avidly at Andover, together with the published tracts and sermons that came in from Great Britain. One such book, Dr. Claudius Buchanan's sermon, *The Star in the East*, describing the Christianizing of India, gave Judson the clue to his life work. "Go into all the world and preach the Gospel to every creature . . ." The words rang with such clearness in his mind that he could no longer hesitate.

At this time four new students, Samuel J. Mills, Jr., James Richards, Gordon Hall and Luther Rice, came to Andover from Williams College where, under a haystack near the grounds, they used to meet at night to discuss the plans of the missionary society which they had organized, prompted by the same fervor that had been working in Judson. Before long he was one of them, together with Samuel Nott, Jr., to whom he had been drawn by the bond of their kindred interests. A few of their teachers were admitted into their confidence and, under their guidance, they presented a petition in June, 1810, before a meeting of the General Association of Congregationalist Churches in the State of Massachusetts. "The undersigned . . ." read the petition, "beg leave to state that their minds have long been impressed with the duty and importance of personally attempting a mission to the heathen . . . and that, after examining all the information which they can obtain, *they consider themselves as devoted to this work for life,* whenever God, in His providence, shall open the way."

Out of this petition, signed by four idealistic youths, and the interest of the General Association, was created the American Board of Commissioners for Foreign Missions. Something else, however, had occurred during the meeting of the Association in Bradford. While the ministers and the young aspirants were gathered together at dinner at the home of John Hasseltine, his youngest daughter Ann waited at table. Adoniram promptly fell in love with her. She was a beautiful, intelligent girl, so full of life and gaiety that her parents, in their concern for her, feared that she would die young. As a child she would often leave the house and go wandering by herself through the woods and fields. "I hope, my daughter, you will one day be satisfied with rambling," her mother reproved her, speaking more prophetically than she knew. Ann was just a year younger than Judson. For some time she had taught school at Salem, an independent step in days when woman's sphere hardly extended beyond her home.

In order to carry out their plans more successfully, it was decided that the Board solicit the cooperation of the London Missionary Society. Adoniram Judson was chosen as their emissary. In 1811, after taking leave of Ann Hasseltine, now his betrothed, he boarded the English ship *Packet*, full of happiness at the propitious working of his aspirations. But the devil was not to let them be without interposing difficulties. On the voyage the *Packet* was seized by the *Invincible Napoleon*, a French privateer. Judson, with the rest, was taken prisoner and transported to Bayonne, where he was thrown into prison to languish for months, perhaps years, had he not been rescued by a man from Philadelphia who smuggled him out under his cloak. As best he could, under the circumstances, he continued his journey to England.

In London the Missionary Society listened to Judson's proposals, yet advised against a joining of forces, both because of the distance between it and the American Board, and the individual nature of the problems that would confront the missionaries from the New World. However, much needed help of another nature had already reached the American Board. The General Association, prior to its incorporation into the Board, had met in Salem, where in March of 1811 Mary Norris, the widow of the Hon. John Norris had died, bequeathing to the Theological Institution of Andover the sum of thirty thousand dollars, and the same amount to the trustees for the benefit of foreign missions among the heathen. It remained only for the missionaries to be ordained, and then America would join the godly forces that had been spreading the Gospel through foreign lands.

Judson, in the meantime, had returned and, as in his many letters, presented to Ann Hasseltine the difficulties that would be his and hers in the missionary field. "We shall no more see our kind friends around us," he told her, "or go to the house of God with those that keep holy day. . . . We shall be weary of the world, and wish for wings like a dove, that we may fly away and be at rest. We shall probably experience seasons when we shall be 'exceeding sorrowful, even unto death'. . . . O, we shall wish to lie down and die. And that time may soon come. One of us may be unable to sustain the heat of the climate and the change of habits; and the other may say, with literal truth, over the grave—

> By foreign hands thy dying eyes were closed;
> By foreign hands thy decent limbs composed;
> By foreign hands thy humble grave adorned. . . ."

Ann loved him and refused to be discouraged by the gloomy prospect. "I hear that Miss Hasseltine is going to India!" one good gossip exclaimed to another. "Why does she go?"

"Why, she thinks it her duty. Wouldn't you go if you thought it your duty?"

The other pondered, and then replied, "But I would not think it my duty!"

Everything was arranged for the departure of the missionaries for Burma, which was chosen because it lay outside the limits of Great Britain's interests and the work would therefore not be duplicated. On February 5, 1812, Adoniram Judson was married to Ann Hasseltine.

The following day the Tabernacle at Salem witnessed the solemn ordination of Adoniram Judson, Samuel Newell, Samuel Nott, Gordon Hall and Luther Rice before the Ecclesiastical Council. The church was crowded with spectators. As the young men stood up before the Council and in thrilling voices told their motives for offering themselves as missionaries, eyes filled with tears. For days all Salem lived in a hush at the noble dedication that had there taken place. On the nineteenth of February, from Salem harbor, the brig *Caravan* squared her shrouds, bearing for the East the first missionaries to sail from America. They were Mr. and Mrs. Judson, Samuel Newell and his wife Harriet, one who like Ann thought it her duty to fulfil her mission.

Before that year was out Harriet Newell, the first American martyr to the missionary cause, was buried in the heathy ground of Mauritius Island, the scene of the pathetic tale of *Paul and Virginia*. In her brief life she had tasted only the pain of her dedication, had seen the corpse of her newborn babe cast into the sea and herself withering away in the blight of the unfriendly climate. But she had been sustained by the glory of the vision that had drawn them all from security and loving friends to a land of strangers. "Oh, glorious intelligence!" she cried in the very face of the death that would have obscured the splendor that she saw beyond.

The subsequent life of Adoniram Judson and his wife in India affords but one of the many examples of devotion of the men and women who followed in their footsteps for a cause that for them justified all pain and anguish, all hardship and persecution. At Rangoon and later at Ava, working hand in hand, they made converts, slowly at first, since it was death for Buddhists to renounce their religion, and with greater success as they learned the language of the people, and could reach them in their own tongue. Early in their work they, too, underwent conversion from Congregationalists to Baptists, after a painful wrestling with themselves. As a result, the Baptist Society for Propagating the Gospel in India and other Foreign Parts was organized in Boston, choosing as their missionaries the Judsons and Rice who had also been immersed in baptism.

Besides the hostility of the Buddhist priests and the viceroys, called appropriately "the eaters of provinces," the American missionaries had to contend with the unfriendliness of the East India Company, which felt its rights infringed upon. As it was, relations had become increasingly delicate between Great Britain and Burma, and the conflict came to a head when the British captured Rangoon. Immediately foreign teachers and missionaries were seized by the Burmese and imprisoned, Adoniram Judson among them. It was only through the devotion of his wife, who in spite of her precarious health pleaded with the authorities for him and other captives, that he escaped certain death.

With nearly a hundred other prisoners, he was thrown into a room so small that the men had to take turns in lying down. Three sets of fetters bound his hands and feet. There was no air but what came through a small barred window looking out on the street. For some recondite reason an unfortunate lion had been shut up among the prisoners and allowed to starve to death—a penalty that bore a mysterious connection with British power. After its death, Judson fell heir to the cage. Through the heat and the stench, amidst sickness and death, he made no complaint, comforted by his wife's love and the knowledge that his work was being carried on in his absence. Under his head, in a pillow that she had smuggled in to him, was the manuscript of his translation of the Bible into Burmese, and it gave him courage—a courage that failed only for a moment when

Ann, pale and weak, held her newborn baby to the bars for its father to kiss.

He remained in prison for two years, when he was released under the protection of the British for his services as translator. His missionary work was resumed with new fervor, Ann standing faithfully by him as before. But her strength was failing. The climate had done its work. After trying in vain to regain her health in America, she returned to her husband—to die.

Two other women joined their lives to Adoniram Judson's in the course of his long career, each raising for herself a monument of faithfulness and devotion. When his life closed in 1850, his achievements transcended the most ambitious aspirations of his youth. He had made a complete translation of the Bible into a language of which he had not known a word on leaving America as a youth of twenty-three. He had compiled a grammar and a dictionary of Burmese to help other missionaries. Most important of all, in a region that on his arrival contained not a single Christian, at the end of his life he left seven thousand converts.

"It is done. I am going." With these last words uttered in the tongue that had become his own, he closed his eyes to behold the splendor of the vision.

For that same vision hundreds of missionaries enlisted in the nineteenth-century crusade begun by Adoniram Judson and his friends, enduring untold sufferings, yielding up their very lives to the end that in lands where there were no Christians there might be no heathen. Throughout India, in the Turkish Empire, in China and Japan, in Persia, in South and West Africa, American missionaries planted their schools and temples till there was not a corner of the world that was without the Bible.

"Who created the science of anthropology?" asked Archdeacon Farrar in an eloquent defense of the work of those who were scornfully known as the "cobblers of God." "The missionaries. Who rendered possible the deeply important science of comparative religion? The missionaries. Who discovered the great chain of lakes in Central Africa, on which will turn its future destiny? The missionaries. Who have been the chief explorers of Oceanica and America and Asia? The missionaries. Who discovered the still more famous Moabite stone? A Church missionary. Who discovered the Hittite inscriptions? A Presbyterian missionary."

North and south, east and west, through fields of snow and stretches of parched desert where there might still be a few heathen to convert, the Word has been made to echo by the humble missionary whose life furnishes the romance of modern Christianity.

Another kind of romance, the romance of red-blooded adventure, lured a wild boy toward the middle of the nineteenth century ten thousand miles from home, to a burial place in a temple where to this day his ashes are worshiped by thousands of Chinese. The adventurous life of Frederick Townsend Ward has furnished the material for many a novel and play, though his name may not be mentioned and the setting be changed to suit the fancy of the writer. Nevertheless, readily recognizable, the inspiration of his vivid career is there.

He was born in 1831 of a generation of fighters and sea captains. The Salem waterfront was his playground; toy boats, first of paper and then of wood, his playthings. As he roamed about the wharves amid the colorful population that came down the flights of stairs leading from the decks of the stately East Indiamen, and as he saw the turbaned Parsee merchant and the slant-eyed Oriental brought over by the Salem sea captains, his imagination ran riot. He longed to grow up and stand upon his own quarterdeck on a ship bound for foreign ports. Wherever sailors gathered he was sure to be, an eager listener to the stories they brought home.

Undoubtedly he heard of the great China ship *Eclipse* whose keel was laid the very year of his birth, and whose bow, carved by the artist Joseph True with the head of a Mandarin, filled the Chinese with such awe that they would come by the hundred to bow down in worship before it whenever she lay in port. Then, after a number of voyages, the *Eclipse* lived up to her name, vanishing from the face of the earth without ever a trace of herself and her crew.

Like the word of a spell, the name of China tolled in Ward's restless head. He could not wait to go there and see the wonderful land for himself. He was barely fifteen when, by pretending he was much older, he sailed for China as second mate on the clipper *Hamilton* from the port of New York. He had only a fleeting glimpse of the land of his desire and then he was called home to be first mate on one of his father's ships that plied to San Francisco.

The routine of shipboard hardly satisfied the craving for adventure that surged in his blood. He must taste life in its depth and variety. For ten full, exciting years, therefore, he was driven by his hunger from one corner of the earth to another, now with Garibaldi, who had been fighting for the revolutionists in Brazil, now with William Walker, whose desperate filibustering expedition was to bring him at last before the firing squad. From San Francisco he occasionally berthed as first officer on some clipper, only to find himself, the reckless soldier of fortune, fighting now in the Crimean War and now for some cause whose ideals he scarcely stopped to question, if only they provided the excitement that was his very breath.

At the age of twenty-seven Ward found himself an officer of a river steamer on the Yang-tze. The Tai-ping rebellion, which had broken out in 1851 when Tien Wang, the pretender to the imperial throne of China had mustered millions of revolutionists to his support, had during the eight years of its progress reached such formidable proportions that both England and France had formed an alliance to defend their trading bases. In spite of their support, the Imperial Government had made no check upon the rebels who, under the leadership of the "Celestial King of the Great Dynasty of the Celestial Kingdom," were running over the land, looting and destroying every city they captured. Not that the foreign allies behaved any differently whenever victory was theirs. The Imperial Government, however, seeking safety at any cost, closed its eyes.

Ward entered at once into the fray, and with the help of Taki, a Chinese banker and the adviser of Li Hung Chang, the right-hand man of the Imperialists, managed to scrape up an army among the deserters and discharged foreign seamen of the waterfront. At first he had no success in his attacks against the Tai-pings, but when he reorganized his army and managed to capture a rebel garrison in Shanghai, the funds of the Chinese Imperial Treasurer were at his command. So too, was the manpower of the Chinese army, the "Imperial Braves," five thousand of whom were added to his nondescript yet hardy fighters.

By 1861 General Frederick Townsend Ward was known as the Invincible, and his army as the Ever Victorious Force. China, of which he had dreamed in his boyhood, became his adopted land, and he who had sunk roots nowhere, married Chang-mei, a Chinese lady and became a Chinese subject. He lived too fast and too perilously. On the twentieth of September when, after many victories, he led his men to capture the fort of Tsze Ki, he was hit by a bullet and died on board the *Hardy*, whose surgeons tried in vain to save him.

Li Hung Chang brought the tidings to the Emperor, who issued an edict for the raising of a temple in Ward's memory at Sung Kiang. Night and day, twelve votive lamps burn in the shrine that holds the ashes of the Invincible General of the Ever Victorious army, and every first of February the Chinese New Year rites commemorate the hero who, according to the inscription on the temple's column, "had sprinkled China with his azure blood."

At the Essex Institute another memorial keeps Ward's fame green in a library of four thousand volumes on China and the Chinese, and in a collection of relics of him and his Oriental wife. The bullet that killed him is also preserved.

CHESTNUT STREET, SALEM

"THE HOUSE OF THE SEVEN GABLES," BUILT BY CAPT. JOHN TURNER, ABOUT 1662.

CHAPTER XIX

## THE PURITAN HERITAGE

WITH justice Salem can boast that the first book in New England was written by the Rev. Francis Higginson, whose *New England Plantations* was printed in London in 1630. Very early in its growth Massachusetts saw the importance of reading and education. "That old deluder Satan," who in former times had kept the Scriptures in an unknown tongue to confound the faithful, was set down for the deceiver he was in the preamble of the Massachusetts Act on education in 1647. The Puritans saw through the wiles of his Satanic majesty. So that "learning may not be buried in the graves of our forefathers in Church and Commonwealth," an unshakeable foundation was laid for education in the various towns, and two presses, one established in Cambridge in 1639, and the other in Boston in 1674, kept the old deluder at bay with the numerous pamphlets that were hurled at his head. It was not till 1768 that Salem owned a press of her own, although from the beginning she had supplied a good part of the matter that went to feed those of Boston and Cambridge. Massachusetts was literate and prolific. Until 1750 more books were issued there than in all the other colonies together.

Though Salem cannot claim her for her own, Anne Bradstreet belongs equally to her literary history as to that of New England. The Tenth Muse, as she was later called, arrived in America on that same ship *Arbella* that had brought Governor Winthrop's party. With her came her husband, Simon Bradstreet, and her father, Thomas Dudley, inveterate hater of tolerance. Both men at different times served the colony as governors, Simon Bradstreet in his old age when he lived in a house on the site of the museum of the Essex Institute. In 1697 the Charter Street burial ground received him at the age of 94—the last of the men and women who had come on that historic ship.

Anne Bradstreet was eighteen when she landed in America. She was intelligent, sensitive and in love with her husband. With the devotion of her fellow Puritans, she made the new land her own; but there was a difference in her adoption. To her, more than a haven of refuge, America was a land of beauty—a beauty which she saw in the shifting seasons and in the songs of the creatures of the field too humble for the notice of the rest whose eyes were turned to God. In the midst of the religious writings of New England, her poems glow with a warmth of emotion that even in our day endows them with life. Change but a slightly antiquated word here and there and her lines to her husband might well have been written by a poet of today.

> If ever two were one, then surely we.
> If ever man were lov'd by wife, then thee;
> If ever wife was happy in a man,
> Compare with me, ye women if you can.
> I prize thy love more than whole mines of gold,
> Or all the riches that the East doth hold.
> My love is such that rivers cannot quench,
> Nor ought but love from thee give recompence. . . .

Yet that poem was penned before 1650, and in Puritan New England.

She was not uninfluenced by the spirit of her times, for like more ambitious poets she, too, wrote religious verses which she undoubtedly considered her most important work. Even in them, in spite of the classical overlaying popular in her day, her true voice is heard, singing of the simple yet wonderful things which she saw about her in the aspects of nature that in most of her contemporaries inspired only mistrust. Read this, from her "Contemplations":

> Some time now past in the autumnal tide,
> When Phoebus wanted but one hour to bed,
> The trees all richly clad, yet void of pride
> Were gilded o'er by his rich golden head.
> Their leaves and fruits seem'd painted, but was true
> Of green, of red, of yellow mixed hew;
> Rapt were my senses at this delectable view.

It is perhaps the first celebration in verse of a New England autumn.

While Anne Bradstreet's anonymously printed poems were still delighting her readers with their fresh and human qualities, Michael Wigglesworth's *Day of Doom* was wrapping New England in the folds of its apocalytic pall. Eighteen hundred copies were sold in 1662, the year of its publication. Every minister thundered from the pulpit the fire and brimstone poetry of the Harvard instructor; every household, not only in New England but in the other colonies, owned copies of it in broadsheets, like ballads, peddled about the country by itinerant vendors.

Throughout the land echoed the voice of Puritanism,

rousing the people from their worldliness to the final judgment when all who refused Christ's offer of saving grace met their condign punishment. Sin and the wages of sin—of such was the kingdom of Wigglesworth, whose vision of doom hung for generations at the bedhead of New England homes. Even the child could prattle the awesome ballad stanzas describing the fate of the unre-deemed.

As chaff that's dry, as dust doth fly before the Northern
     wind,
Right so are they chasèd away, and can no Refuge find.
They hasten to the Pit of Woe, guarded by Angels stout,
Who to fulfil Christ's holy Will, attend this wicked rout.

With Iron bands they bind their hands, and cursèd feet
     together,
And cast them all, both great and small, into that Lake
     forever,
Where day and night, without respite, they wail, and cry,
     and howl
For tort'ring pain which they sustain in Body and in Soul.

Thus early did the dourness of Puritanism combat in literature the expression of mankind's gentler feelings to-ward the material world.

On July 4, 1804, in a house that was no longer new when Judge Hathorne had sat in judgment on the witches of Salem, was born one of his descendants whom the heritage of Puritanism was to pursue like a ghost. Nathaniel Hawthorne came at the flowering point of the nation. He was to live through its expansion when two oceans formed the boundaries of east and west; he was to see that nation attain its place among the great powers of the world; he was to behold it severed and bleeding in a bitter civil war that made Americans like himself leave their lifework and take sides as their conscience dictated, carrying their convictions to the very forefront of battle. The struggle and the pain of growth were to clamor at the barriers of his self-absorption, yet through it all he was to live solitary and apart, the artist concentrated on the inner life whose vividness made but a shadow of the reality about him.

Ever since Judge Hathorne with his fellow magistrates had sent those nineteen men and women to their death in 1692, the family believed itself to be suffering under a curse. Indeed, tradition had it that when, irrevocably, Judge Hathorne had condemned Rebecca Nurse for the third time, the poor woman looked into his face with blazing eyes, and in the despair of her innocence, cursed him and his blood forever. With a strange fatality the substance of the family began from that day to melt away, each generation inheriting less than the one preceding. By the time Nathaniel was born in the house which his grandfather, "bold Captain Daniel," had bought near the wharves to be within sound of the sea on quitting the quarterdeck, the family possessed little besides their pride in their name. Disaster dogged them, the last stroke falling in 1808 when to that same house in Union Street came the news that Captain Nathaniel, the child's father, had died of a fever at Surinam.

It was no uncommon end for a sea-faring man of Salem, but his young widow never recovered from the blow. With her three children she left the house, echoing with the unbearable memory of her brief happiness, and went to live in her girlhood home on Herbert Street where, in the back garden that linked the Hathorne and the

Manning dwellings, she had allowed herself to be wooed by the handsome Nathaniel. Perhaps it were truer to say that she went there to die, for although in the body she survived her loss, she died with the husband whom she had loved with a painful intensity that had given to all his homecomings the rapture of stolen bliss. The child Nathaniel and his two sisters scarcely knew her—that ghost which now and then revealed itself before the living, only to return with morbid eagerness to the room where it dwelt in the company of the dead whom a tenacious imagination persisted in keeping alive.

In the Salem of the day the Hathorne family was taken for granted as poor but eminently respectable. Mr. Manning, the widow's brother, provided for her and the children. No one questioned Madame Hathorne's seclusion. In the close, almost Brahminical society of the aristocratic little town, it was nothing unusual for a woman to hide herself away in a dreamy semi-invalidism that set her apart as a thing too precious for daily living. Outside, the sun might shine on healthy, joyful men and women. For the recluse the true life resided in the mistiness of a room with closed shutters and the curtains drawn. Intellect and the spirit via Boston from the East were coming to their own.

With such a background it is hardly remarkable that Nathaniel grew to be the man he was. As a child the habit of solitude was fostered in him. In time it became his chosen way. There were happy intervals in his boyhood when the large-eyed, beautiful lad with a face already marked with melancholy left the dreary Salem home to live a more normal life at Manning's Folly, the house built by his uncle in Maine near the shores of Lake

Sebago. Yet even here the lonely boy liked nothing better than to hide in a cabin and before an unshared fire, read Walter Scott and the thought-provoking novels of William Godwin, the philosopher who could out-Radcliffe Mrs. Radcliffe. But Nathaniel, accustomed from earliest childhood to stronger fare than *Caleb Williams*, accepted the tale of sin and conscience as part of the well of inner experience from which he was to draw.

The years he spent at Bowdoin College left intact the core of his essential self. He made friends of Franklin Pierce, the future President, and of the devoted Horatio Bridge; he met Longfellow. But always, even in his intimacy with those who came closest to him, there was a veil that nothing could tear away, because without it life among people would have been impossible for him. It protected that inner self from corruption, but unfortunately it also kept him from the warmth of human contact that might have melted the film that was slowly freezing over his heart.

For nearly ten years after his graduation from Bowdoin in 1825, he lived with his mother and sisters in Salem. Herbert Street had hardly changed since his childhood except perhaps that the houses seemed a little older, and the one in which he lived had taken on the age of his birthplace, which he could see from his window in the southwest corner of the third story. The small garden where his mother and father had carried on their brief romance put on with every spring the freshness of ageless things; yet a somberness hung over the atmosphere like the shadow of Salem's past. Things became venerable early under that spell. As if to clutch at a fleeting immortality, he carved his name with a diamond in a pane of his chamber window.[1]

The family, if such a disunited group could be called one, had withdrawn to an even stricter seclusion during the years that had passed. Now Madame Hathorne appeared only at rare and weighty intervals, like a visitant from some supernal region. Her daughters led their own lives in their self-imposed apartness, going nowhere and receiving no one. Although both were attractive—Elizabeth, the elder might have been called beautiful—no one came to court them; they wanted no one. With their mother's youth, their happiness had been immolated on the altar of the living dead.

Perhaps to put up a defense between himself and the unhappy Hathornes, Nathaniel while at Bowdoin had formed the habit of spelling his name as we now know it. The unconscious ruse fooled the fates and gave the name immortality. But it changed not a hair of that beautiful head which used to make strangers turn to look at him, nor did it serve to lift one corner of the cloud that had hung over his birth.

He lived like a hermit. As the family never met, even at meals, his food was brought on a tray and laid behind his door which, in the tradition of the household, he kept locked as if such precaution were needed to guard a privacy that had always been sacred to him. There, in his solitude, with the blinds drawn so that nothing of the outside world might distract him, he dreamed and brooded of the past, reviving the legends that had surrounded his childhood and endeavoring to give them permanent form.

[1] The pane is preserved in the Essex Institute.

At night, when the last window had winked out its light in the sleeping town, he took long walks along the seashore listening to the beating of the surf that had been as the pounding of a heart in the commercial life of Salem. Now the stately ships no longer lay three deep in the wharves; the East India trade had all but ebbed away. No more rollicking music came out of Kit's dance house; everything was subdued as in a place where death is expected. It was the end of Salem's sea-glory that was sobering the sailors, who with the strange intuition sharpened in them by long months at sea, saw the old warehouses converted to tenements, the splendid white sails folded forever, and the harbor darkened with coal barges. Even the Custom House, massive and silent in the night, seemed like a tomb, and the flights of stairs in the shipyards like the mocking ruins of something that had once been great but now lived only as an ironic comment on human ambition.

Hawthorne observed everything with an almost morbid detachment. Always he was outside of things—the spectator. But he was also the artist. In his room he succeeded in completing seven tales drawn from his native past, and a novel, *Fanshawe*. The tales never found a publisher and saw light only in the blaze of the kitchen stove. *Fanshawe*, which was brought out by Marsh and Capen of Boston in 1828 at a cost of a hundred dollars to the author, might have been burned as well for all the impression it made. Disappointed in his "dream of undying fame," he found satisfaction in the fact that the novel, which he later came to regard as little as his public, had been published anonymously.

He kept on writing, nevertheless, and in an effort to

come closer to a life in which he had walked a stranger, he struck up a friendship with a young man by the name of Conolly who lived in some mysterious relation with the middle-aged Miss Susan Ingersoll, a distant cousin of Nathaniel's. Together with the family pride of the Hathorne's, Miss Ingersoll had inherited the fine old many-gabled house which she occupied with her protégé. There Hawthorne came to see his friend, as it was out of the question to bring him to the dismal nunnery where his mother and sisters presided. The house drew Hawthorne as much as did its occupants. Often, when tired of brooding in his room, he would walk the short distance to Turner Street, inhaling the night air laden with the tang of kelp and eelgrass from the nearby sea, and enter the narrow doorway to the dim, low parlor weighed down by the beams that divided the ceiling into squares.

It was no cheerful dwelling, no more than the home on Herbert Street, but it had an air of romance that the other had not. The mantel was laden with delicate old glass and Delft. In the cupboard bits of Chinese jade and ivory from India were dominated by great vases brought home from the Orient by Miss Ingersoll's father. She talked often of her ancestors, and Hawthorne's stock of legends grew. Somehow it seemed as if somewhere in the melancholy old place a story lurked that he must bring to light. On one of his visits Miss Ingersoll told him that the house had originally had seven gables. "Seven gables," he repeated. "The House of the Seven Gables—that sounds well."

It was not till many years later that his novel of *The House of the Seven Gables* was written, embodying the mystery with which it filled him, and the obsessive tradition of the family curse. Other Salem houses have since come forward to claim the title. It is still to the Turner-Ingersoll house, however, restored in 1909 and made into a neighborhood settlement, that the pilgrim, haunted by visions of the pathetic Hepzibah and her "cent shop," pays tribute. With it, too, are linked *Tales of a Grandfather's Chair*.

There was another Salem house to which Hawthorne began to turn his steps with greater frequency after 1838. Number 53 Charter Street could lay no claim to distinction, except perhaps in that it bordered Burying Point and contained the dust of grim old Judge Hathorne of witchcraft fame. It was not reverence for his stern ancestor that brought Hawthorne to Charter Street, but a frail, invalid girl of twenty-six. He was in love, deeply, unalterably in love for the first time in his thirty-four years.

## CHAPTER XX

# NATHANIEL HAWTHORNE

SOPHIA PEABODY was not beautiful. Neither was she plain. Her eyes, now dulled by the headaches that had tortured her since adolescence, now brightening as a word or a thought touched her sentimental fancy, preserved her from the commonplace. Small, slight, poised in her movements from her long habit of invalidism, clad in her flowing white wrappers and toying with a flower in her pale hands, she was just the woman for whom, indefinitely, Hawthorne had been waiting.

The whole household exuded an air of transcendental culture. Sophia herself was versed in the new philosophy that was blowing like a fructifying breeze from Concord and Boston through New England. In her it assumed a sentimental classicism that turned Hawthorne to an Apollo and a Hyperion—names which she repeatedly gave him—and removed their love to an altitude that made possible an engagement of four years. In her room—she too had the habit of the recluse—Sophia had fitted up a studio where she modeled, painted, read and studied Hebrew and Greek. Learning was expected of her in a home where the youngest daughter, Mary, was an expert on educational systems, and the oldest, Elizabeth, one of the founders and expounders of transcendental thought.

Emerson had taught Elizabeth Greek. She had kept a school in Boston and lived in the home of the famous

Dr. Channing, the apostle of Unitarianism. In 1826 she took up the cause of transcendentalism. Six years before Margaret Fuller, that foremost of American bluestockings, had held her *conversazioni*, Elizabeth gave a series of lectures in public. Bronson Alcott paid her the compliment of one of his poems, apostrophising her as "Daughter of Memory, Mythologist!" In her old age her admirers dubbed her affectionately the Grandmother of Boston.

When she drew Hawthorne into her fold for the stories which he had been publishing anonymously in the Boston magazines, her career was still in the making. It was in 1839, an important year for transcendentalism, that Dr. Nathaniel Peabody, no less remarkable than his daughters, moved to Boston, where at 13 West Street Elizabeth founded the bookstore which became the rendez-vous of the intellectual flower of the age. Emerson, Thoreau, Alcott, the mystical Jones Very, Theodore Parker, George Ripley and James Freeman Clarke all frequented the cozy West Street parlor where the solid world vanished and they walked in eternities and infinitudes.

Hawthorne, sitting somewhere aloof or looking out of a window, was often one of the party after leaving his duties as collector of the Boston port—a position which he had obtained through the efficient wire-pulling of Elizabeth Peabody, who was not too much exalted by the rarefied atmosphere for mundane considerations. It was an unromantic post, but it offered the regular employment that Hawthorne had been seeking, and provided besides the steady income which would enable him to assume the responsibilities of a household.

So far his literary efforts had brought him little money. Very few had heard of him, and only the initiated knew that he was the author of the extraordinary stories that for some years had been appearing in *The Token*. Yet he had won high praise. Park Benjamin, piercing Hawthorne's incognito, mentioned him by name in the *American Monthly Magazine* and termed him the equal of Washington Irving. "In this dismal chamber FAME was won," Hawthorne set down in his Herbert Street cell.

Meanwhile, in the name of transcendentalism all kinds of cults and fads were being hatched for the furthering of the perfect life. Everyone had his notion of a transcendentalist Utopia. It remained for Dr. George Ripley, recently resigned from a Unitarian pulpit, to launch it on a paying basis by the typically New England means of a joint stock company. Both Dr. Ripley and his wife were faithful supporters of the Transcendental Club; it was therefore to its members that the plan of Brook Farm was presented.

Couched in admirably abstract terms, Dr. Ripley's prospectus left the earthly facts so vague that it seemed as if the eternalities had already been attained. One thing emerged from the noble rhetoric. If a "more moral union" were insured between intellectual and manual labor than was actually in existence, the transcendental millennium would be just round the corner. To hasten its coming Dr. Ripley and his wife were establishing a milk farm in Roxbury, once the scene of Dr. Eliot's missionary work with the Indians. Here might man, especially intellectual man, know the lovely face of honest labor and in a union with her, bring forth transcendental fruit.

Emerson, to whom the prospectus was sent, approved of the scheme but would invest none of his money in it. Margaret Fuller preferred to watch the new society as an outsider, rather than as a member of the inner circle. One after the other, the Transcendentalists gave reasons why they considered themselves unfit for the experiment. One man, the one who would have seemed the least likely, encouraged Dr. Ripley's plan to the extent of investing in it a thousand dollars, saved from the wages of his Boston Port job.

Hawthorne had other motives, however, than those of preparing himself for the true and perfect life. The prosaic routine of his post had stagnated his creative vein. He must leave his uncongenial work or suffer the consequences in sterility and a sleepless conscience. Moreover he felt that he must at last marry, and therefore looked to Brook Farm as perhaps offering the independent life he sought. But he must first try it alone.

Accordingly, one day in April, which, with the inconsistency of New England weather treated the earth to a February snow storm, he arrived at Brook Farm ready to become the true Adam by means of pick and shovel. He was soon put to work. Such strength and zeal did he show that gins and other machines fell to pieces under his hand, threatening to bring the Utopian paradise to bankruptcy.

Giving him a pitchfork, an implement that could bear hard use, Dr. Ripley led the recruit to a hillside where, in competition with it, loomed a pile of manure. Hawthorne went to work with a will, assuming, no doubt, that the meanest tasks most exalted the soul. "I shall make an excellent husbandman,—" he wrote to Sophia when he saw with what gusto four clergymen who had joined themselves to the Farm, applied their energies to ridding the physical and moral man of the vices incurred in a false state of society.

Chopping wood, planting and hoeing, turning the grindstone and milking cows, Sophia's Hyperion became a shepherd of the new Arcady. Alas, the creative mind that should have awakened with the exercise of the physical man remained dormant. Worse, it grew so weary that it seemed to Hawthorne as if he would never again pick up a pen. He had no admiration of the Transcendentalists about him. Emerson, who sometimes visited the Farm, he respected but could not worship. Margaret Fuller, with her incessant talk and her contentious mind, he disliked. Even her heifer, which was herded with the Farm's eight cows, called forth his criticism. "She is very fractious, I believe, and apt to kick over the milk pail," he wrote Sophia. "Thou knowest best, whether in these traits of character, she resembles her mistress."

Under the circumstances it came as no surprise to Sophia to learn that Hawthorne was quitting the Farm to return to Salem. "I was beginning to lose the sense of what kind of a world it was," he wrote reminiscently, "among innumerable schemes of what it might be or ought to be." Still, the time he spent with the good Dr. Ripley and his community of aspirants to perfection was not wasted. Deep in his mind and in notebooks that did full justice to the experiment, was the material for the *Blithedale Romance*, Hawthorne's only realistic novel to which both Henry James and William Dean

NATHANIEL HAWTHORNE, 1840
Painting by Charles Osgood

Howells were to assign the highest place among his works.

In July, 1842, Hawthorne and Sophia Peabody were married in the West Street home in Boston, and went to live in Concord at the Old Manse left empty on the death of its superannuated owner, Dr. Ezra Ripley. Before the Revolution the house had been built by Dr. William Emerson, who had seen from his study window the memorable first engagement at the bridge between the embattled farmers and the redcoats. Ralph Waldo Emerson had also occupied the house in which he had written his first essay on Nature. Neither historical tradition, however, nor literary association, had prompted Hawthorne to select the Old Manse. He had wanted a place where he could live apart, and he found it, though now it was a seclusion *à deux*.

Sophia was ideally happy with the husband whom she could not too much admire. Here was their Eden—this plain two-storied gable-roofed dwelling set in the midst of the Concord landscape and margined by the slow Concord River whose current, like the pulse of age, could scarcely be determined. Nothing old and decayed was suffered to remain in the rooms they occupied. Decrepit chairs, dusty portraits of stern divines that looked to Hawthorne like so many bad angels, all were sent to the attic to molder in peace. On the lower floor the old minister's bedchamber made an attractive parlor with bright hangings and the wedding bric-à-brac, while his study in the upper southwest corner shone with pale yellow paint and paper, dappled in the afternoon with the shadows of trembling leaves. Here, surrounded by his familiar bachelor furniture, Hawthorne was to dream his dreams, and in the cheery sunlight renew the flourishing of an old and tired stock.

Marriage accomplished a release in his closed, inhibited life. Now through the beneficent influence of Sophia, who acted as contact between himself and the world, his Concord neighbors were suffered to visit him. Emerson came, unlocking his word hoard on nature and friendship and compensation, and irradiating his thoughts with that peculiar slow smile that was like the emerging of the sun from behind a cloud. Hawthorne listened, rarely breaking in upon that talk with a word or a question.

And Thoreau, who was then part of Emerson's household, sometimes accompanied the philosopher and sat in the Hawthorne parlor, hardly listening because of the thoughts that surged within him, and rousing himself to a pleasant reality when Sophia, who feared he was bored, played for him her little music box, one of her wedding presents. Instantly the inward-seeking eyes brightened and the face that had seemed so ugly to the lover of beauty assumed a soft loveliness. Slowly friendship ripened between the shy poet and the shyer Hawthorne, who surprised even himself on finding that he enjoyed the calm gliding of Thoreau's Musketaquid along the Concord and the climb to the hills that for the first time in America were rousing the nature worship of poet and philosopher.

Hawthorne, too, like Sophia, knew happiness in the heart of that Concord where, as Mrs. Peabody told her daughter, "native Apollos and Platos spring up in your everyday walk." There was no dearth of them, what with the forcing-house power of Transcendentalism and Emerson's delight of discovery. For three years, broken by visits to Salem and Boston, the Hawthornes mingled in that current of simple living and high thinking.

The pinch of poverty wakened them to the necessity for change, and again Hawthorne cast about for some government employment that would give him and his family, now increased by the birth of a daughter, a security which he had not known since his marriage. Moreover, he was dissatisfied with his literary output. He had hoped to establish himself with a sustained work, but found that at the end of three years he had produced only a volume of sketches which were published with the title of *Mosses from an Old Manse*. They were first-rate work, containing such pieces as "Rappacini's Daughter," "Young Goodman Brown" and the fantastic "Feather-top." But was there anything that surpassed the best stories in his *Twice-Told Tales*,—anything with the grim power of "The Minister's Black Veil" or the moving beauty of "The Gentle Boy"?

In the nick of time, through the influence of his political friends, Hawthorne was appointed Surveyor of the Port of Salem with an income of twelve hundred dollars a year. The Old Manse was abandoned and the little family went to live with Madame Hathorne in the old Herbert Street home, that to the married pair now became "Castle Dismal." Years had not changed the habits of the aging Madame Hathorne. Nathaniel and Sophia scarcely saw her, and only baby Una, whose laughter brought a ray of light to the old face, was suffered to cross her threshold.

In the pillared Custom House, at an unpretentious wooden table, Hawthorne took up his duties with a will, as Sophia had given birth to their second child, a son whom they named Julian.

Salem's days of glory as a seaport had faded. The square riggers for the East Indies had one by one begun to fold their sails. Sumatra and other ports of the Orient were becoming more and more the evocations of memory. Even the Manila trade was at an ebb. Salem merchants still carried on commerce with the Philippines on a smaller scale, but now their vessels set out from Boston. The opening of the Erie Canal and the development of the railroad which, in 1838, had laid its tracks in Salem and set in motion its frail-looking, four-wheeled coaches modeled after the old-fashioned stages, had deviated commerce to the larger centers. Now the huge edifice, built in the days of Salem's prosperity, housed a staff of antiquated sea-dogs with little to do and an inclination to do still less. To Hawthorne it looked like a sailors' refuge where the old hulks were suffered to decay in peace.

In that sluggish atmosphere it seemed as if Hawthorne's creative brain were drugged. Or was it rather the effect of "Castle Dismal"? In search of more congenial quarters, the Hawthornes moved first to a house on Chestnut Street and then, in September, 1847, to the square wooden building at 14 Mall Street, in a front room of which, on the third story far from the noise of the street, Sophia furnished her husband's study with all the things that associated themselves with his literary life. He wrote again, slowly and painfully at first, and then with renewed impetus as he saw the theme forcing itself out of the mold of the short story to a novel.

The germ of *The Scarlet Letter* had been growing in

the depths of his subconscious mind ever since, years earlier, he had written the story of "Endecott and the Red Cross." There the scarlet letter of adultery figured only as a detail in a supernumerary character mentioned like many others to lend color to the tale; but the story that might be derived from it had preyed on his mind for nearly ten years. "There was likewise a young woman," he had written of the prototype of Hester Prynne, "with no mean share of beauty, whose doom it was to wear the letter 'A' on the breast of her gown, in the eyes of all the world and her own children. And even her own children knew what that initial signified. Sporting with her infamy, the lost and desperate creature had embroidered the fatal token in scarlet cloth, with golden thread and the nicest art of needlework. . . ."

Essentially *The Scarlet Letter*, Hawthorne's masterpiece, is a poetical handling of sin and the wages, as well as the consequences, of sin. Rebellious artist that he was, though inescapably still a Puritan, he had taken the obsession of his life and turned it over in the light of his imagination until, as through a prism, all the hidden colors were drawn out of it. Perhaps one might read in the gradual spiritual growth of Hester Prynne after her sin with Dimmesdale the message that through the expiation of her fault she had attained to a higher life than she could have achieved without it. But we are treading on dangerous ground, as Hawthorne himself draws no conclusions and presents no thesis. Suffice it that in *The Scarlet Letter* he wrote a work of ever-living fame that can hold its own with the masterpieces of world literature.

And here we must take leave of Hawthorne and his

life in Salem, which he found unbearable on losing his Custom House post in 1849, the same year that caused the greatest exodus from Massachusetts to the West at the cry of "Gold! Gold!"

A workman at Sutter's Mill, California, had discovered nuggets of the precious metal in January 1848 while working on a roadbed, and the shout of his discovery had been ringing across the continent, starting caravans on the westward trek on land and sea. Everywhere, throughout Massachusetts, men stilled the power in the mills, farmers threw down their spades and merchants pooled their resources to form emigrant companies for the golden shores.

Many of them performed the weary journey by the overland route. Massachusetts, true to her maritime tradition, spread her sails to the winds and made the voyage round the Horn. Rubbing their eyes, Hawthorne's old cronies of the Salem Custom House looked out on the sudden activity at the port and could scarcely believe themselves awake. Was that Salem's barque *Eliza* casting off from Derby Wharf? Were those Salem men, piling her deck, and singing strange words to the tune of "Oh! Susannah"? Incredulous they listened as the song that was to become the hymn of the gold seekers, sounded in the air:

> I came from Salem City,
>     With my washbowl on my knee,
> I'm going to California,
>     The gold dust for to see.
>
> It rained all night the day I left,
>     The weather it was dry,
> The sun so hot I froze to death,
>     Oh! brothers, don't you cry.

Oh! California,
That's the land for me!
I'm going to Californi-a
With my washbowl on my knee. . . .

It was short-lived activity. The clipper ship, which was to reach its zenith from 1850 to 1854, was not destined to be part of Salem's history. As an important seaport she had ceased to exist, although for still half a century, until the *Mindoro*, the last of her merchantmen was docked in Derby Wharf, to be stripped of her sails and degraded to the humiliating service of a coal carrier, she occasionally followed the compass to the old trading bases. More and more her merchants, like Colonel Francis Peabody, who established a linseed oil and jute factory in 1841, were putting their money into industry and manufacture, leaving the building and sailing of their great ships to Boston and New York.

So it was that the clipper, *Surprise*, commissioned by the Salem Lows, who had established themselves in New York, was launched in Boston, setting a record by making the voyage round the Horn to California in ninety-six days. The triumph was not Salem's, nor was it her joy to see the maiden flight of those coursers of the sea, the *Stag-Hound* and *Mastiff*, or of the floating beauties, *Flying Cloud*, *Lightning*, *Great Republic*, and *Glory of the Seas*, the masterpieces of Donal McKay's shipbuilding art.

Hawthorne had nothing more to hold him in Salem. Except for brief visits there he spent his remaining years abroad as consul at Liverpool and as a traveler in Italy, where he rounded out his literary life with the writing of *The Marble Faun*. After 1860 he returned to Concord, renewing old friendships but guarding jealously from all but his wife, his essential self.

Life touched him not at all, so removed did it seem from that somber world which he carried about with him everywhere. While the issues of Abolition were at their height and he was living in the very nest of the Anti-slavery movement, he remained without powerful convictions—indeed without any convictions at all but for a vague belief in the ultimate settling of the question by some unlooked for means. "There is still another view, and probably as wise a one," he could defend his indifference. "It looks upon slavery as one of those evils which Divine Providence does not leave to be remedied by human contrivance, but which, in its own good time, by some means impossible to be anticipated, but of the simplest and easiest operation, when all its uses shall have been fulfilled, it causes to vanish like a dream."

The means impossible to be anticipated turned out to be the Civil War.

To the end his aloofness wrapped him like a cloak. In 1864, while traveling in search of health, he died as he had lived, alone, in a hotel in the White Mountains. On the twenty-third day of May, mild and bright, he who had shunned human contact to remain his alienable self was borne to his grave at Sleepy Hollow by Emerson and Longfellow, Lowell, Holmes, Agassiz and other great men of his day. Frankin Pierce, once president, remained with Sophia and her children.

"I thought him a greater man than any of his works betray," wrote Emerson, the day after the burial.

## CHAPTER XXI

## OTHER SALEM LITERARY FIGURES

AMONG the young men who buzzed about Emerson like bees round the source of the honey of wisdom, was a Salem youth of striking appearance. Of him it could not be said that he buzzed, however. The philosophic slowness of speech, the abstracted air of the seeker into mysteries beyond human ken were more consonant with Jones Very. The long narrow face, hollowed even in youth by asceticism, was surmounted by a vast forehead over which the scant hair drooped. The nostrils of the long sensitive nose quivered easily, but as if to control too great a show of emotion, the lips were habitually pressed to a straight line. Under overhanging brows the eyes looked out like those of sea captains accustomed to gazing on long, shining distances; Jones Very's gaze was fixed on even farther bournes.

There is little to tell of his life except that he "lived and died at 154 Federal Street," as the Salem guidebook will tell one with notable succinctness. Outwardly few events marked the life that began in 1813 and ended in 1880. But there was much that Jones Very experienced within himself, although even of that life he has left but a slight record.

Like most studious youths, he entered Harvard. Then, after leaving college, he attended the inevitable Divinity School—the soil of his religious growth. For two years

he taught Greek at Harvard. The midnight lamp, however, burned not over ancient texts but over the poems
and essays which he felt inspired to write under the
impulse of the literary awakening that was taking place
in New England. In 1838, taking his courage in his hand,
he submitted a sheaf of his poems to the oracle of Concord.

Emerson liked to foster genius. Moreover, he discerned
something of a religious mood akin to George Herbert's
that marked young Very as out of the common run of
bardlings. "The sentiment which inspires your poetry is
so deep and true," he encouraged, "and the expression
so simple, that I am sure you will find your audience very
large."

For once Emerson proved no prophet, as the sale of
Very's *Essays and Poems*, published in 1839 through his
patronage, revealed through the years. It was the only
edition that was to reach the public during Very's life-
time.

Of the essays—on epic poetry, on Shakespeare, on
Hamlet—there is little to say except that they portray
the scholar and the man who walked hand in hand with
a religion that was almost a mystical experience. It was
in poetry, especially in his sonnets with their strangely
lengthened last line, that Very excelled. In both his
poetry and his prose one idea, more truly a conviction,
obsessed him: that the aim of the human soul is to identify
itself with God, as only in such mingling can true happiness be found.

He lived too close to Concord not to feel the power of
nature that was turning Emerson and Thoreau to stream-
and-mountain worshipers. To Jones Very this worship

afforded the only ecstasy he ever knew from mortal things, and it is therefore in his nature sonnets that he is most truly the poet. Perhaps we cannot better take leave of him than with his lines, "The Columbine":

Still, still my eye will gaze long-fixed on thee
Till I forget that I am called a man,
And at thy side fast-rooted seem to be,
And the breeze comes my cheek with thine to fan.
Upon this craggy hill our life shall pass,—
A life of summer days and summer joys,—
Nodding our honey-bells 'mid pliant grass
In which the bee, half-hid, his time employs;
And here we'll drink with thirsty pores the rain,
And turn, dew-sprinkled, to the rising sun,
And look when in the flaming west again
His orb across the heaven its path has run;
Here left in darkness on the rocky steep,
My weary eyes shall close like folding flowers in sleep.

William Wetmore Story, as unlike Jones Very as if they had belonged to different worlds, was born at 26 Winter Street, the house that his father, Justice Joseph Story, had built for himself in 1811. Here, in the cradle that had held the father, the son was laid, out of respect to an honored tradition. And here, when the child was five years old, the great Lafayette was entertained on his second visit to Salem. Perhaps long afterwards under the sun of Italy, William Story recalled how torrents of rain had fallen during the visit of the great man; how he had watched the parade of the children and the sailors in uniform; and how, in the evening, Lafayette had stood with Judge Story on the front steps of the Winter Street house, shaking hands with the long line of admirers who came to pay him homage. Perhaps he recalled, too, that

Judge Story had received as much honor as the great Frenchman.

The boy was brought up amidst the best that New England had to offer, in a home of learning and refinement, softened by the graces of a charming and accomplished mother who could on occasion forget that she was a lady to give what is known as a piece of her mind. The wayward son never forgot the particular piece which she flung at him at a critical moment of his career. "Well, William, I've known in my life many a fool, but I've never known so great a one."

The usual routine of education was taken for granted by Judge Story for his son: Harvard, then Harvard Law School, and then an honorable career at the bar. It remained but for William to follow in his own footsteps. William made no objection. By the time he was twenty-one his formal preparation had been accomplished and he was admitted to the Massachusetts bar, where he showed himself to be a worthy son of his distinguished father. Judge Story was proud of him and smiled indulgently when, after the briefs were laid aside for the day, the youth shut himself up in his room and pottered about with lumps of wet clay.

An artist in the family? Judge Story's smile was slightly rueful as he recalled the year 1804 when, at his son's age, he had published a poem in heroic meter by the title of *The Power of Solitude*. He had thought it a great work then, and had been very proud when he had held the first copy in his hand. A beautifully printed volume it was, the best of the Salem imprints and with an adequately melancholy illustration on the cover by the artist Cornè. Later, when he had reread the verses with the eye of age, he had burned every copy he could find. How thin and unimportant, how adolescent it had seemed against the weighty tomes on jurisprudence that had followed it!

William Story's dabbling with clay did not interfere with his producing the solid books that were expected of him. By 1844 he had published a two-volume *Treatise on the Law of Contracts*, followed three years later by a *Treatise on the Law of Sales of Personal Property*, both works of such value that they are still in use as text-books. Judge Story never saw the second book in print, for he died in 1846.

That year marked the turning point of William's life. Upon his father's death a public monument was decreed to him, and to William's astonishment, he was chosen to execute it. At first he would not hear of it. It was one thing to give up early morning hours, before his office called him, to his modeling; it was quite an-other to undertake such a commission—and of so eminent a man as his father. The committee, however, insisted upon its choice. On condition that he would first be permitted to go abroad to study, William consented. He sailed for Italy in October of 1847 and remained on the continent until he had finished his preliminary sketch.

On his return the committee approved the design and Story executed it, writing, in the meantime, a biography of his father. But he was no longer happy in New Eng-land. He had tasted Italian life in the studios of Rome, where men gathered in the worship of art, and he dreamed of returning. Briefs and contracts, bench and bar seemed to belong to a dead past, and he was alive with ambition to create such works as he had seen in churches and museums, in the very streets of the city that called him. In 1850, in spite of his mother's prayers and finally her anger at what she thought his madness, he gave up law to devote himself to art.

From then on, except for brief absences, he lived in Rome—one of the earliest American pioneers of that boundless realm of art inhabited by willing expatriates from all over the world. His studio became one of the most frequented in Italy. The Brownings, Walter Savage Landor, old Mrs. Trollope, visiting American and English artists, poets and musicians, elbowed one another up the stairs of his tower. Margaret Fuller and her young Italian husband, Marquis Ossoli, were frequent visitors before they sailed for America with their infant child, only to be shipwrecked within sight of the shore they were never to reach. Hawthorne came often to the studio and stood in silent admiration before Story's statue of Cleopatra. In vain the sculptor listened for an expression of what Hawthorne must feel. But how delighted he was when in *The Marble Faun* the reticent author broke his silence to describe the siren of the Nile— "fierce, voluptuous, passionate, tender, wicked, terrible and full of poisonous and rapturous enchantment."

Italy released Story's creative energy. Besides his sculptures, imbued with the passion that had inspired the canvases of Delacroix, he published several volumes of poetry, *Fiammetta*, a novel, *Roba di Roma, Conversations in a Studio, Excursions in Art and Letters* and many fugitive pieces, all of which spread his reputation. Of his sculptures, *Semiramis* was bought by the Metropolitan Museum of Art in New York. His portrait busts and monuments are found in London, Baltimore, Cambridge,

Boston, Washington and other cities of Europe and America.

As a man, he possessed a rare cultivation and charm that made Europe marvel at such polish in one of those reputedly uncouth Americans. Henry James in *William Wetmore Story and His Friends* tells a delightfully appropriate anecdote at the expense of a Frenchman who could not overcome his astonishment at Hawthorne's excellent manners. "Il sortait de Boston, de Salem, de je ne sais quel trou—"[1] he exclaimed to James with subtle implication—and here he was, a model of perfection! How often must that observation have been made of Story whom his friends, after his death in 1895, remembered as one of the most urbane men they had ever known!

Out of the same *hole*, as the Frenchman had been pleased to call Salem, and from exactly the same background of law, came William Hinckling Prescott who, with John Lothrop Motley and Francis Parkman, formed the triumvirate of the great American historians of the nineteenth century. Prescott, the son of a prosperous lawyer, and grandson of the Col. William Prescott who had commanded at Bunker Hill and whose monument Story modeled, was born on May 4, 1796. His native Salem was not to hold him long. At the age of twelve he was taken from the Salem school to continue in Boston, which became the permanent home of his family.

Like Justice Story, Prescott's father intended his son for a career at the bar, but an untoward accident to the boy at Harvard College was to determine otherwise.

[1] Trans. "He came from Boston, from Salem, from I don't know what hole—"

During some rough play in the Commons Hall, someone flung a hard crust of bread across the room, hitting young Prescott in the eye. Eventually the injury deprived it of sight. Nevertheless, Prescott obtained his degree and entered his father's law office. Soon the uninjured eye showed signs of coming blindness. The afflicted father consulted doctors and specialists, all of whom agreed that on the youth's general health depended whether or not he would lose his sight. Travel in a mild climate was prescribed.

From the spring of 1816, therefore, to the summer of the following year, Prescott traveled through England, France and Italy, making up for his impaired vision by beginning on that discipline of his memory which, in later life, when he was almost totally blind, enabled him to retain whole chapters for dictation to his assistants.

The year's travel made no improvement in his sight. The law career had perforce to be abandoned. He had no regrets, however. Other plans, as yet remotely associated with the civilizations he had seen abroad, were beginning to shape themselves in his mind. At college he had tried his hand at composition. After his marriage to Miss Susan Amory in 1820, he set to work earnestly at literature.

His beginnings were modest—an article, a review here and there, an essay, the while he renewed his studies of the Romance languages in which he was to pursue the research for the work he was planning. His system was that employed by the blind. With the help of a noctograph he made notes, which his assistants in turn read aloud to him until the mass of material was assimilated by his phenomenal mind.

He turned to the writing of history. But it was not history as it was known in his day. He had too much contempt for the pedantic, biased, pseudo-patriotic productions that filled the shelves of public institutions for him to want to add to them. History with him was to be a literary achievement. William Robertson, the Scottish historian whose *Charles the Fifth* had been one of the most widely read books of Prescott's youth, furnished the model. Mably's *Essai sur l'Étude de l'Histoire* suggested the method.

He worked slowly and painstakingly, partly because of his deficient sight, yet chiefly because he had no respect for hurried work. Time was at his disposal, and immortality perhaps within reach. It was not till Christmas Day of 1837, therefore, that his *Ferdinand and Isabella* appeared. It had been well worth the labor. The dramatic story of the Spanish Empire, its conquest of Naples and of the arrogant Arabs who had long dominated Spain, the strengthening of the power of the church through the Inquisition, the discovery of a vast new continent in the West, gave ample material for Prescott's inspired pen. Overnight the book made him famous, not only in Boston but in Europe where it became the sensation of the year.

From Spain in Europe Prescott turned to Spain in America. Here was an almost unexplored field. It was nearer to him. The dramatic light and shade of the epic tragedy of conquest stirred his inmost being. Bold Cortez on the one hand, proud Montezuma on the other, the conflict of passions, the pitting of one civilization against another and the final humbling of one: what mightier themes could a historian seek? Prescott wrote the *Con-*

*quest of Mexico*, the book that was to make him immortal.

When it appeared in 1843, its success equaled that of *Ferdinand and Isabella*. Posterity, however, has given it first place over its predecessor and over the two great books that followed it—the *Conquest of Peru* and the *History of Philip II*. When the first two volumes of *Philip II* were published, their reception overshadowed that of Prescott's previous work. For four years he labored in total darkness on the third and last volume of what contemporary critics acclaimed as his masterpiece, but death overtook him in 1859 before he could write the word *Finis*.

Lesser literary lights glowed and faded in Salem in the course of its history. They are for the curious to seek out and enjoy. Two men have become classics in their special field of history—the delightful Rev. Joseph B. Felt, whose *Annals of Salem* no lover of that storied town can afford to miss, and the Rev. Charles Wentworth Upham, whose *Salem Witchcraft* has not yet been superseded.

Of the two, biography has left scant record in the case of the Rev. Joseph Felt. Of Upham, however, we know that besides divinity he pursued politics, making an inveterate enemy of Hawthorne, who used him as a model for his Judge Pyncheon in *The House of the Seven Gables*, as a revenge for the clergyman's activity in depriving him of the Custom House post. In time the Rev. Mr. Upham was elected to Congress and served as Mayor of Salem, which had risen to the rank of a city in 1836 under the first mayoralty of the Hon. Leverett Saltonstall.

Besides the many notables who were born in Salem or chose it as their place of residence, there were many who visited it and left records of their impressions. George Washington, who greeted the enthusiastic populace from the balcony of the Town and Court House in 1789 and who unconsciously served as a model for a profile bas-relief by McIntire, had many gracious things to say of his reception as well as of the beauty of the dark-haired New England women. A year earlier Brissot, who was to become a leader of the Girondists and, at their downfall, meet his death at the guillotine, praised Salem comfort and Salem hospitality. Other distinguished visitors did not fail to succumb to its beauty and antique charm in compliments that the Rev. Joseph Felt religiously recorded.

One disgruntled foreigner alone came, saw, and was not pleased. It was E. J. Kendall, who in his account of his travels made a number of pronouncements, one of which in particular roused the champion in Felt. "The inhabitants have drawers under their dining-tables," Kendall wrote, "into which to thrust the dishes, in the unwelcome event of a stranger's visit."

Felt's retort is pointed, unwittingly humorous and thoroughly New England. "If ever there was the mere semblance of fact for such a fabrication, we dare warrant that it was on one of our washing-days, when commendable economy induces us to gather up our cold fragments, so that time need not be taken from our cleansing operations, and set them before our families as a sufficient meal for them, but which custom would consider as uncivil for strangers. Under such circumstances, some good dame of our community, on the point of congratulating herself that all would go on smoothly, the repast soon be ended and washing recommenced, when some one with the form and dress of a man, but with little manliness of heart and conduct, called at an unseasonable hour, to be refreshed, and thus keep his purse undiminished by the charges of an inn. That she might save her establishment from the appearance of being poorly supplied, she might have put part of her least palatable fare into the drawer, intending, that if the visitor remained, she would make exertion for some better food. Now, so far from construing this as parsimony, it should be construed as proper economy for the family, and a suitable regard for strangers."

For this, in spite of its Augustinian grammar, if for nothing else, the Rev. Joseph B. Felt deserves a place among Salem's worthies.

## CHAPTER XXII

# TOWARD THE TWENTIETH CENTURY

THE history of the nineteenth century is a record of moral and material advance, of sundered boundaries and liberations, of enlightenment and progress. The names of many celebrated men adorn its pages, not in accounts of wars and conquests, but for achievements so marvelous that in their light the ambitions of Napoleons and Bismarcks are dwarfed to insignificance. It is the modern age that in its span of a hundred years accomplished more than all the centuries preceding it. Scientific experiments curb space and light to man's uses. Steam and electricity are harnessed to his needs. Darkness is abolished. The railroad and the telephone make nothing of distance. The whole world is brought into intimate relation.

In the vocabulary of science many new words find place to designate the many things, no longer strange, that have come to man's knowledge. There is the theory of gases and that of molecules and of atmospheric dust. There is the science of geology that can determine the age of the world and from the markings of a stone decipher the history of mankind. There is the discovery of the Roentgen ray, the beginning of experimentation on radium and of the uses of anaesthetics that have eliminated much of the world's pain. In other fields inventors have been breaking through barriers and opening up new realms. How little did the Rev. Mr. Felt know, as he set down the first fumblings of scientific man in his *Annals*, that not even the antechamber of the palace of science had been entered!

"A balloon 18 feet high and 54 feet in circumference, ascends from the premises of the Assembly House," he noted among the pastimes and amusements of the day. "It fell near Baker's Island." Not in his wildest dreams could he have envisioned a giant craft of steel and as yet undiscovered metals, riding the clouds as a ship rides the sea.

"Mr. Perrette, machinist of Paris," he recorded with reference to a so-called self-moving carriage, "advertised . . . that he should experiment with such a carriage at Washington Hall." Did any of the curious who paid 1/6 a ticket to see the queer contraption dream that a time would come when a self-moving carriage, Latinized into automobile, would devour space at the rate of sixty miles an hour?

Later Felt described with real pleasure the exhibitions of a phantasmagoria and of a kaleidoscope—"an object of great curiosity to most of our community in 1818." For him, as for the rest of Salem, the wonder ended there in the play of shadow and shifting color. What would they have said to phantoms on a screen that moved, and talked? Would they have run out of the room in terror like many of the first spectators at the earliest projection of the cinematograph?

For the most part, people everywhere inclined to scepticism at the innovations that were being wrought before their very eyes. In 1789, the year of Felt's birth, when Danvers River was the scene of a peculiar experiment, the crowd on the shore looked on with much shaking of the head as Nathan Read tried out his paddle wheel for a boat. In 1817, when the steamboat *Massachusetts* first came into Salem port, Felt with the rest of his townsmen showed curiosity—and diffidence.

"She had come from New York, and was bought by a company here," he dutifully noted. "She sails on an excursion in the bay. Each adult is charged $1 for a passage and each child 50 cents." We may be sure that he did not permit his curiosity to get the better of his prudence. "Being found far more trouble than profit," he continues with some satisfaction, "she was offered at auction in the fall, and finally set out for Mobile, to be sold there, but was cast away at Little Egg Harbor. Thus wrecked, she was disposed of so that her owners realized very little of what they paid for her. . . ." It might seem as if with the ill-fated *Massachusetts* were cast away all hope of navigation except by spar and canvas. Yet the day was not far off when vessels larger than the Salem Custom House would make from a harbor on one hemisphere and, in any wind and weather, clear a port three thousand miles away in less than a week.

The triumph of the nineteenth century, however, was a moral one, when four million slaves were freed in the United States. True, their shackles had to be severed by the sword after the nation had been brought to the brink of destruction. But the force that secured their freedom was the conscience of that nation, awakened by the moral indignation of New England at the existence of such evil among a people that held "these truths to be self-evident: that all men are created equal; that they are endowed by their Creator with certain inalienable rights; that among these are life, liberty and the pursuit of happiness." Long since, when the preamble of the Declaration of Independence was drawn up, the far-seeing Tom Paine would have inserted a clause including the Negroes among the beneficiaries of the divine endowment. The slave owners, however, fought against it and won.

From earliest colonial days New England had opposed the importation of slaves. But the traffic proved profitable and a few Massachusetts shipmasters engaged in the Guinea trade, as it was called, in spite of the abhorrence in which it was generally held. Dr. Bentley preached against it in vain so far as notorious Salem offenders were concerned. "It is reported," he wrote in his diary under the date of November 12, 1790, "that Sinclair has returned from a Guinea voyage with the loss of all his crew. Notwithstanding the laws of the Commonwealth, there is not one man of spirit to stand forth and make inquiry into these detestable practices. I am informed that this daring wretch who has made so much mischief is engaging in another such voyage."

Doubtless the daring wretch did set out on that voyage and on many another, although in 1783, by the decision of the Supreme Court of Massachusetts, slavery had been abolished according to the interpretation of the clause, "All men are born free and equal" which had found its place in the State Constitution three years earlier. In the very year when Dr. Bentley made his despondent entry, Massachusetts alone of all the states in the Union returned only free persons in the first census held in the United States.

Nonetheless, the Sinclairs of the seaport towns persisted in their illicit trade. Negroes constituted articles of merchandise and as such they fell under a code of instructions issued by the trading company and duly followed by the captains of slave ships. It was to their mutual advantage that the merchandise did noϲ deteriorate on the voyage.

"As slaves," read one set of instructions issued to the command of a brig in 1785, "like other articles, when brought to market, generally appear to the best advantage; therefore too critical an inspection cannot be paid to them before purchase; to see that no dangerous distemper is lurking about them, to attend particularly to their age, to their countenance, to the straightness of their limbs, and, as far as possible, to the goodness or badness of their constitution . . .

"Male or female slaves, whether full grown or not, we cannot particularly instruct you about; and on this head shall only observe, that prime male slaves generally sell best in any market. No people require more kind and tender treatment to exhilarate their spirits than the Africans . . . When you consider that on the health of your slaves, almost your whole voyage depends . . . you will therefore particularly attend to smoking your vessel, washing her with vinegar, to the clarifying your water with lime or brimstone, and to cleanliness among your own people, as well as among the slaves. . . ."

As the reward of his venture the captain was to have four slaves out of every hundred, and four more at the place of sale, together with a salary of two pounds eight shillings a month, and eight hogsheads to relieve the tedium of the nights at sea. Not a bad profit as ventures went.

The eighteenth century closed and the nineteenth drew on toward its first thirty years before the one man of spirit whom Dr. Bentley sought stood forth to condemn slavery. William Lloyd Garrison was only twenty-four when he roused the country's sleeping conscience with a jolt. A son of Massachusetts—he was born in Newburyport, December 10, 1805—he inherited the courage of New England from his sea-captain father and a profound moral sense from his Baptist mother. As a boy he tried his hand at many trades. Then he became a printer, and because he found he had much to say, an editor. Youth was no obstacle in those days. If a man could write—and Garrison developed early a clear, trenchant style—he had no trouble finding a vehicle. In 1829, therefore, young Garrison was invited by Benjamin Lundy of Baltimore to become co-editor on an Antislavery paper, the *Genius of Universal Emancipation*.

He had not been there long before he was sued for libel for an article in which he denounced a Mr. Todd for transporting in his vessel a cargo of Negroes from Baltimore to New Orleans. The Court fined Garrison fifty dollars, and because he could not pay it, he was sent to jail. The case stirred up the country. Whittier, Henry Clay, the foremost men and women throughout New England, found themselves partisans in a question to which until then they had given little thought. Arthur Tappan, a merchant in New York, paid the fine and Garrison was released, knowing now what his work was to be.

At first he thought of establishing his Antislavery paper in Washington, but since the North was as yet far from having any crystallized convictions on the question, he made Boston the base of his operations. On the first day of 1831 Garrison launched his *Liberator* on the troubled waters of the nation.

He was fearless and he spoke without faltering. He had conviction enough to set ablaze a whole continent and he did not spare the spark. Conscience told him that his was the task to plead for the millions inarticulate in their bondage. Hence, from the dingy hole of his office that contained both his printing press and his bed, he lifted up his voice till, like the first shot of the Revolution, its echo rolled down the years. Even today the opening address of the *Liberator* throbs with the man's terrible earnestness.

"I am aware that many object to the severity of my language; but is there not cause for severity? I *will* be as harsh as truth, and as uncompromising as justice. On this subject I do not wish to think, or speak, or write, with moderation. No! no! Tell a man whose house is on fire to give a moderate alarm; tell him to moderately rescue his wife from the hands of the ravisher; tell the mother to gradually extricate her babe from the fire in which it has fallen—but urge me not to use moderation in a cause like the present. I am in earnest: I will not equivocate; I will not retreat a single inch—AND I WILL BE HEARD."

And he was heard. At his reiterated plea for the emancipation of the Negro, Abolitionist societies sprang up in emulation of the first Antislavery group organized by Samuel E. Sewall in 1831. Within ten years nearly two thousand such societies formed working centers for Liberation.

Unhappily, organizations for the opposition set up their own bulwarks throughout the South and in the North as well. Tremendous interests were involved in the issue of Abolition, so tremendous that in spite of the constant agitation carried on by Garrison and his followers, there were times when it seemed as if centuries must pass before the idea could triumph.

First of all, slave owners in the South had no desire to surrender property in manpower that was worth millions and millions of dollars. Again, supposing they consented, what was to become of the emancipated Negroes? If they were sent out of the country, as some idealists had proposed, where could the workers be found to take their place? If, on the other hand, they were allowed to remain at large, who was to provide for them— and who would prevent the insurrection that would undoubtedly break out?

As the slave owners dominated Southern politics and therefore the politics of the nation, there followed a period when, to strengthen their position, they proceeded to wholesale aggressions through control of Federal power. Texas, which belonged to Mexico as a Free State, was annexed in 1845 that it might be divided into four slave states; a Fugitive Slave Law was passed which made it possible for escaped Negroes to be seized even in the North; and the Missouri Compromise, that prohibited slavery north of a certain parallel, was repealed. It looked as if the South were out to win, all the more since it could dictate to the moneyed interests in the North which from the beginning, on the ground that the agitation against slavery was undermining the Union, had stood solidly against Abolition.

Five years before the war broke out Emerson warned prophetically: "The hour is coming when the strongest will not be strong enough. A harder task will the new revolution of the nineteenth century be than the revolution of the eighteenth century. I think the American Revolution bought its glory cheap. If there were few people, they were united, and the enemy three thousand miles off. But now vast property, gigantic interests, family connections, webs of party, cover the land with a network that immensely multiplies the dangers of war."

For thirty years the moral conflict raged between the Abolitionists and the enemies of emancipation. In the course of the fight Garrison's life was often in danger from the mob till he could find safety only in prison. Riots occurred in which one man, the Rev. Elijah P. Lovejoy, was murdered for defending his press from destruction. Brother was pitted against brother; one half of the nation turned against the other. It made no difference that in 1852 Harriet Beecher Stowe's Abolitionist novel, *Uncle Tom's Cabin*, had found its way to millions of homes not only in the United States but throughout the world, where the question of emancipation had become as burning as in America. A solution could be found only through armed conflict.

The American Civil War, one of the most tragic in history, broke out in 1861, the year that saw the emancipation of forty-seven million serfs in Russia under the imperial ukase of Czar Alexander II. If legislation had succeeded in accomplishing the same purpose in the United States with the Negro slaves, thousands of lives would have been spared. It was what the Abolitionists had sought from the first. The slave powers willed otherwise.

By April of the year, after the attack on Fort Sumter, the fife and drum began to be heard again through New England as during the War of 1812. Washington called for troops and the Governor responded by gathering the militia to the towns. Antislavery passion rose. Those who so far had been lukewarm spoke out. Throughout Massachusetts many a man echoed the sentiments of Wendell Phillips when he cried: "I rejoice for the first time in my Antislavery life; I stand under the stars and stripes and welcome the tread of Massachusetts men." They were not tardy in defending their "noble Republican government," and volunteers went to fill the quota for the state.

Salem contributed her share. During the four years of the war more than three thousand of her men and boys fought in the Union ranks; two hundred of them never returned. One, General Frederick West Lander, was brought home for burial early in the war.

As a civil engineer Frederick Lander had distinguished himself in carrying out a number of projects for the government in connection with the extension of the railroad, an enterprise which, in America, had germinated in the brain of Gridley Bryant of Scituate, after reading of the proposed railroad in Liverpool. But let him tell his story in his own words: "I had . . . purchased a stone quarry . . . for the express purpose of procuring the granite for constructing [the Bunker Hill Monument]. This quarry was in Quincy, nearly four miles from water carriage. This suggested to me the idea of a railroad . . . Accordingly, in the fall of 1825, I consulted Thomas H. Perkins, William Sullivan, Amos Lawrence, Isaac P. Davis, and David Moody, all of Boston, in reference to it. These gentlemen thought the project visionary and chimerical . . . I awaited the meeting of our Legislature in the winter of 1825-26, and after every delay and obstruction that could be thrown in the way, I finally obtained a charter, although there was great opposition in the House. The questions were asked, 'What do we know about railroads? Who ever heard of such a thing?' "

Gridley Bryant set out to instruct their ignorance, and succeeded in awakening their wonder when on October 7, 1826, he started the first train of cars on the four miles of the Granite Railway. Today his large-wheeled box wagons, drawn by straining horses, would rouse the laughter of the irreverent, who find it hard to imagine that from such an infantile beginning developed the continent-girdling giant of the modern railway. Ridicule was not spared Bryant in his day, but men of foresight were not wanting who saw a future in the railroad idea.

Replacing the granite bed of Gridley's road by less obdurate material, and the horses by steam-power, the Massachusetts road builders put in motion their first locomotive on the Boston and Worcester tracks in March, 1834. Salem lost no time following in the heels of progress, and her first lines were laid through an enterprise that was chartered in 1836 as a result of the initiative of William H. Foster, George Peabody and later of Captain David A. Neal. By 1841 the *Monthly Chronicle* for June could boast: "The magnificent system of railroads, extending from a common center at Boston, throughout the State of Massachusetts, and reaching to four of the adjoining States, is now nearly completed."

However magnificent the three hundred odd miles of road might seem to the men of the 1840's, they were but a beginning to the ambitious citizens of the following decade. Thus, when Frederick Lander was ready to give his services to the nation, it was to study the facilities for stretching a railroad across the continent to the Pacific. The project got under way. With a group of engineers and surveyors Frederick Lander engaged in numerous expeditions meeting untold dangers in unexplored territory. From one such exploit he was the only man to return alive. Subsequently he helped to construct the wagon line that paved the way for the future railroad, and made himself so invaluable to the government that he was entrusted with missions of the greatest importance.

In 1861, when Fort Sumter was fired upon, he was in Texas on an embassy from Washington and returned to the capital just in time to bring important information. Meanwhile, to General George B. McClellan had been confided the charge of the Army of the Potomac that was to capture Richmond. Frederick Lander, receiving his commission as brigadier, hastened to his command on the upper Potomac.

For some time the army made scarcely any progress, the cautious McClellan studying every move before risking the lives of his soldiers. The more ardent Union men, in exasperation at his slowness, nicknamed him "Tardy George."

"What are you waiting for, George, I pray?" they taunted in anonymous verses,

To scour your cross-belts with fresh pipe-clay?
To burnish your buttons, to brighten your guns;
Or wait for May-day and warm spring suns? . . .
Is the mud knee-deep in valley and gorge?
What are you waiting for, tardy George?

Action came all too soon for the enterprising General Lander. While reconnoitering at Edward's Ferry he received a wound in the leg which, though it looked trifling at first, failed to heal. On the third of March, the following year, General McClellan announced the death of one of his most valued men.

War sentiment and patriotism ran high in Salem after the stirring reports of that first year of the war. When General Lander's remains were brought home for burial, the ceremony became a public occasion. The body lay in state at the City Hall, where grateful Salem accorded it the homage due to a hero. Then it was buried from the South Church with such honors as had not been witnessed within the living memory of the General's fellow citizens.

In him they were honoring those Salem men whose blood sowed the battlefields of the South.

## CHAPTER XXIII

## SALEM AND THE TELEPHONE

TOWARD the fall of 1873 a tall, very dignified young man with black side-whiskers and a drooping moustache which gave his otherwise handsome face a rueful expression, would get off the train that linked Boston and Salem, and with long, quick strides, make his way toward the white clapboard house at number 292 Essex Street, on the site now occupied by the Y.M.C.A. building. Behind a window overlooking the street and with his nose flattened against the pane, a little boy of five watched the passers-by. The moment he spied the familiar black whiskers and the sober dark clothes usually worn by much older men, he dashed down the stairs to the front door, waving his hand, on which he wore a glove.

Soon the two were sitting together and an animated conversation was going on about all the sights and sounds that would interest a child. The young cheeks glowed, the eager eyes sparkled. Questions were fired in quick succession and answers given. But there was something strange about the communication of the two. The youngster spoke little, and in a monotone, and often pointed to the glove on his hand. Looking closely, one could see that letters and words were inked on it and that by means of an ingenious method of finger-spelling, he was able to make himself understood. Little George, the son of Thomas Sanders, a wealthy financier of Boston, had been born deaf. Gradually Alexander Graham Bell was giving him speech.

There were other reasons, however, that brought Bell every evening from Boston to the house of Mrs. Sanders, the child's grandmother. For a time, after he had undertaken to teach George to speak, he had had his little pupil live with him at his boarding house in Boston. Since the arrangement proved inconvenient, Mr. Sanders suggested that Bell live in Salem with the boy. There, in more commodious quarters, he could both continue teaching George and carry on his experiments on the multiple or harmonic telegraph in which Mr. Sanders had an interest.

Professionally Alexander Graham Bell was a teacher of speech, a career which had been followed both by his father and grandfather first in their native Scotland and later in England. Melville Bell, Alexander's father, had obtained such success with his invention of Visible Speech as well as with his *Standard Elocutionist*, that he was summoned to lecture in Boston. At that time Alexander, who had been teaching at his father's school in London, showed signs of developing the tuberculosis that had carried away his two brothers, whereupon to save him the family migrated to Canada. Meanwhile, the elder Bell's lectures had been so well liked in Boston that he was invited to teach at the School for the Deaf, later the Horace Mann. As Melville Bell had other engagements in Canada, he suggested his son for the position. Hence in 1871, at the age of twenty-three, Alexander Graham Bell started upon the work that was eventually to lead to his great discovery.

Inventions were in the air. Every day applications for

patents poured into the Washington office and inventors young and old made pilgrimages with their models in their hands and visions of millions in their eyes. Bell, too, had his visions, but they were not alone of money, though money, he knew, would make him a more acceptable suitor in the eyes of Mr. Gardiner Greene Hubbard with whose daughter, Mabel, Bell had fallen in love.

Mabel Hubbard was one of his pupils. At the age of four she had lost her hearing after scarlet fever, and although Mr. Hubbard had left no method untried to give her normal speech, it was not till she became Bell's private pupil that there was any sign of real progress. She was a quiet young girl whose looks, as is often the case with the deaf, expressed what she could not say. It was to her that Longfellow, a Cambridge neighbor, addressed the verses, "Maiden with the meek brown eyes . . ."

Before long Mr. Hubbard showed as much interest as his daughter in young Bell, especially after he became better acquainted with the multiple telegraph on which the elocution teacher had been working and in which Mr. Sanders had such confidence that he had taken a financial interest in it. Mr. Hubbard was a man of vision. Together with Mr. Sanders, he took the promising inventor under his wing, but waited till definite results were achieved before he gave his consent to his daughter's engagement.

Meanwhile, in the Essex Street house in Salem, before the astonished eyes of old Mrs. Sanders, all sorts of experiments were going on which sometimes made her doubt the sanity of her guest. There was the time he had strung wires across from his windows to his neighbor Richards' to determine goodness only knows what. Nevertheless, whatever it was, it must have turned out the way Bell had expected, for the war dance he performed in the best manner of the Canadian Indians was both exuberant and long. Then there were those other times when with his assistant, Thomas A. Watson, a few years younger than himself, he would indulge in all sorts of extraordinary antics, exchanging signals from the cellar to the attic, singing a note over the piano till it gave one a case of the vapors, or moping over gadgets and machines. Then always the war dance at the first sign of success.

One March day in 1875, Bell, in his most elderly and dignified garb, set out for Washington carrying a bulky apparatus. He had something tangible to show the world, and as the world in his case meant an authority on the subject, he sought out the Secretary of the Smithsonian Institution.

Professor Joseph Henry, one of the foremost physicists of his day, whose name is perpetuated in the "henry" or unit of inductance, was then a very old man. Yet he found time to see the unknown whose card, "A. Graham Bell," meant absolutely nothing to him. For half an hour the young man spoke, describing his multiple telegraph and telling of other experiments which suddenly made the eighty-year-old physicist sit up and take notice. "I told him," Bell recorded, "that on passing an intermittent current of electricity through an empty helix of insulated copper wire, a noise could be heard proceeding from the coil."

The following day, with the help of his apparatus, he demonstrated his experiments before Professor Henry, who listened absorbed while Bell adumbrated his vision of the electric telephone.

Difficulties were to beset the inventor before he could proceed to the working out of his ideas. Mr. Hubbard and Mr. Sanders were primarily concerned with the multiple telegraph in which they saw surer prospects of making money; therefore Mr. Hubbard particularly discouraged any deviation that took time from the main work. No multiple telegraph, no Mabel, he would say in so many words whenever he caught Bell experimenting on the electric telephone which he, Hubbard, looked upon as an amiable but inconvenient aberration of the young Scotsman's brain. A machine that would transmit speech by telegraph? That would enable one to talk to a person miles away? Impossible! Regardless of the fact that Bell's classes were growing smaller through his neglect of them for the sake of the ideas that occupied him day and night, and unmindful of the youth's frayed shirts and shining coats, he gave him no more money than permitted his construction of the various parts of the multiple telegraph. For nearly a year Bell lived, or rather existed, on his allowance for teaching George Sanders.

The time came when he could not bear to give a moment to the multiple telegraph, so great was his urge for the new invention. Essex Street was the scene of many a curious happening. Hardly a week passed but Mrs. Sanders' house sprouted wires that descended sometimes from Bell's upper study window to her best parlor, sometimes to the next-door music studio of Dom Manuel Fenellosa, who allowed the mad young man to run a current of electricity through the strings of his pianoforte. What did it all mean? What was the peculiar Mr. Bell seeking?

Those experiments were not enough. In Boston, with the indefatigable Watson, Bell worked in Mr. Williams' shop at 109 Court Street, or late into the night in the two rooms at number 5 Exeter Street which Bell had engaged for privacy. He had been told that inquisitive and suspicious-looking strangers were in the habit of stopping in the shop before the electrical parts that Watson constructed for him. Already Elisha Gray had had priority over him with the multiple telegraph. Bell must keep his telephonic experiments secret.

By the middle of June, 1875, through a series of fortunate accidents, Alexander Graham Bell conceived the model of the apparatus that was to transmit speech. "Before we parted that night," Watson recalled years later, "Bell gave me directions for making the first electric speaking telephone. I was to mount a small drumhead of gold-beater's skin over one of the receivers, join the center of the drumhead to the free end of the receiver spring and arrange a mouthpiece over the drumhead to talk into." It was a simple device and quickly constructed. What was the frenzied joy of the inventor whom none but Watson had believed in, when, through the first telephone wire ever stretched, his voice was heard across space as he had predicted!

More intensely than ever, cutting down on food and sleep, Bell worked to perfect his invention and draw up the patent specifications for the Washington office. Mabel and he, through the cooperation of Mrs. Hubbard, were now engaged. He could work with a freer mind. Finally the model of the telephone was improved to the satisfaction of the sceptical Mr. Hubbard, but the wording of the patent specifications still failed to satisfy Bell. There must be no holes, no dubious phrasings affording leeway to the inevitable litigants who always come up to claim successful inventions.

One night, long after the Hubbards with whom he was staying had gone to bed, he discovered his omission and inserted a clause covering his experiments in variable resistance. On February 14, 1876, a few weeks before Bell's twenty-ninth birthday, his patent specifications for the electric telephone were filed—in the nick of time. A few hours later Elisha Gray submitted his caveat, or description of his theories on the transmission of speech by electricity.

It was the year of the Republic's centennial and a great exposition was opened that May in Philadelphia's Fairmount Park to celebrate the occasion with fitting pomp and ceremony. For five years the sponsors had collaborated with all the nations of the civilized world. Throughout the many acres marvelous edifices had sprung up with the magic of an Aladdin's lamp. Tree-lined avenues led from exhibition to exhibition out of the glare of the summer sun, and fountains, not the least wonderful of which showed Moses striking water from a rock, refreshed those visitors who had not already quenched their thirst at less innocent sources. Wines, tobaccos, coffees, the arts, trades and sciences of the whole world were submitted before a body of judges, while bands played and red, white and blue festoons and ingenious transparencies enlivened the avenues.

Many distinguished guests had come from all quarters of the globe. Most splendid of them, and most pic-

turesque with his blonde beard and imposing frame, was
Dom Pedro, the Emperor of Brazil. Day in and day out,
indefatigable and enthusiastic, he accompanied the reception committee from building to building, showing
his appreciation of one exhibition after another.

On an unbearably sultry Sunday toward the end of
June, Dom Pedro, with the committee, stopped before
the education exhibition of Massachusetts, arranged by
Mr. Hubbard. There, squeezed in between the Visible
Speech charts of Melville Bell and the unfortunate multiple telegraph, was Alexander Graham Bell's extraordinary contraption that was said to transmit the human
voice electrically. As usual, Bell had temporized in the
cause of perfection and as his model had arrived late,
it had not been included in the electrical exhibit.

The judges were about to walk out, exhausted, after
what they considered the last demonstration for the
day, when the zealous Dom Pedro caught sight of Mr.
Bell, whom he had met in Boston and with whom he
had held a lively conversation on teaching the deaf to
speak. On learning from Bell the nature of his exhibit,
Dom Pedro must have it shown then and there. The
judges perforce deferred to their distinguished guest.
Mr. Bell was requested to set to work on his electrical
telephone, and the demonstration began.

"To be or not to be," declaimed that scion of Scotland's far-famed elocutionists into the telephone transmitter, while from the other end his assistant handed the
receiver from one man to another, who listened spell-
bound to Bell's recital of Hamlet's soliloquy from a
distance of more than five hundred feet.

"I will now go and talk," volunteered one of the

judges, Sir William Thomson, who had been knighted for his part in the laying of the Atlantic cable ten years earlier. Professor George F. Barker took the receiver. Bell, after his soliloquy, had begun counting, "One, two, three . . ." Suddenly there was a moment's silence and then Professor Barker cried out, "Sir William is now speaking!"

Elisha Gray, who might have invented the telephone, so near had he come to it, then put the receiver to his ear and heard the ironically appropriate words: "Aye, there's the rub."

From an obscure exhibit Bell's telephone became the highlight of the exposition, but only among scientists and engineers. To the people at large it was just another toy. The *New York Tribune* echoed their note. "Of what use is such an invention? Well, there may be occasions of state when it is necessary for officials who are far apart to talk with each other without the interference of an operator. Or some lover may wish to pop the question directly into the ear of a lady and hear for himself her reply, though miles away; it is not for us to guess how courtships will be carried on in the twentieth century."

Bell did not let the grass grow under his feet. The invention was only in its infancy; it must be developed to become a commercial utility. So far only the transmitter could talk to the person at the other end, who had to telegraph back his answers. The apparatus must be made to work both ways. Tirelessly Bell and Watson resumed their researches, perfecting the mechanics of the telephone and testing it over longer and longer distances through the courtesy of various companies which lent the inventor their wires for his tests.

One such experiment utilized the wires of the Eastern Railroad, from Boston to Salem. It was a complete success. "All those at the Boston end of the line," reported the Boston *Post*, "held free and easy conversation with the Salem office . . . A remarkable instance of the extreme delicacy and faithfulness of the instrument was shown in the fact that when Mr. Hubbard first addressed the listener at the Salem end of the line, Mr. Watson instantly recognized his voice and called him by name before replying."

On February 12, 1877, in the Lyceum Hall of Salem, the Essex Institute and its guests gathered for an historic occasion. Alexander Graham Bell, in a Prince Albert coat and his best platform manner, was ready to deliver a lecture on telephony, to be followed by a demonstration from his instrument, planted on the platform under the flaring gas light. Salem ladies in plumed bonnets and wide ruffled skirts, keeping their hands warm in little barrel muffs, sat beside dignified gentlemen with smoothly combed square beards and stove-pipe hats which they held politely in their laps. The three sections of the hall were occupied to the last seat. Toward the rear some of the spectators were sitting on the raised steps. It was distinctly an occasion.

Bell began in his fine, resonant voice. First he described the telephone and the principles on which it worked. Then, talking into the transmitter of the apparatus, which was connected with his rooms in Boston where a body of scientific men and reporters were taking notes of the proceedings, he said, "Mr. Watson, will you speak to the audience?"

The ladies started. The gentlemen sat up. It was a little like magic. They were not left long in suspense. "Ladies and gentlemen," came a blurred yet comprehensible voice from the machine, "it gives me great pleasure to be able to address you this evening, although I am in Boston, and you are in Salem!" The whole house burst into applause. True, the words were made out distinctly only by the people in the front rows, but how marvelous to hear the distant voice at all!

The demonstration continued, this time with members of the audience participating. The news came from Boston that the engineers of the Boston and Maine railroad were on strike. "Are the trains running?" asked General Cogswell.

Clearly the answer came from the machine: at that time, half-past five, they were tied up.

Then Bell introduced the Rev. E. C. Bolles who said, "I shake hands with you cordially in imagination twenty miles away." The people in Boston returned his greeting.

The Rev. E. S. Atwood then asked from Salem, "Does it rain?"

"It does not in Boston," Watson answered.

Lyceum Hall thrilled with excitement, especially when Watson closed the program by singing "Hold the Fort" which, with the popular but doleful "Gypsy's Warning" comprised nearly the whole of his musical repertory.

Bell was eighty-five dollars the richer by this lecture. It was, so far, the only money that his invention had brought him. Mr. Hubbard, however, now saw the commercial possibilities for it and gave his consent to

Bell's marriage to his daughter. In July, 1877, the young inventor took his bride on a visit to his parents in Canada and then they both sailed for Europe.

The rest of Bell's life pertains not only to Salem but to history. Before the close of the century his telephone patent justified its being called the most valuable single patent ever issued. Rivals discovered its worth, and one suit after another was brought to court against Bell by serious inventors like Gray, Dolbear and Edison, as well as by a host of cranks and deluded men who thought they showed a clear title to the invention.

The culmination came with the gigantic Pan-Electric scandal in 1885, when men high up in government sought to get rich by the most audacious stock swindle ever perpetrated at the expense of an honest inventor. The swindle, happily, was exposed, and Bell went on with his numerous activities, that ranged from the invention of a telephone probe, first used in an attempt to locate the assassin's bullet that killed President Garfield, to the founding of an Aerial Experiment Association when flying was thought as remote as speech transmission had been in the early days of his researches.

In 1915 Bell saw, through the efforts of such able engineers as Theodore N. Vail and John J. Carty, the perfection of development to which his invention had been brought with the opening of the coast-to-coast telephone line, a distance of thirty-four hundred miles. "Hoy! Hoy! Mr. Watson! Are you there? Do you hear me?" he asked from New York. The faithful Watson from San Francisco answered, "Perfectly."

Through the World War Bell lived, seeing the realization of flight—and its abuse as a dealer of death when bombs were hurled down from the sky on defenseless women and children. He survived the overthrow of monarchies and the rising up of new forms of government. Honored with degrees and titles from the whole civilized world, he died on the second of August, 1922, in an era wherein science had made miracles a commonplace.

## CHAPTER XXIV

## SALEM TODAY

INEXORABLY, with the passing of time, industrialism encroached upon the dreamy town of Salem clinging to the memories of its past, till by the end of the nineteenth century it had become a city of factories huddled about the olden center whose quiet, unchanging, beautiful dooryards still held inviolate their ancient secrets.

The population altered, imperceptibly at first, with the infiltration of the persecuted Huguenots in the seventeenth century, and in the shifting of people from colony to colony. As wars and revolutions racked Europe, its people sought peace and opportunity in the New World. Stubbornly the original stock of New England held to its purity; the grafts would not take. Nevertheless, as the transplanted of other nations took root, their influence made itself felt, as plants in a garden will bear upon the character of the original seed. In Salem, however, an ever-narrowing circle kept itself aloof from foreign infiltration. Clannish, proud of its blood, it still survives in white-haired spinsters and unmarried last sons who would rather put an end to the race than graft it unworthily. Behind the dignified porticos with their urned gateposts and green-shaded doorways many an old name is dying.

Meanwhile the foreign population lives its busy, prolific life in the tenements which once were warehouses and in the cheap cottages without beauty or tradition that have sprung up about the factories. Salem has not yet become reconciled to the immigrant, although a spirit of Christian charity strives to make the best of an unwelcome fact, as instanced by the following observations published by Joseph B. Saunders, in 1926: "Immigrants of many classes have, in their time, created new and grave problems and added to the always present duty of molding them to the ideals of the Fathers . . .

"Policies in religion, education and government have been fruitful of dissension, but the democratic trend and force of the day has broadened religion and diffused education . . . The evils of democracy are not a few but, in its perfection, democracy is 'the sense of manhood in the individual, and the spirit of brotherhood in the community.' For this sense of brotherhood we should in the future strive, and in considering the racial elements now composing our population, we may hope under proper guidance for an enrichment of our community life."

In the town itself where for many years only one church and one manner of worship were tolerated, temples have been erected whose names speak volumes for the religious tolerance that has since prevailed. There is the Church of the Immaculate Conception on Walnut Street, where Roman Catholics go to mass at the summons of its three-thousand-pound bell, the largest in Salem. And there is St. James Church on Federal Street, also Roman Catholic, with its huge and powerful organ. Then there are the Church of St. John the Baptist for Polish Catholics, and St. John's Ukrainian, for Greek Catholics; St. Joseph's for French Catholics, and St. Mary's for the Italian. At the corner of Webb Street and Forrester stands St. Nicholas' Russian Church, and at Essex and Herbert streets, not far from Hawthorne's birthplace, the Sons of Jacob Synagogue. While the descendants of the early founders faithfully worship at the First Church, rebuilt for the fourth time in brick in 1826, the foreign population celebrates marriages and births and deaths according to the beliefs of their fathers in the Old World. Freedom to worship God holds for all.

In the populous sections living has its risks and hazards, as the most recent "great fire" proved on June 25, 1914. Early that afternoon some chemicals exploded in a leather factory in Blubber Hollow, on Boston Street. Far into the night the flames raged, snapping up like so much tinder the wooden cottages of the foreign workers and the ill-built factories that knew no such thing as fireproofing. Nearly two thousand buildings were destroyed before the flames, spread by a high wind, were under control. Fifteen thousand persons found themselves on the streets, their homes burned down, their few possessions turned to smoke and ashes. As the fire occurred during the day, when most of the people were awake or at work, only three lives were lost. The property damage was reckoned in the millions.

Fortunately nothing of historical interest was touched, as the fire occurred in the newer section of Salem. Hence today the visitor can still see houses that were standing during the dark years of the persecutions of Quakers and witches. Indeed, the home of Jonathan Corwin, that was built in 1635 and survives as the Witch House, shows still the lines of its ancient architecture in its sloping roof and overhanging second story. Successive generations and the hand of commercialism have altered its primitive dignity, but it does not take too great an effort of the imagination to transport it and oneself to the year 1692, when across its sanded floor paced the impatient witch examiners, while through its narrow rooms echoed the cunning answers of Mr. Parris' Tituba and the defiant denials of Bridget Bishop, maintaining her innocence before God and man. There is many a thing that the old house could tell.

Of the proud mansion of the greatest of early colonial shipmasters, Philip English, nothing remains, although its many gables and soaring stories were the pride of seventeenth-century Salem. Hawthorne knew it as a youth and his knowledge of it may have entered into his descriptions of *The House of the Seven Gables*. Of the original, torn down in 1833, not a fragment of its leaded glass gives sparkle to the dust.

For the curious, a number of houses of the same period still survive. There is the Pickering House at 18 Broad Street with its typical roof and ever-present gables, and the Narbonne House at 71 Essex, that was built in 1671 and yet outlives the younger "Great House" of Philip English.

Through the door of its little lean-to a hundred years ago, the children of Salem used to pass, clutching their pennies in their hands as they looked about the "cent shop" presided over by some aging Hepzibah. Jim Crows and gingerbread men with eyes of raisins and sugar frosting trimmings, tempted the boys. There were also jars of "lozengers" in beautiful colors that melted on

the tongue in sweetness and tartness and every taste at
once; and delicious Gibraltars, that far-famed Salem
candy, beloved of sweet-toothed spinsters and old ladies;
and rock sugar that looked like icicles. And for the girls
there were strings of red sealing-wax beads, and worsted
of many colors, and porcelain dolls as big as their little
fingers. They were strange dolls with moveable arms
and legs and a fixed stare out of black, unevenly painted
eyes. Then there were bolts of brilliant India cottons,
printed shawls, clasps, buttons and odds and ends for the
women—pins and needles, thimbles and the many trinkets
which long ago peddlers used to carry in their packs.
Poor little humble "cent shop"! Like the last Indiaman,
it too has vanished out of Salem life.

It is the architecture of the eighteenth century, car-
penter-architect era, and of the period following the
Revolution, that brings the connoisseur to Salem. Perhaps
nowhere else in New England are there so many fine examples of the art to be found, and in such perfect preservation. With the expansion of Salem's markets and
the resulting wealth, merchants began to take pride in
their homes. Primitive designs seemed no longer appropriate to house the treasures that came from the East
with every ship that touched port. Thus European plans
were imported and modified to suit New England taste.

Externally the houses had a noble solidity emphasized
by simple lines and harmonious proportions. Generally
wood was employed, until Richard Derby constructed
his mansion in brick, which may still be seen on Derby
Street, and McIntire gave it the seal of approval in the
hip-roofed houses of Chestnut Street. Within, the rooms
exhibited all the art of the ship carpenter. Fine carved

paneling covered the walls. Newel posts spiraled in cable forms, matched by the delicate rods of the balusters, each a masterpiece of the ship carver's art. Wide, broken staircases gave the mansions stateliness and grace. Here were homes for easeful living, demonstrating to the courtly foreigner that where the wilderness had been, a new culture had arisen.

Of the post-revolutionary mansions perhaps the best example is the Peirce-Nicholls house at number 80 Federal Street. Jerathmeel Peirce, the wealthy East India merchant, had had it built in 1782 from the designs of Samuel McIntire. It took twenty years to finish, room by room, each cornice and mantel lovingly carved by the hand of the master artist. Outwardly, the white clapboard mansion shows the usual square proportions of the period—the three stories with the last foreshortened, and a balustrade bordering the low roof—a classical translation of the deck-roof to which the shipmaster used to clamber, spyglass in hand, to pick out the incoming sails of his ventures. A fence borders the street, to the gateposts surmounted by urns. Behind them opens a dignified Doric porch.

It is its interior that gives the Peirce-Nicholls house claim to being the most beautiful wooden mansion in New England. Well-proportioned, each room, whether in cornice or fireplace, contains some example of McIntire's art which he here exhibited from his early Georgian to his late Adam style. Today the mansion is owned by the Essex Institute.

Nothing of Salem's past has been lost. Although some historical landmark, like Hawthorne's beloved town pump, may have vanished, records of it are to be found in that thesaurus of Salem lore, the Essex Institute, whose museum occupies the site of Governor Bradstreet's house. Lovingly preserved, every phase of Salem's history has its documents or its actual examples in the many buildings, like the Pingree House, owned by the Institute. Its library is one of the largest in New England; its collections of Essex County documents and pamphlets are perhaps the most complete in the nation. Every precious scrap of tradition, from the sampler of Governor Endecott's wife to the old pine desk on which in his Custom House days Hawthorne scratched his name with his thumbnail, are appropriately enshrined, to the eternal gratitude of the race.

As if the treasures of the Essex Institute were not enough for a city of Salem's size, there are public buildings, libraries and societies that have collections of their own. It is to the Peabody Museum, however, that everyone goes who is interested in Salem's maritime past and in the natural history, Oriental and ethnological collections that have grown out of the curiosities brought home by the far-wanderers. So rare are some of the specimens that scholars from other lands come to the Peabody Museum for their researches. Besides cases containing literally "the riches of the Indies," and ship models wrought with tender care by the old mariners, there are walls covered with portraits of those intrepid seamen, the Crowninshields, the Derbys, the Peabodys and the Silsbees, uncomfortable in their formal stocks against a curtained interior in which, that their shadows might rest in peace, the artist has opened out a window showing far sails on the sea. Vaguely their eyes gaze from the canvas upon remembered distances.

In spite of its modernity, there lingers still over Salem a palpable enchantment. Unlike other American cities that have survived their centuries, Salem, the essential Salem, has come through unchanged, perfect and whole, like those bits of life imprisoned in amber that her sailing men used to bring home for waiting wives and sweet-hearts. Time has in a sense built a protective wall about her, preserving inviolate that lofty yet achievable culture that is New England's contribution to the world.

THE END

# INDEX

B